THE STORY OF
CALTON JAIL
EDINBURGH'S VICTORIAN PRISON

THE STORY OF

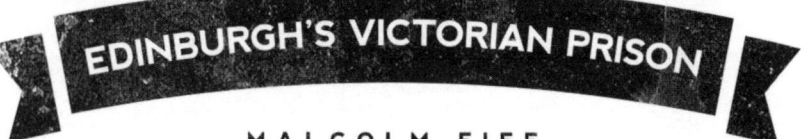

EDINBURGH'S VICTORIAN PRISON

MALCOLM FIFE

*In memory of Thomas Pressland (died 8 August 2011),
Lothian and Borders Police and Park Patrol Superintendent
from 1975 to 1992*

First published 2016

The History Press
The Mill, Brimscombe Port
Stroud, Gloucestershire, GL5 2QG
www.thehistorypress.co.uk

© Malcolm Fife, 2016

The right of Malcolm Fife to be identified as the Author
of this work has been asserted in accordance with the
Copyright, Designs and Patents Act 1988.

All rights reserved. No part of this book may be reprinted
or reproduced or utilised in any form or by any electronic,
mechanical or other means, now known or hereafter invented,
including photocopying and recording, or in any information
storage or retrieval system, without the permission in writing
from the Publishers.

British Library Cataloguing in Publication Data.
A catalogue record for this book is available from the British Library.

ISBN 978 0 7509 6224 7

Typesetting and origination by The History Press
Printed in Great Britain

Front cover image: Calton Prison viewed from Calton Hill.
The East Wing features prominently in the picture, which is thought to
have been taken between 1862 and 1873. (Courtesy of Jan Weijers)

CONTENTS

	Introduction	6
	About the Author	8
1.	The Need for a New Prison	9
2.	The Bridewell	13
3.	The Construction of Calton Prison	20
4.	Prison Life	27
5.	The Prison Governors and Warders	31
6.	Public Executions	36
7.	Executions in Calton Prison	48
8.	Down and Out – Beggars, Tramps and Vagrants	56
9.	Women on the Wrong Side of the Law	60
10.	Boys and Girls in Trouble	65
11.	The Long Arm of the Law	74
12.	Transportation	76
13.	The Railway	83
14.	Sailors in Deep Water	90
15.	The Criminally Insane	97
16.	Heavenly Matters	104
17.	Political Unrest	108
18.	Crofters in Rebellion	112
19.	Irish Terrorists	116
20.	Suffragettes	119
21.	Foul Deeds in the Highlands	122
22.	Prisoners from Foreign Lands	126
23.	Deaths and Suicides at Calton Prison	132
24.	Escapes	138
25.	The Cell Doors Close for the Final Time	149
	Appendices	152
	Bibliography	174

INTRODUCTION

In Victorian times, passengers arriving at Edinburgh's Waverley Station could catch sight of towering stone walls and castellated towers on top of a cliff face next to it. Those not familiar with the city would sometimes assume this to be Edinburgh Castle. It was in fact Calton Prison, which occupied a prominent position in the city centre. Jules Verne, the French novelist who visited Edinburgh in 1859, likened it to a walled medieval city.

Up until the end of the eighteenth century, criminals were locked up in the Tolbooth in the Royal Mile. However, by this time it was becoming increasingly antiquated and overcrowded and the decision was taken to build a bridewell on Calton Hill in which persons who had committed minor offences were detained. In the early nineteenth century a prison was established next to it. Although primarily intended to serve the needs of justice for the local county, it was also the intention that it should be the National Prison for Scotland.

Detained within its high stone walls were numerous high-profile criminals, including the bodysnatchers Burke and Hare while awaiting their trial. When public execution was abolished, this gruesome practice was undertaken behind closed doors at Calton Prison. Political prisoners were also locked up here, including suffragettes and socialists who were thought to be a threat to the country during the First World War. Irish terrorists, fraudulent bankers and smugglers rubbed shoulders with drunks, beggars, pickpockets and other minor offenders, who were by far the most numerous category of prisoner. In the early years of the twentieth century it was decided that the facilities at Calton Prison were becoming increasingly dated and that Edinburgh needed a new prison. By 1926 it had closed, being replaced by Saughton Prison on the edge of the city.

Despite its impressive appearance, with its castellated walls and towers, almost all of the prison was demolished. Although many old buildings in Edinburgh were torn down in the last century, this could be considered to be one of its greatest losses. In its place was built St Andrew's House, a large art deco building which now houses government offices. The only reminder of this prison, which housed

INTRODUCTION

many of Scotland's most notorious Victorian criminals, is the Governor's Tower, which clings precariously to the clifftops of Calton Hill.

Few prisons in Britain would have witnessed such a motley collection of humanity pass through their gates. Its memory has all but been extinguished from the minds of most of Edinburgh's citizens, with its buildings torn down and a meager amount of its records escaping destruction.

In its early history, Calton Prison was usually referred to as a jail or gaol. The term prison was more commonly used from around the mid-nineteenth century onwards. In official reports it was usually known as Edinburgh Prison from this time onwards.

Malcolm Fife, 2016

ABOUT THE AUTHOR

Edinburgh-born Malcolm Fife has an MA in Geography from the University of Edinburgh and is the author of *The Nor Loch: Scotland's Lost Loch*, *Scottish Aerodromes of the First World War* and *British Airship Bases of the Twentieth Century*. In addition he has produced a number of illustrated features for *Scots Magazine*. He worked for the Parks and Recreation Department of Edinburgh Council for eighteen years before becoming a freelance photographer.

1

THE NEED FOR A NEW PRISON

In the late eighteenth century Edinburgh was experiencing unprecedented expansion with the construction of the New Town, which previously had been confined within the old city walls. Society itself was also undergoing a rapid transformation with the growth of the middle class. Traditional conventions were now coming under scrutiny – including the way that criminals were treated.

The late Georgian era saw the rise of a movement that questioned the effectiveness of punishments for offenders. There was also concern about the conditions in which they were held in prison. One of the leading protagonists was John Howard, who travelled the length and breadth of Britain inspecting its prisons.

For centuries Edinburgh's main prison had been the Tolbooth, situated on the High Street immediately west of St Giles' Cathedral. Known popularly as the 'Heart of Midlothian', it was built in 1561 but incorporated part of an older example. As with tolbooths in other Scottish towns, initially it was used for a number of functions including as the town hall and customs office. In the sixteenth century the Scottish Parliament also met in it.

For a time prisoners were also held in the spire of St Giles' Cathedral. In 1562 a room was prepared to house fornicators known as 'Wobsteris Hous'. Bored prisoners, however, had the habit of dropping objects onto the congregation below and eventually this practice was abandoned.

Confining offenders to long periods of imprisonment was, until recent centuries, relatively unknown. Persons were only locked up until their fate was determined. They would then be banished, flogged, fined, or worse, hung.

By the eighteenth century, the Tolbooth had relinquished its other functions and was used solely as a prison. Externally, it resembled little more than a large house. Its limitations were by this time becoming increasingly apparent: the security was poor as there was no boundary wall and it was on a public street. Political prisoners and rioters had to be held in Edinburgh Castle as there was a possibility sympathizers could storm the Tolbooth. Many prisoners were able to escape. Once through the front door they could mingle with the crowds in the Royal Mile.

Prison regulations included a ban on the inmates undertaking any form of work while in the prison. This was increasingly at odds with the thinking of prison reformers of the time. Worse still was the fact that the gaoler had a licence to sell ale and port to those confined in the building. Local citizens could often be found drinking with the prisoners in the common room. It was not, however, all happiness and merriment. Some prisoners were allowed to mingle freely but others were confined to their rooms. Three of the apartments were furnished with stocks in which the inmates could have their movements restricted. One of their legs was pinned in the stocks and they were held in this manner for long periods. Worse still was the cell for condemned prisoners who were sometimes held in iron chains for periods of up to six weeks before being removed to the scaffold.

Historian Hugo Arnot visited the Tolbooth in the late eighteenth century and recorded that it was kept in a slovenly condition with the eastern quarter being the worst part. Here the stench was intolerable. Three boys, one about 14 and two about 12, were confined in the cell usually reserved for criminals awaiting execution. In one corner there was a pile of old rags and straw that had been used by prisoners to sleep on. On entering another cell they found a further two boys not even 12 years old. So bad was the smell from it that Hugo Arnot could not even enter it. The small-scale nature of the prison is apparent, as in June 1781 there were only nineteen debtors and twelve criminals housed in its fourteen apartments.

Aware of the shortcomings of the Tolbooth, in 1782 the Lord Provost and the sheriff depute Archibald Cockpen drew up a report detailing plans for a new prison and bridewell. It was their intention that an attempt should be made to reform the characters that were sentenced to be locked up, inspired by the teachings of John Howard. They related that there were few prisons in the country more at odds to the ideas of this prison reformer than that of Edinburgh's Tolbooth. To remedy the situation they envisaged construction of a jail and workhouse or bridewell next to each other. They would be laid out in divisions so that young offenders could be kept apart from hardened criminals. A courtyard would be located in each division. Conversation among all inmates would also be frowned upon. For this scheme an area of around 3 acres was needed. All the buildings were to be laid out inside a perimeter wall. The structures were to be placed upon arches so that if any escape attempt was made it would be easily seen. The perimeter wall was to be 30ft in height and 4ft thick and security would be further enhanced by parapets at regular intervals along it. The Governor's House would be placed in the centre of the complex and was to be three storeys high. On the second floor there would be a large room for management meetings and examination of prisoners. In addition, from here the governor would be able to view all the divisions to see what was going on.

The entrance gate would be made out of iron in case of any assault on the prison. This would also enable guns to be fired through it by prison staff. More unusually a turret was to be placed at each corner of the perimeter wall. On them were to be placed swivel guns that could be pointed at the prison buildings in case of insurrection or to repel any attack from without by raking the wall with fire. Interestingly this may gave a clue as to why the Bridewell and Calton Prison when built were surrounded by a wall and towers that would have done a medieval fortress justice. It was perhaps not only to keep the prisoners in but to fend off an attack by potential rebellious subjects.

Work on the Bridewell commenced some ten years after the report by the Lord Provost. Calton Hill was already in public ownership by this date and made an obvious choice for such a scheme. Edinburgh would, however, have to wait till 1817 before it got a new prison. In the intervening period there was little improvement in conditions at the Tolbooth.

Until the eighteenth century, Calton Hill was known as Craigingalt, meaning crag on the hill or wooded hillside. The name Calton was adopted from a local settlement and used for this physical feature from around this time onwards. The name is thought to be Celtic in origin, meaning 'place of or at the groves'.

Calton Hill is now woven into the fabric of Edinburgh, with roads and buildings clinging to its slopes. These somewhat disguise the rugged features of this landmark. Around 350 million years ago volcanoes erupted across the region, their lavas transformed into rocks that now form many of the hills in and around Edinburgh, the best-preserved example being Arthur's Seat. Calton Hill – with old lavas some 600ft thick – is a displaced fragment of a long-extinct volcano. Glaciers in the last Ice Age gouged out a deep valley next to it and transformed its western slopes into cliffs and craggy rock faces.

Unlike the other hills of Edinburgh, Calton Hill seems to have been shunned by prehistoric man – there is little evidence that there were ever forts or settlements on it. Until relatively recently in history its upper slopes were completely devoid of both trees and buildings. Its steep cliff faces and marshes to the east probably did much to contribute to its isolation. There was an old legend that a fairy boy, who was a drummer to the elves, held a weekly rendezvous at midnight on the bare and desolate top of Calton Hill.

A more sinister occurrence was the erection of a gibbet for a public execution on Dow Craig near the summit in 1554. Duels were also fought out of the sight of prying eyes at the extreme eastern end of the hill at Quarryholes. At its opposite end a Carmelite monastery was constructed at Greenside around 1520 next to the church of the Holy Cross. It was recorded that in 1534, David Straiton and a priest named Norman Gourlay were burnt at the stake for heresy not far from it. This was no means an isolated occurrence as other persons accused of being witches and sorcerers were also punished in a similar manner on the northern edge of Calton Hill.

The Reformation in Scotland brought an end to the monasteries. In the closing years of the sixteenth century the buildings of the monastery at Greenside were converted to a hospital for lepers. Its position in what was then open countryside was ideal for this purpose. Harsh regulations were imposed on those inflicted with this dreadful disease. A gallows was erected at one end of the hospital to hang those that disobeyed them. Even to open the gates between sunset and sunrise was punishable by death.

2

THE BRIDEWELL

The term bridewell originates from St Bride's Well, a holy well in London near to which King Henry VIII had a house. The residence was donated by Edward VI for use as a hospital but turned into a house of correction. An Act in 1575 deemed that each county in England should establish a house of correction to accommodate vagrants and the work-shy.

The prestigious architect Robert Adam was given the task of designing a bridewell for Edinburgh in the late nineteenth century. He submitted a number of different designs, some inspired by classical architecture and others resembling feudal fortresses. All of them, however, incorporated the latest thinking about prison design. After much deliberation, a castle-style building was selected which included the concept of a panopticon or inspection house.

This was the idea of Jeremy Bentham, a British philosopher, for a new type of prison. It entailed a circular building with a central observation room from which all the cells were visible but from which the observer could not be seen. Prisoners did not know when they were being watched. This made supervision easier as well as requiring fewer staff, making the prison more economic to run. Robert Adam's final design only partially implemented this, much to the annoyance of its inventor. It also included side wings on either side of the Bridewell that would have provided a debtors' prison and a lunatic asylum, along with houses for the governor, surgeon and chaplain which were to be built into the southern boundary wall. Due to financial constraints they were not built.

In August 1791, an Act of Parliament was passed to build a new prison. Some £5,000 was received from the government towards the building of a bridewell, a house of correction and prison in the city. Only the first was constructed, at a cost of £11,794. A grand procession was formed on 30 November 1791 to lay the foundation stone to the Bridewell. It was composed of the Lord Provost, followed by the magistrates, the sheriff depute and the noblemen of the county. Behind them was the Grand Master of Freemasons, the Earl of Morton, and members from many lodges. On reaching the site of the Bridewell, the Grand Master gave three knocks on the foundation stone with a mallet. Then, according to an ancient ceremony, oil, corn and wine were poured over the stone and the following words were uttered over it: 'May all-bounteous author of nature bless this city and country with abundance of corn, wine and oil and with all necessities, conveniences and comforts of life and may the same almighty power preserve this city and country from ruin and decay to the latest prosperity.' After a speech by the Lord Provost, two crystal bottles were deposited by the foundation stone. One held coins of the reign and the other the names of the city magistrates and a copy of each newspaper published in the city. The *Caledonian Mercury* newspaper was less than enamored by the choice of site, protesting at the time, 'Why should the Bridewell be built on Calton Hill? It is certainly reverting the order of things by putting a rogue above a gentleman.'

In early September 1795, the new Bridewell received its first inmate when Janet Symington was committed to a cell to undergo six months' solitary confinement and hard labour. At that time it was suggested the jail in Edinburgh could eventually be dispensed with and culprits sentenced to long terms housed in the proposed new prisons at Glasgow and Perth. It was reported that serious crimes such as murder and highway robbery in the County of Edinburgh were almost unknown. Stealing from houses, however, along with the theft of potatoes, turnips and poultry, were then common occurrences. Most of the petty thefts were committed by boys aged between 8 and 18 years old.

Mr Murray was appointed the first governor of the Bridewell. He was highly thought of, often spending his own money to buy the prisoners tobacco and snuff as a reward for good behaviour.

The report from the 'Committee on Petition of the Royal Burghs of Scotland Respecting the Providing of Jails' ordered by the House of Commons contained a lengthy account on the state of the Bridewell on Calton Hill in 1817. It perhaps gives the best contemporary insight of life in this institution:

> The prison consists of four stories or flats, besides the attic story, which is the hospital. In each of the four principal flats there are thirteen working cells, with an iron grating in front, looking inwards to the chapel and central inspection tower and thirty-six sleeping apartments, looking towards the exterior of the prison, there are thus in all fifty-two working cells and one hundred and forty-four sleeping rooms but of the latter a considerable portion are used for solitary working cells, for such prisoners as are specially sentenced to solitary confinement. The working cells are separated from the sleeping and solitary apartments by a vaulted passage running along the whole of the semicircular range in each flat, the whole is built of stone and each cell being arched over, there is no wood used in the construction of any part of the fabric except the door and the roof.
>
> The form of the house is very similar to that of the letter D, the cells occupy the semi-circular part and the rectilineal part is taken up by the stair cases, in the

centre is a semicircular tower, from the windows of which, looking across the chapel the prisoners are seen at work in the front working cells, without being aware when they are so inspected.

The kitchen and wash-house are separate buildings, placed on each side of the main entrance and immediately in front of the principal building. The Governor's House is upon the northern boundary wall and the space between the latter and the prison is laid out in gardens, courts and airing ground for the prisoners. The prison is supplied with water from the city's general reservoir which is received in two large cisterns situated at the top of the building, one on the east and the other on the west wing, from whence it is distributed in pipes to the several flats and offices.

Each of the sleeping cells is furnished with an iron bedstead, a straw mattress, a pair of blankets, a sheet and a woollen rug. When prisoners are committed, they are stripped of every article that belongs to them, their hair cut close, bathed, cleaned and habited in the clothing of the prison, this consists of a coarse linen shift. Apron and cap, woolen petticoat, gown of drugget [a course fabric of blue and white cotton], coarse woollen stocks, list shoes and a night cap, for the male prisoners.

The articles they bring in with them (of which a regular inventory is made in presence of the prisoner) are cleaned, washed, labelled and safely kept till the expiry of their sentences, when they are all returned.

The allowance of provisions to each prisoner is as follows:- bread, from wheat ground over all without any of the bran being taken out, made up in loaves of the size of twelve to the weight of a quartern loaf (i.e. about 5¾oz each), two of these loaves to each prisoner weekly, viz, one on Wednesday and the other on Saturday, to dinner. Prisoners sentenced to be fed on bread and water only, have three of these loaves daily:- Oatmeal, two thirds of a pound avoirdupois, per diem for each prisoner, one half made into a chopin (quart) of porridge for breakfast and the other half into a similar quantity for supper:- Barley, four ounces avoirdupois, per diem, for each prisoner, made into a Scotch pint (two quarts) of broth for dinner, six days in the week, when potatoes are not in use, but only three days weekly during the potatoe season:- Potatoes, three pounds avoirdupois per diem, three days in the week, during the potatoes season, made into a Scotch pint of soup for each prisoner:- Cheese, four ounces avoirdupois to each prisoner every Saturday for dinner, the quality to be equal to soft Kanter or Dutch old milk:- Beer, one half pint English measure per diem to breakfast and one English pint every Saturday, for each prisoner to dinner:- Salt, one ounce per diem to each prisoner six days in a week and half an ounce to each on Saturday, cheese and beer being given out that day for dinner:- Flesh, usually cow or ox heads, at the rate of thirteen pounds Dutch weight, for every prisoners on Sundays and the same quantity for every thirty prisoners on Wednesdays, or as near as possible to these respective quantities, the broth and potato-soup during the rest of the week are made from the fat skimmed off the Sunday and Wednesday's dinners:- vegetables, from the garden as necessary and as in season.

The prisoners are employed in spinning, knitting stockings, picking oakum, weaving linen, cotton and woollen stuffs, making list shoes, sewing, etc. When prisoners bred to handicraft trades are in custody, they are employed as required for the use of the prison, in carpenter-work, cooper-work, smith-work, shoe-making, painting, white-washing. Some of the most trusty of the female prisoners are set apart for cooking, washing and cleaning the prison and the garden is also cultivated by the labour of the prisoners; almost all of it is made up by them.

Whipping or other corporal punishment for any misbehaviour or offence committed within the prison is not permitted by the Act without a warrant from the magistrates of Edinburgh, the sheriff or one or more of the justices of the peace for the county, proceeding upon a written complaint at the instance of a governor and a regular proof on oath in presence of the prisoner complained upon; but to preserve subordination, the governor is empowered to punish refractory prisoners by a temporary diminution of the ordinary allowance of provisions, solitary confinement on bread and water, putting in fetters, etc., but the last seldom occurs.

The chaplain performs divine service once every Sunday and Wednesday and during the Lord's day, the prisoners are employed in catechizing, reading the Bible, etc., in classes of six or eight in a cell. They have then also an occasional relaxation, when the weather permits, by being allowed to walk in one of the courts of the prison, in such numbers as the governor directs, under the charge of the turnkeys. When the chaplain visits the prison on Wednesday, he gives an exhortation and a prayer; and those prisoners who are considered to be in a dying state, he reckons it an important part of his duty to visit often and specially. Many youths of both sexes are prisoners who cannot read; The utmost pains is taken to instruct them as far as can be, every attempt is made to improve the morals of the prisoners in general. Prisoners are occasionally to be found fitted to instruct young persons in reading but in order to produce uniformity and method, it has been judged more expedient to hire a person to teach them regularly two hours every day.

The governor has a discretionary power to reward prisoners who are exemplary in their conduct and industrious, by an extra allowance of provisions, while in custody and a small gratuity in money or clothes at liberation, where no money is due upon their accounts.

Seclusion from friends being a principal part of the punishment intended by the Bridewell, no person is permitted to visit a prisoner without a special order in writing from one of the commissioners or the magistrate by whose warrant the prisoner was committed and that only on one day of the week, between the hours of ten and twelve forenoon, nor are supplies of provisions or other articles allowed to be brought in or sent by the friends and relatives of prisoners, that all may be on a footing with respect to diet and clothing.

The Bridewell attracted a number of distinguished visitors who were interested in prison reform and the welfare of those confined in them.

James Neild inspected it in the early years of the nineteenth century and Joseph Gurney, accompanied by his sister Elizabeth Fry, made the following observations after their tour of it on 5 September 1818:

From the Jail we passed on to the Bridewell, the two buildings being situated close together – The latter we saw under great disadvantage, for in consequence of its being under repair, the prisoners were shut up in their sleeping cells, instead of being at work as is usually the case. The plan of this prison is very celebrated, on account of its affording an opportunity of inspection into the several apartments, in which the prisoners work and pass the day. This important object has been effected by the prison's being built in the form of a semicircle, in the centre of which is a watch tower.

Joseph Gurney went on to make the following suggestions for improvements:

The first is, that the semicircular arrangement of the working cells, at the same time that it is so well calculated for the purpose of inspection, enables the prisoners to see out of one cell into another and thus gives the opportunity, notwithstanding much watchfulness on the part of the keepers, of improper or dangerous conversation. The second is that the doors and windows of every two night cells are so near to one another that the prisoners can converse freely together after they are locked up for the night. This of course they do and without … detection or prevention. The third and principal source of evil is the inadequacy of the prison in the point of size. There are in it only 52 working rooms and 144 sleeping cells; it being not intended for not more than 144 prisoners; but the persons committed to the Bridewell are at all times so very much more numerous, that both sleeping and working cells are very improperly crowded.

This gives rise, of course, to much evil communication and greatly impedes the system of labour, on the regularity of which the use of the Bridewell mainly depends.

To meet this exigency, additional buildings are absolutely necessary. Were the present Bridewell appropriated to females and another house of correction built for men, the existing want of accommodation would be remedied and that complete separation between the sexes, which is of such essential consequence, would in the best possible manner be effected.

Much benefit might also arise both in the Bridewell and the Jail at Edinburgh, from their being regularly visited by a committee of benevolent and independent persons, who might provide instruction for the ignorant and employment for the idle and might exercise over the prisoners individually that kind and Christian care, which would be the most likely means of introducing them, not only into serious reflection, but into habits of virtue and respectability.

In 1822 treadwheels were installed which could provide 'employment' for thirty prisoners sentenced to hard labour. One of their functions was to assist in the manufacture of corks. At that time there were plans to double this number.

A report by the Committee on the Bridewell stated that the average number of prisoners confined in it during 1828 was 162, compared with 287 in a similar institution in Glasgow. The previous year it had been 184. It related that, 'It was believed that a great deal of good was accomplished among the prisoners by the zealous exertions of the teacher, whose time was now wholly devoted to the improvement of the unfortunate beings who are consigned to that penitentiary.' There were, however, signs around this time that matters were beginning to go seriously wrong. In 1827 it had been stated that the Bridewell was in a deplorable state and there had been no improvement in the following year. There was a great shortage of room and prisoners were obliged to sleep two to a bed. Discipline was difficult to enforce, solitary confinement was impossible, and the inmates could speak to each other despite being in different cells.

While in its early years the Bridewell appears to have been well run, its management came under investigation in early 1829. Serious allegations were also made in the *Caledonian Mercury*, including that an old man from Sweden was confined in his cell for twenty days without a change of linen. It was claimed that he had eventually died in his cell. Another female foreigner was believed to have been kept for sixty days in the Black Hole (punishment cell) with only straw to lie on. During her confinement she did not receive breakfast and was threatened with discipline by whipping. Another prisoner, John Russell, was put in the Black Hole while suffering from diarrhoea, where he lay for three days and three nights on the cold stones. He was thereafter removed to the hospital ward but died six days later. A boy named John Ross was also confined in the Black Hole for eight days with buckets of water being thrown over him as a punishment.

There was, however, no doubt about the treatment of a young man named John S. Todd who was brought to the police office on 1 May 1829. Here he was physically examined after spending thirty days in the Bridewell for begging. What was discovered was shocking: the former inmate was described as being an entire mass of disease. From head to toes he was covered in vermin and was in a state of extreme debility. While in the Bridewell, Todd received no change of linen, nor did he receive water to wash with. Furthermore, he was also unable to shave. At one stage the prisoner became sick and was in great distress but the turnkeys denied his request for medicine.

At the police office he fortunately received much better treatment. They gave him water and soap to wash with and the clerk of police collected donations so the unfortunate man could be gifted with new clothes.

As a consequence of these disclosures the governor was removed and replaced by James Kirkwood, captain lieutenant of police, on 1 July 1829. The following year the visiting justices to the Bridewell reported that it was well managed and that the prisoners had no complaints. There were fifty-one males and fifty-three females in the institution when it was inspected. Neither the Bridewell nor Calton Prison would suffer from such mismanagement again.

3

THE CONSTRUCTION OF CALTON PRISON

In the early years of the nineteenth century, the proposal for a new prison for Edinburgh received a new momentum when the government offered £10,000 towards its construction. The intention was to establish a national prison for Scotland. The obvious choice for its location was on Calton Hill next to the Bridewell, as the council already owned the land here.

An alternative proposal was put forward in a report by William Rae, the sheriff. In his report a number of sites were examined, including the possibility of locating it in the Old Town behind Parliament House or on the northern slopes of Castlehill next to Ramsay Gardens. However, a location on the sloping bank on the south side of Princes Street and near Canal Street was thought most appropriate. Its advantages were that it faced south and was easily accessible. The sheriff recommended that the Courts of Justice could also be located here with an ornamental entrance on Princes Street at the junction with South St David Street. It was suggested that the new prison could be situated behind it, on the lower slopes, making it less visible. Objections were raised and letters were written to the press pointing out that this ground, formerly occupied by the Nor Loch, was damp and unhealthy. It was near the valley bottom, which limited the amount of sunlight that would fall on the prison. This was an important factor when considering the location for as 'so very little fire can be allowed, the admission of the sun is essential to both health and comfort'.

The town council opted for Calton Hill despite its distance from the law courts next to the High Street, and in February 1814 preliminary steps were taken for placing the new prison on its slopes.

The building was designed by the Edinburgh architect Archibald Elliot, whose previous work included Stobo and Taymouth castles. It is hence not surprising that his plans for Calton Prison resembled a castle in the reign of Edward I, with a massive gatehouse facing onto Regent Road. Immediately behind it was a large symmetrical prison block. The whole site was enclosed by a curtain wall. On the south side it clung to the clifftop and large drum towers rose at intervals. The climax of the composition was the Governor's Tower, today the sole surviving part of the structure.

Lord Cockburn, however, was less than impressed with the scheme, commenting that, 'it had been a piece of undoubted bad taste to give so glorious an eminence to a prison'.

On 23 September 1815, 'the most brilliant procession which ever adorned the annals of masonry' assembled in the High Street. The dignitaries and representatives of over twenty Masonic lodges then set off to first lay a foundation stone for the Regent Bridge, which was going to cross a steep valley which had restricted access to Calton Hill. Once this was done the procession of round 2,500 persons made their way to the intended site of the new prison.

A foundation stone with a plaque was laid on the ground. The bands played tunes and songs were sung including 'Great Light to Shine'. Several speeches were made and the Lord Provost stated that:

> There is perhaps no city where it was more difficult than at Edinburgh, to find a proper situation for a prison, keeping in view the great object of attention to the health and special regard to the morals of those whom it is indispensable necessary for the preservation of order in society to confine them in.

Calton Prison was opened for the reception of prisoners in 1817. Regent Bridge on the road leading to it was not completed for a further two years when it was hurriedly opened for the entrance of Prince Leopold into the city. On the morning of Monday, 14 September 1817, twenty-five prisoners were removed from the Tolbooth and taken to their new home. A further four who were under sentence of death were placed in the new Lock-Up House, an annex of Calton Prison in the Lawnmarket. An area of ground to the east of the Bridewell had been set aside for building a separate debtors' prison. It was hoped that its construction would commence in the next few years. As an interim measure the Governor's House was to be used but this proposal does not seem to have been adopted. Various designs were drawn up but the scheme was hampered by a lack of funds.

In 1824 a 'royal inmate' arrived in the form of the equestrian statue of Charles II, which had stood in Parliament Square. It was later returned to its original position in 1835, where it still stands to this day.

At a general meeting of the Justices of the Peace in 1829, it was declared that there was adequate accommodation for the criminal prisoners in Calton Jail but not for the debtors who were in need of a separate prison. No money, however, was forthcoming from the council for a new building. Ten years later in late 1838, matters were reaching a crisis point. Governor Rose wrote a letter to the council drawing their attention to the crowded state of the prison. There were 206 prisoners and only fifty-eight cells. Consequently, as many as fifteen prisoners had to sleep in the day rooms and the same number in the chapel. Part of the problem was due to the great number of prisoners awaiting trial being confined with its walls. Some remained there for several months before their case was even heard in court. It was decided to transfer the debtors to the jail in the Canongate Tolbooth to alleviate the problem. Further relief came with the opening of the general prison at Perth in 1842. This in some ways superseded Calton Prison's role as the National Prison of Scotland. Prisoners sentenced to long jail terms would now be sent here. Throughout its history, only a very small number of those that ended up inside Calton Prison spent more than a few months at a time inside it. Those convicted of serious crimes were transported overseas and, when this form of punishment came to an end, they were dispatched to a convict prison, often in England.

In the early 1840s the architect Thomas Brown was given a brief to design a debtors' prison for the vacant ground to the east of the Bridewell. He specialized in prison buildings and his other work included Ayr, Dornoch, Dunfermline and Inverness prisons. Construction commenced on Calton Hill in 1844. An advertisement appeared in *The Scotsman* newspaper for plumbers, gas fitters, plasterers, masons, carpenters, glaziers and smiths. The new structure was built to resemble a medieval fortress like the earlier prison. It had a huge gatehouse with towers at its eastern end. The idea of this was to provide a separate entrance for the debtors from the criminal prisoners. The new structure, however, became part of Calton Prison with only a small part of the new accommodation being given over to debtors. During its construction Thomas Brown had a dispute with the local prison board, who desired the battlements to resemble those of the earlier prison buildings. The architect, however, wished them to be plain and, as a consequence, leading Scottish architect David Rhind – whose work included designing commercial banks and churches – was left to finish the project. It was rumored that Thomas Brown had contemplated replacing the Bridewell with a central round tower or keep not unlike that at Windsor Castle, forming a commanding centrepiece to the whole group of buildings. *The Scotsman* newspaper in September 1850 was full of praise for the completed scheme:

> We have often gazed with high admiration and all the feelings which natural and artistic picturesqueness can suggest on the grand fortress-looking mass of buildings which crown the precipices of Calton Hill. In no other city in the world does an abrupt precipice rise up from the centre of a mass of houses of dense population to give such a rock its characteristic crown of a vast embattled fortress which might be supposed in old feudal days to have protected and commanded the town.

No sooner had the new east wing to Calton Prison been completed than consideration was given to further increasing its capacity. The Lord Provost of Edinburgh blamed the ever-increasing numbers of those locked up 'on the fact that the present discipline in our prisons was of such a nature that the criminals entertained not the slightest dread but on the other hand courted punishment'. He believed it was all owing to the comfort with which criminals were treated. 'Unless some check were put on this system they would soon find one half of the people of Scotland in and the other out of prison.' The architect Mr Rhind drew up alternative plans in early 1854 to provide additional cells by either taking down the Bridewell and erecting a new building which would provide seventy cells or construction of a new block behind it with a 120 cells. The pressure on accommodation in Calton Prison, however, was alleviated with the passing of the MacKenzie Act, in which public houses in Scotland became regulated and were no longer allowed to open on Sundays. So effective was this measure in reducing crime that the average daily numbers of prisoners dropped from 579 to 359 and there was no longer a pressing need for further cells to be added to Calton Prison.

A fire broke out at the prison on 29 June 1858. Two fire engines arrived promptly and within an hour the flames were extinguished. While the washing and cooking department was extensively damaged, fortunately no one was injured. The cause was believed to have been one of the kitchen fires overheating.

As far back as the 1830s there had been criticism of the accommodation provided for female prisoners held in the Bridewell. One authority then described it as a 'cauldron of contamination'. Eventually the Home Office was drawn into this controversy, writing to the Edinburgh Prison Board in 1870 and complaining about the unsatisfactory accommodation in large parts of Calton Prison. Particular attention was drawn to the small, badly ventilated cells in which many women were held. Often there were two to a cell, when regulations stated that there should only be one. In defence, Edinburgh's Lord Provost retorted that the prisoners were well kept and that is was no punishment at all to be shut up in its cells! Matters, however, were brought to a head when in the early 1870s new prison regulations came into force which required cells to have 800 cubic feet of space for each prisoner. Ever reluctant to spend money on new prison buildings, the County of Edinburgh Prison Board did everything they could to delay any improvements. They protested to the Secretary of State in 1880 that the claim of inadequate accommodation in Calton Prison was erroneous.

Eventually, the government got their way and the Edinburgh Prison Board was forced to undertake major reconstruction work on its buildings.

Architect and engineer to the Scottish Prison Department, Major-General Collinson was given the task of enlarging and redeveloping Calton Prison. He was formerly responsible for planning Barlinnie Prison at Glasgow. In 1879 he submitted a report on Calton Prison's potential for improvement and then a review of the current state of its buildings. It provides a good account of the structures that comprised the prison in late Victorian times:

> The Calton Prison is situated on the South Side of the Calton Hill at a level of about 230 feet above the Sea, overlooking the ravine separating the Old Town from the New Town. Towards the ravine the rocky ground falls precipitously from the prison walls but on the other side the Calton Hill rises to 350 feet. On the west side is an old burying ground. Thus the prison is well situated as regards access and open space around it; but it has the disadvantages of being overlooked from the Calton Hill which is open to the Public. The total area now occupied by the prison is about 3 1/3 acres.
>
> The Calton Prison consists of 4 distinct blocks of buildings, The centre or Bridewell, The West Division, The Little Prison and the East Division.
>
> The Bridewell was the first prison building erected on this site, about 1792 and the Town agreed to give 6 acres for the purpose; it appears to have cost nearly £12,000 which the Government contributed.
>
> The plan is a Semicircle, having a central hall open to the roof and 4 tiers of cells on the circumference, having the ends to the hall filled in with iron bars: behind these and divided by a narrow passage are small cells for sleeping only: the prisoners being intended to work by day in the larger front cells. It is therefore not suited to the separate system of confinement, the back cells being too small and the front cells admitting of a certain amount of association. Moreover the back cells are imperfectly warmed by stoves in the passage and ventilated only by windows and it would be expensive to alter the building to remedy these defects and after all it would be an inconvenient and imperfect prison. There are no means of communication between the prisoners in their cells and the warders.
>
> I consider therefore that if the Calton Prison is retained, the whole of this building would have to be removed and replaced by a proper prison. [This recommendation was undertaken.]
>
> The West Division was erected about 1816 by the Town and County Prison Authorities at an expense of about £28,000 including boundary walls of which the Government contributed £10,000. The whole area now enclosed by the prison walls was enclosed about the same time and in 1842 the Town acknowledged the right of the Prison Board to that area, based on the original grant by the Town.
>
> It is a building of three stories and an attic, a central passage in each storey with cells on each side; each passage is sealed with stonework and as the ventilating chambers pass along in the ceilings, this cannot be easily altered.
>
> The warming is from coils of hot water pipes on the ground floor by which each passage is heated and the air is led from them into the cells above under the cell floors. The extracting flues are near the ceilings in the inner walls and

led under the passage of the floor above, to a general shaft in the centre of the building at the bottom of which is a fire. The windows all open. The warming of the ground floor requires improvement which can easily be done. There are no means of communication between the prisoners and warders and no regular water closets. A hundred of the small cells could be converted into fifty good cells for about £200.

The Little Prison was erected about the same time as the west block, for a treadmill on the ground floor and a storey of cells above. In this floor there is a central passage with cells on each side. The cells are all small and the only ventilation is the window, the passage is warmed by a cockle stove in the basement and there are small holes above each cell door to let the warm air in.

The East Division – This was erected about 1846, it was begun as a civil prison and the east gate was constructed to give it a separate entrance.

The building cost about £12,000. There is a central hall extending the whole length of the building and three stories high with corridors or galleries to each tier of cells. The cells are all of good size, well lighted and warmed and ventilated.

They are warmed by hot water pipes under the floor of hall, with separate channels to each cell opening near the floor in the outer wall. The extracting flues in each cell are near the ceiling in the inner wall and go up to a general shaft at the east end of the building, at the bottom of which is a fire grate.

The communication between prisoners and warders is by wire and label at each cell with a gong on each floor. There are no regular water closets.

(Excerpt from Edinburgh (Calton) Prison, memorandum by General Collinson on reconstruction, 1879 (HH8/12) reproduced with permission from the National Records of Scotland)

The decision was taken to upgrade Calton Prison rather than establish a new prison on the outskirts of Edinburgh as suggested by Major-General Collinson.

To make way for the new buildings, the elegant Bridewell was torn down and in its place two large rectangular cell blocks erected. Much of the stone of the demolished buildings – which included the Little Prison – was incorporated in the new works. In February 1883, workmen unearthed the foundation stone of the Bridewell along with a bottle of coins that had been place beside it. After some discussion it was decided to deposit them back in the ground, underneath the new buildings. *The Scotsman* newspaper was full of praise for the new buildings:

Externally both blocks reproduce the leading architectural characteristics of the surrounding buildings but the Scottish Baronial Style has been followed in a more ornate degree. Internally, on the other hand, the buildings are constructed in accordance with the most recent ideas of prison administration. The cells rise in tiers or storeys on each side of a spacious central corridor which is lighted from the roof and from mullions and transomed windows at either end. Entrance from the cells is obtained from galleries, run on brackets, at different floor levels and reached from the corridor by staircases on each side. Especial attention has been given to the subject of ventilation and the square corner turrets which give a great deal of character to the exterior appearance of the buildings are made to serve the purposes of shafts, through which the vitiated atmosphere is drawn off.

The West Division, which was the original jail, was reconstructed to increase the room for the female prisoners that were to be held in it. The East Division, on the other hand, required few alterations.

The other major change was that to the boundary wall next to Regent Road, which was taken down and reconstructed by a more elegant piece of masonry some 18ft in height. A new gateway was constructed to the east of the former one. To increase security an inner gateway was added. Between the two there was space to accommodate a prison van. The outer door would be closed before the inner door was opened so that a 'rushing' of the gates would be out of the question. A high wall was also erected next to the old Calton burial ground to enhance security.

After seven years of reconstruction, some of the new buildings were ready for occupation in late 1887, with all work being completed in the following year. This would be the final form of Calton Prison. No more major work was undertaken to its structures until its closure nearly forty years later. The enlarged prison was now the only one of any significance in south-east Scotland as those at Haddington, Linlithgow and Selkirk had been closed.

In the autumn of 1890 it was again reported that there were more male prisoners than cells for them!

4

PRISON LIFE

Joseph Gurney and his sister Elizabeth Fry visited Calton Prison in addition to the Bridewell on 5 September 1818 while on their tour of northern England and Scotland. At this time the prison had only been open for a year. They recorded their impressions of this jail, which has given a useful insight into life inside it:

> The plan of this new and extensive building is very similar to that of the prison in Horsemonger Lane, London. The ground-floor is divided into seven each containing a good day-room and a courtyard, the court-yards meeting in a point, at which is placed an octagonal watch-house. Above the watch-house, on a steep hill impending over the prison, is the Governor's House, from which there is a complete inspection over several yards, but not into the day rooms of the seven compartments, one is attached to the infirmary, one is for debtors, one for women criminals, one for untried men and three for male convicts. In the upper stories of the building are the night cells ranged on both sides of long galleries. These cells are airy and the bedding sufficiently plentiful. Some of them are allotted to prisoners under sentence of death and are distinguished from others by a long iron bar fixed in the wall, to which these persons are fastened by chains. The jailer considers this provision necessary to his own safety: the experience, however, of almost all other prisons is sufficient to prove him mistaken; and so cruel a mode of confinement appears to be particularly objectionable in Scotland, because in that country six weeks elapse, in capital cases between condemnation and execution. On being introduced to the kitchen, which is much too small for its purpose, we tasted the food prepared for the prisoners and found it excellent. They have porridge and half a pint of beer in the morning, porridge again in the evening and for dinner broth composed of barley, other vegetables and ox-head. Besides their food, they have three pence per day in money and are allowed firing; also shirts, stockings and shoes, but no other articles of clothing, except in cases of emergency. The prisoners in this jail are not ironed, except in case of refractory conduct and when under sentence of death. The infirmary is commodious and

is regularly attended by the surgeon – there is also a small room fitted up for the reception of infectious cases.

A Bible is placed in every sleeping cell; the clergyman attends twice a week to officiate in the chapel and care is taken that those who are ignorant of reading should have the opportunity of being instructed. Much pains are taken in this prison to ensure cleanliness. The prisoners wash themselves every morning and have a change of shirt weekly, their blankets are cleaned monthly. The whole prison is white-washed once every year: it appeared to us in all parts exceedingly clean and neat.

The divisions of the building on the ground floor afford very considerable opportunity for classification which however does not appear to be carried to so great an extent as is desirable.

The juvenile offenders, of whom we were much concerned to observe a large number, were not separated from those of maturer years and more confirmed criminality. Neither was there any classification attempted with the women who were all together day and night; for in consequence of their night cells being so placed as to afford the opportunity of conversation with the men, they were under the necessity of sleeping in their day-room. This was an evil of no small magnitude and I am happy to understand, is now corrected.

Much as there is in this large prison of order and good management, it is quite deficient in one great point of vital importance. There are no work-rooms in it and no provision for the employment of the prisoners. The consequence is, that they pass their tedious days in total idleness; and as they are necessarily kept in companies, there is no criminal in jail, who has not the fullest opportunity of corrupting and being corrupted.

In August 1831, the *Reading Mercury* reported: 'A Scotch tourist after remarking upon the filthiness which unfortunately prevails in many parts of the country but especially in the Highlands declares that the gaol at Edinburgh is the cleanest place he met with on his journey.'

As that decade drew to a close, new regulations were introduced setting the standards for the remainder of the century. Much of the corruption and bad practices – including gambling, swearing, drunkenness, cheating and stealing – among the prisoners had been suppressed. A silent system was introduced to reduce conversation; a common complaint among those that visited the prison had been the level of noise in it. Such a measure was only partially successful as inmates were still able to converse with each other. A few years later a prison inspector commented on the amount of talking, whistling and singing that went on in the female quarters. A prison uniform was made compulsory and no one was now allowed to retain their own clothes. Visits were restricted and the sale of food and liquor was banned. By the early 1840s, the original prison buildings were improved and upgraded.

Gas lighting had now been installed throughout the complex. Up until then most prisoners got up before daylight in the winter and went to bed at four o'clock in the afternoon. Some of the criticisms made by John Gurney had been rectified. The additional cell accommodation allowed for the classification and separation of prisoners. Inmates were put to work instead of lying idle all day. This initially included oakum picking, which was a task sometimes used as a punishment for disobedient prisoners. It involved inmates being given quantities of old tarry rope that they had to painstakingly unpick into individual strands for recycling. There was also stocking weaving, with seventeen looms in operation in 1843. Other employment included mat making, shoe making, tailoring, knitting, sewing, and stone breaking. There was, however, little opportunity for outdoor work due to the confined site of Calton Prison. Some of the inmates were involved in its reconstruction between 1881 and 1888. For their work, the prisoners received a small payment. Many were very glad of the opportunity to earn some money. The prison staff also ensured that their charges got adequate exercise outside in the airing yards. In 1843, both a regime of military exercises and a diet recommended by the General Board of Prisons were introduced. During the early years of Calton Prison it was not unusual for some public-minded person to give donations towards giving the prisoners a special dinner at Christmas and New Year. Governor Sibbald received mutton, bread and vegetables on 1 January 1820 from a gentleman who had made similar gifts in previous years. Two pounds was received in early 1827 to provide additional clothing for the poorest inmates. A small library was established in 1840 to encourage literacy among the prisoners. Prior to this there was a meagre collection of books in the prison.

While whipping was frequently used as a punishment in mid-Victorian penitentiaries, it was almost unknown in Calton Prison. A treadwheel had been installed for such purposes but was done away with by the late 1840s as they fell into disrepute with Scottish prison officials. Around the same time the Dark Cell, in which prisoners who proved troublesome were placed, was also abolished.

The favoured form of punishment was the crank machine, of which there were six in number by 1851. This involved turning a lever in a revolving motion on a machine that had no function other than to exhaust its operator! An example of its effectiveness as a deterrent to criminals was given three years later in a report quoted in the *John O'Groat Journal* of 2 June 1854. One ex-offender who had spent about sixteen years of his life in Calton Prison had:

> ... after a first experience of the crank, remained absent four months during which time the wooden bed had been introduced, after the expiry of his next sentence, he bade the Governor 'Good Bye', complaining bitterly of the hardship of being obliged to change his profession and work for his bread after spending so many years of his life so comfortably.

The Prison Inspectors' report for 1868 stated that all the cells possessed lighting, heating and ventilation. The inmates rose at six o'clock and went to bed at nine o'clock. Most were put to work during the day, with some being employed in cooking and cleaning. All convicted prisoners were required to sleep on a guard bed – which had pillows made out of wood – for the first month unless exempted by the surgeon. He reported that:

> I attend the prison every day and visit all who are complaining and inspect all the prisoners twice a week, the general health of the prisoners has been very good and no epidemic has taken place during the year. The provisions are of good quality and the general dietary sufficient in ordinary cases and not more than sufficient, for those employed in hard labour, the clothing and bedding are sufficient, the warming and draining are satisfactory.

The chaplain performed three services on Sunday and read prayers to the prisoners on the other days of the week. He called on the prisoners in their cells frequently and the sick in hospital daily. Throughout the nineteenth century, church ministers from parishes around Edinburgh played a major part in the life of Calton Prison, visiting it often to provide advice to its inmates and support the work of the chaplain. In 1868, a schoolteacher and schoolmistress provided daily lessons to the prisoners, many of whom could hardly read or write.

By the end of the nineteenth century, there was criticism that conditions had been improved to such a degree that the prisoners were living a life of luxury. At a meeting of Falkirk Town Council in 1898, Bailie Cook Rennie said he had visited Calton Prison during that year: 'It was in splendid condition and the prisoners were well treated – in fact too well treated and they all seemed happy. The Prison was like a palace.'

David Lyon, who retired in 1923 after fifty years' service as depute town clerk, recalled visiting the debtors' apartments in Calton Prison:

> ... where he said was to be seen the same kind of life which Dickens [the novelist] described. All kinds of people were there in a great common room where their friends were allowed to supply them with food. He had seen them before a well set board, sitting down to a grilled steak with a bottle of beer while others played cards.

Debtors were classed as civil prisoners and the regulations for them were far more lax than that for criminal prisoners. They were not, for example, obliged to undertake any work while confined in prison.

5

THE PRISON GOVERNORS AND WARDERS

Thomas Sibbald was appointed the first prison governor of Calton Prison when it opened in 1817. Previously he had been in charge of the old prison in the Tolbooth. Unfortunately, however, he died suddenly on 21 May 1822. According to the *Caledonian Mercury* newspaper:

> In discharging the duties of his office, Mr Sibbald was remarkably humane and conscientious. He was father to the prisoners under his charge and grudged no trouble to serve them. His familiarity with misery had not in the least degree hardened the natural tenderness of his heart which was continually displayed in acts of kindness to the wretches, so that his death may well be considered as a public loss. His active and unaffected benevolence where benevolence is so much wanted will not be easily supplied.

At a meeting of the town council on 29 May 1822, James Young, lieutenant of police, was unanimously appointed as the new governor of Calton Prison. Two years later he was at the centre of a court case in which Peter McFarline, a lieutenant in the 91st Regiment, attempted to sue him for £1,000 in damages.

While imprisoned for debt he alleged that on 10 June 1822 he was dragged out of bed and assaulted by two men on the instructions of the prison governor, James Young. Further to this he was locked in a cell for common criminals without bed or bedclothes for two days. The jury, however, ruled in favour of James Young. Over the next few years there was a series of escapes from Calton Prison for which Governor Young was held responsible. In 1826 he was transferred to the much smaller Canongate Prison, which was located in the Tolbooth not far from Holyrood Palace.

With accommodation becoming increasingly scarce in Calton Prison, in 1838 the town council decreed that the Canongate Tolbooth should in future act as a relief for it and only house debtors. Captain Rose replaced James Young as the governor of Calton Prison in 1826. He continued in this position until the Bridewell and Calton Prison were merged in 1840. It was then decided that a new governor should be appointed and John Smith became the governor of the newly enlarged prison in 1842. Unlike most of the men appointed to this position – who were military men nearing the end of their careers – he was an unusual choice: born in Hawick, Smith originally served an apprenticeship as a joiner. Later he came to Edinburgh, where he was soon appointed one of the city missionaries and thereafter was made governor of the House of Refuge.

Smith's appointment to the post of governor turned out to be a shrewd choice. Smith may well have been the most enlightened of all the governors of this prison; he investigated the reasons as to why people ended up as criminals. Alcohol was attributed to be one of the main causes and he took part in campaigns to curb its influence. Meanwhile the number of children imprisoned in Calton Prison was substantially reduced by the late 1840s.

With the establishment of a national prison service in Scotland, many staff took the opportunity to move to new appointments in other regions. Not so with John Smith. He served as governor of Calton Prison for thirty-three years. When he died suddenly on 7 November 1875, at the age of 71, he was still working despite being in poor health. The *Edinburgh Evening News* wrote the following in his obituary:

> All along he took great interest in the prisoners under his charge and exerted himself to reclaim them from their vicious habit. He had always a word of kindly encouragement to say to them and knowing that one of the best means of reclaiming a man from his vicious ways was to put him in the way of earning an honest livelihood, he exerted himself to find employment for those who expressed a desire to reform their lives. In this way he was the means of restoring very many to respectable positions in society who would otherwise have gone on to swell the criminal ranks. His success in this good work was most apparent amongst those who had just entered a criminal career. Many lads he assisted to emigrate and not a few kept up regular correspondence with him from their adopted homes.

When the Bridewell and Calton Prison were merged in 1840, it was not only decided to have one governor but also one surgeon, chaplain and schoolmaster in place of two. Dr Simpson was appointed the medical officer for the city, including the Lock-up House and police cells. His salary was to be £80 per year. Mr Hislop, a member of the established church, was appointed chaplain to the united prisons. For this he was to receive £120 per year on condition that he devoted all his time to prison work. Mr Mitchell, the chaplain of the Bridewell, could not be considered for this post as he had been a Dissenter. Instead he was appointed schoolmaster on a salary of £80 per year. Provision was also made for an assistant with a remuneration of £35 per year. To look after the female prisoners a matron was appointed. Her pay was £75 per year. New warders were employed and the old system of placing a felon to look after a felon abandoned. In 1841, there were sixteen male warders. Their remuneration was between 14s and 16s a week. For this they had to work fifteen hours a day and seven days a week. There were an additional nine female warders. Other prison staff consisted of two watchmen, three clerks and four cooks. An extract of the inspectors' report on Scottish prisons that appeared in the *Caledonian Mercury* on 20 September 1841 stated:

> The Governor reports highly both of the matrons and states that all the warders, males and female and other subordinate officers are to the best of his knowledge, and belief, truthful, orderly and to the greater extent industrious, good-natured, kind and firm but some are not very intelligent. Others have no knowledge of a trade and that two of the female warders could not write. That upon the whole very few subordinate officers come up to the standard in the circular letter on the appointment of officers, which appeared in the second report of the General Board of Directors of Prisons and that eight of the male warders and five of the female warders are certainly below that standard, chiefly as respects intelligence.

With new legislation, the operation of Scottish prisons was becoming organised along increasingly professional lines and the level of standards raised.

In May 1868 the governor of Ayr Prison, Robert Sutherland, was found lying dead in his room at a public house in London. He had cut his throat with a razor. On the table nearby were notes lamenting that he had been living a life of wickedness, although there is little evidence of this, and he also stated that his brain and mind seemed paralysed. James Taylor, head warder and deputy governor of Calton Prison, was appointed the new governor of Ayr Prison.

After the death of John Smith in 1875, there were ninety-five candidates for the post of governor of Calton Prison. The Edinburgh prison board unanimously elected a Captain Christie to the post. He had served through the Indian Mutiny, taking part in the relief of Lucknow, Fort Rooyah, and other engagements. On leaving the army, Captain Christie was appointed deputy governor of Chatham Convict Prison in 1872.

In October of the same year the death of poet James Reed was announced. He had been born in Hawick in 1799 and after serving in the army moved to Edinburgh in 1825. For around ten years Reed had worked as a warder in Calton Prison before returning to his trade as a slater and eventually dying in poverty. The popular songs 'The Good Rhine Wine', 'The Stout Old Brigadier' and 'The Slogan of Freedom' were all penned by him.

One Saturday morning in April 1878 cleaner Mary McIntyre became a victim of crime after leaving Calton Prison. James McKay and John McAlpine approached

Mary and asked if she was a discharged prisoner, which she denied. Without warning the men dragged her back to the prison gate and put the same question to the warder on duty. The assailants said they wanted to know if she was a woman named Mary Lee for whom they had paid 7s 6d. For this action James McKay and John McAlpine ended up in Calton Prison themselves, being sentenced to a term of sixty days each. It was stated in court that it was not unusual for persons to prowl about the vicinity of the jail and set upon discharged prisoners when liberated.

Physical assaults on prison staff appear to have been relatively rare in the late nineteenth century and early twentieth century. One such instance, however, did occur in December 1901. John King, a stoutly built man, was walking in the exercise yard when one of the warders told him off for looking at the other prisoners. King took exception to this and grabbed the warder by the throat and struck him. The warder fought back and hit King with his baton. Other prison staff came to his assistance, one of whom was bitten, and it took six or seven warders to bring the situation under control. The prisoner had just about completed a sentence of six days when he launched this assault. At his trial it was disclosed that he had no less than twenty previous convictions for assault and had undergone sentences varying from a few days to three years' penal servitude. To this he could now add one of twelve months' imprisonment with hard labour. On hearing this, John King exclaimed to the judge, 'Thank you, sir. That is only a sleep for me. You will have to get a coffin for me yet.'

After twenty-five years as governor of Calton Prison, Captain Christie retired in 1900 at the age of 66. It was stated that 'during his tenure of office, he has effected many improvements for the welfare of the prisoners. Under his supervision, the average earnings of the prisoners has trebled and the cost of their upkeep has consequently been much reduced.'

Colonel Campbell, the governor of the general prison at Perth, was appointed to fill the position. Born in India some fifty-eight years earlier, he had followed a military career and developed an interest as a naturalist. While in pursuit of his studies he even made several expeditions into Tibet when it was a closed country. Unlike the previous century, the governors of Calton Prison only held their posts for a relatively short time. In 1907, Colonel Campbell was presented with a handsome cabinet at his retirement ceremony. He was praised for his efforts in trying to get work for discharged prisoners.

Campbell was replaced by the governor of Dundee Prison, Major William Stewart, who had at one time served in the Bengal Lancers. After he became ill and died in 1918, Major Raymond Munro – whose career started in the Highland Light Infantry – filled the position in 1919. He hade taken up prison work in 1909 and his first appointment was as deputy governor of Barlinnie Prison. During the First World War, Major Munro returned to military service and fought at the front in 1916. At the end of the conflict he resumed his career in the prison service with his appointment at Calton Prison. After returning from a holiday, on 5 July 1924 he too died suddenly from an illness that he had contracted while on active service.

Like Governor John Smith, first-class warder George Mears spent most of his working life at Calton Prison. He was a native of Weymouth, Dorset, and at the age of 20 he joined the Royal Navy. After five years' service he left and was appointed warder in the Scottish Prison Service at Edinburgh. Here he remained for thirty-six years until he retired in June 1913. During his career he had been present at no less than five executions: that of Chantrelle, the poisoner; of Jessie King, the baby farmer; of Herdman, who murdered his paramour in 1897; and of Vicars and Innes, the Gorebridge poachers. The three governors under whom he served thought highly of him owing to his humane and kindly disposition in this treatment of prisoners. During his thirty-six years' service, around a quarter of a million prisoners passed through the gates of Calton Prison. Commenting on the changes he had witnessed, George Mears stated that the harsher methods of the former days had given way to more humane treatment.

6

PUBLIC EXECUTIONS

When Calton Prison replaced the Tolbooth as the main prison of Edinburgh, it presented a problem for the authorities when it came to carrying out capital punishment. In the early nineteenth century the scaffold was erected on the west front of the old prison. Condemned prisons could walk directly from their cell through an opening in the wall and onto it. When it was decided to continue to carry out public executions in the High Street, a site was selected at the head of Liberton Wynd. A small prison known as the Lock-up located close by was constructed and administered as an annex of the new Calton Prison. Over the next half-century almost all condemned prisoners were transferred to it the night before their execution. It was not, however, its only function as it also accommodated a small number of criminals on short sentences. There were eight cells, four of sufficient size for the confinement of four prisoners in each and two prisoners in the others. It also possessed a kitchen and quarters for the keeper.

Robert Johnstone, aged 22, was the first of over twenty condemned persons to spend the last night of their life in the Lock-up House. At 2.40 p.m. on 30 December 1818, he was removed from it and stepped up onto the scaffold. His crime was to participate in a street robbery on John Charles, a candle maker. The death sentence still existed for many less serious crimes, including sheep stealing, in the early years of the nineteenth century. When the drop fell, Johnstone managed to rest his toes on the platform, as the rope was too short. The crowd responded by throwing stones at the executioner, and officials on the scaffold fled the scene. One of the spectators climbed onto the structure and cut Johnstone down; the crowd then carried him away. Order was only restored when soldiers arrived from the castle, but not before ten policemen had been injured. The condemned man was found and revived, only to be placed on the scaffold again. This time the hangman's rope was too long and Johnstone had to be raised up while it was shortened. When the drop came, he struggled for several minutes before expiring.

Five months later George Warden was also executed. He was a post office clerk and sentenced to death for stealing money from letters. This time a barrier lined by a large number of policemen had been erected around the scaffold to prevent a reoccurrence of the previous fiasco. While in Calton Jail he was visited frequently by his mother and 5-year-old sister. The Revd Porteous, the prison chaplain, accompanied Warden to the scaffold. A few seconds before the drop was opened, Warden fainted and was left swinging on the rope. The executioner quickly responded by pulling the lever for the drop.

In the opening days of 1820, the Lock-up House was used for its first double execution. Brine Judd and Thomas Clapperton, both in their early twenties, had broken into a house at Roadmains, near Borthwick. They attacked its owner and stole a silver watch, banknotes, a deposit book and a can of butter. Shortly before their execution they thanked the prison governor for the way he had treated them. During their confinement in Calton Prison they were kept in separate rooms so that they could perform their religious devotions according to their different faiths: Clapperton was a Protestant and Judd was a Roman Catholic.

On Tuesday, 4 January they were removed to the Lock-up House. On entering it the two men stopped for a few minutes beside the fire but then requested to be taken to the iron room, where they were to be chained for the night. Here they slept for a few hours before getting up at 4 a.m. when they received some tea and toast. Rain discouraged a large crowd from gathering to watch the execution.

Samuel Maxwell died on the scaffold on 17 January 1821 for breaking into a house near Neilston with several accomplices and stealing a gold watch, £9 in banknotes and other items. Initially they were held in Glasgow Prison but in early December 1820 were transferred to Calton Jail to await trial. A former soldier, Maxwell was the only member of the gang to receive the death sentence. On the night before his execution he wrote a brief record of his life.

Two years later, William McIntyre stood trial for breaking into a house belonging to Thomas Riddell in Grey Street and another in George Square, Edinburgh, with several other youths. The Lord Justice Clerk at their trial stated that 'it was absolutely necessary in their case to set an awful example to the youths who [were] instigated to these crimes by older people in order to screen themselves from punishment.' McIntyre, who was aged about 17, was sentenced to hang along with Charles McLaren, Thomas Grierson and James McEwen, who were all said to be about 14 years old. While in Calton Jail the latter three received a reprieve and had their sentences commuted to transportation to New South Wales for life. In the end only William McIntyre had to take his final steps up the scaffold on 26 February 1823.

Just under a year later there was a double execution, this time of John Wilson and Duncan Fraser. Both had pleaded guilty to breaking into a shop in St Mary's Wynd and stealing some articles of clothing. When executed, Wilson was aged 22 and Fraser 16. On hearing of the death of his son, Wilson's father lost his mind and had to be taken to an asylum.

The following month the local newspaper questioned the suitability of the Lawnmarket as the most appropriate place for public executions. It went on to argue that they should be held in Calton Prison. The scaffold, which was stored in sections under the North Bridge, had to be re-erected every time there was an execution. Its assembly during the night prior to an execution often kept the residents in its vicinity awake.

In February 1825, it was reported that a petition had been forwarded to the King for a reprieve for two young men under sentence of death. There were, in fact, numerous cases of prisoners who were awaiting their imminent demise in Calton Prison having their sentences commuted to transportation. The turnkey did not want the hopes raised of these two men and kept details of the petition secret. They, however, found out as their cells faced onto Calton Hill. Their friends climbed up on it and, using their fingers as a telegraph, put them in possession of the facts. Throughout the history of Calton Prison persons standing on the high ground opposite often passed information to prisoners in a similar manner or by simply shouting in their direction.

While walking home on the road from Dalkeith to Edinburgh from the Lauder Fair on 18 April 1826, James Hunter was attacked by three men who struck him from behind. He fell to the ground and they pulled out notes and silver from his pockets. Two women who were with him attempted to hold onto one of the attackers but were threatened and were forced to let him go. The following day James Renton and Andrew Fullerton were apprehended as suspects. Only the latter was found guilty at the trial and as robbery, like housebreaking, was then a capital crime he was sentenced to death. While in Calton Prison he was visited on several occasions by his wife and other relatives. He also devoted much of his time to reading the Scriptures. On the eve of his execution on 16 August he was removed from Calton Prison by coach to the Lock-up House. Here Andrew Fullerton spent a sleepless night. Just as the executioner was about to open the drop in the platform he passed out. Aged only 22 at the time, it was thought that he was the least guilty of the three robbers.

The practice of hanging those convicted of minor thefts faded away around 1830. Only those who had committed murder or other serious crimes now faced capital punishment.

William Adams was the last person to end up on the scaffold in Edinburgh for a minor theft. He was hanged on 17 March 1830 for robbing Michael Firnie of £1 4s and a tin of snuff. Although he was well known to the police he only had one previous conviction, for which he spent some time in the Bridewell. When the death sentence was passed leniency was requested in view of the age of the accused, who was only 20. The Lord Justice Clerk retorted, 'that from the way and manor [sic] the crime was committed, in the very centre of the city, it was absolutely necessary for public safety that an example should be made.' On the evening of his execution he was visited in the Lock-up House by his parents. During the night he woke up shivering but this was attributed more to the cold of the building than fear. After being taken out of the Lock-up House the hymn 'The Hour of Departure Has Come' was sung at the condemned man's request. He then gave a short speech to the crowd, imploring them not to keep bad company and to attend church. His last words were 'God bless you all'.

In 1832, the Punishment of Death Act abolished the death sentence for most crimes that did not involve murder or treason.

While the previous executions received little attention in British newspapers, in the late 1820s there were a number of horrific crimes committed in and round Edinburgh that shocked the nation. The most notorious were those of the body-snatchers William Burke and William Hare, who murdered no less than sixteen people in order to supply doctors with bodies to dissect. After their trial, Burke and his mistress Helen McDougal were removed to the Lock-up House, followed by Hare and his wife, Margaret Laird, who were lodged in a different apartment. Burke had hardly been seated when, looking round, he said to the officers who had him in their charge, 'This is a **** cold place you have brought me to.' When preparations were made for his removal to Calton Prison he requested the officers to visit him there. On being informed that there would be no admittance to him, he said, 'Well! Well! though I should never see you again, you will see me on the 28 January 1829 at the head of Liberton's Wynd. I have now only five weeks to live and I will not weary greatly for that day.' While in the Lock-up, he expressed his dread of being secured in iron chains in the condemned cell.

Hare and his wife were also transferred to Calton Prison where they were kept in close confinement in separate cells. They were liberated in early February after Hare gave evidence against his criminal associate, Burke. The *Durham County Advertiser* reported the following:

> As proof of the hardened indifference of Hare – on a visit of a party to the Jail lately he was walking in the yard. We had almost supposed this society would have been shunned even by felons but two other prisoners were walking with him. His companions pointed him out saying 'Here's Hare', looking at him. And when the eyes of the party were directed upon him, the wretch himself exclaimed in a tone of impudent levity 'Pitch a shilling this way, will ye.'

William Burke, Calton Prison's most famous prisoner, spent his last days reading books left by his spiritual advisers and talking freely about the murders he had committed. Heavily manacled and confined to the murderer's diet of bread and water, he was said to display an astonishing calmness. At the time it was reported in the *Sussex Advertiser* that he was also suffering from an unspecified excruciating disease.

One gentleman who visited him remarked that his cell was very cold. William Burke responded that 'since matters are come to this, I must just bear it all.'

On the morning of Tuesday, 27 January, he was removed to the Lock-up House in a coach accompanied by Governor Rose and an assistant. On having his iron manacles removed he exclaimed, 'So may all earthly chains fall from me.'

He slept soundly on the night before his execution and remained calm and composed to the end. A huge crowd said to number about 20,000 came to watch the execution. Once at the scaffold they yelled abuse at the condemned man, with cries of 'Burke him and do the same for Hare'. When the drop fell, Burke, dressed in black, struggled for several minutes, gasping for breath until he expired. On every convulsion, a large cheer arose from the crowd. The rope, perhaps, may have been deliberately too short.

Only a few months later, the citizens of Edinburgh were treated to a double execution, unusually of a husband and wife. It drew almost as large crowd as that of Burke's. John Stewart and Catherine Wright had been condemned for the murder of Robert Lamont on board the *Toward* steamboat on a passage between Tarbet and Glasgow. The couple had mixed a quantity of laudanum in his drink so that they could rob him, but before they could disembark the ship's captain detained them. There were allegations that John Stewart and Catherine Wright were responsible for several other robberies in which their victim had succumbed to poison. When John Stewart's first wife died in 1825, he embarked on a life of crime. Initially sheep stealing was his boldest enterprise but he then fell in with a gang of forgers. Deciding that there was less chance of detection alone, he cut his links with them and settled in Dumfries where he made his own molds to produce counterfeit currency. In a chance encounter with a former companion in crime, John Stewart was informed that a more profitable way to obtain money was to drug his victim and then rifle his pockets. His second wife Catherine Wright usually mixed the poison in the drink. Both were brought from Glasgow to Calton Prison for their trial, which took place on 14 July 1829. The couple were found guilty and sentenced to hang on 19 August. They were transferred from the prison to the Lock-up House in a coach accompanied by the governor. On meeting her husband again, Catherine Wright, who was only 22, wept and sobbed for hours. The following morning John Stewart complained of the cold in the building despite wearing a coat. Tea was offered to them and both were allowed to smoke tobacco from a pipe.

The couple were then lead to the scaffold dressed in black clothes given to them by the prison governor, Catherine Wright audibly repeating, 'Amen, amen'. Her face was then covered and the rope put about her neck. She expressed a wish to embrace her husband but, this being impossible, they shook hands, she saying, 'John, I trust we shall meet again in heaven.' When the fatal signal was then given, the crowd remained silent in the driving rain. The *Cambridge Chronicle and Journal* reported:

When all was ready and both were placed side by side upon the drop, they shook hands twice in an affectionate manner, bidding each other an eternal farewell upon earth. The unhappy woman expressed a desire to salute her husband. Stewart then offered up a short prayer, repeating again and again the same form of supplication, after which his wife prayed with great fervour and expressing her hope they would meet again in the regions of eternal bliss. When she had ended, at half past eight o'clock her husband gave the signal (by dropping a handkerchief) and in an instant they were launched into eternity, both dying almost without a struggle.

A horrific murder took place later in the year of a Mrs Franks and her 15-year-old daughter Madeline at their cottage, a short distance from Haddington. A neighbour who became concerned about them found Mrs Franks lying dead in the pigsty with her throat cut and Madeline lying in a room with the top of her head in pieces. John Lloyd, Superintendent of Police, found bloody shoe marks made by an iron heel and these were traced to Robert Emond, the murdered woman's brother-in-law. She had given him some boxes for safekeeping and a dispute had erupted over them.

At his trial Robert Tait, a prisoner who had been confined in the same cell in Calton Prison as Robert Emond, stated that in his sleep his companion frequently exclaimed, 'Oh, that wretched passion'. He had told him that for a long time he had had a comfortable life but he had recently quarrelled with his wife. Tait asked Emond if he had committed the murders to which he replied, 'Oh yes. But don't speak to me of it for it goes like a knife to my heart whenever I think of it.' At the conclusion of the trial Robert Emond was confined in the Lock-up House. Here he begged the turnkey for a drink of water and some bread, which he ate greedily. Later he was transferred back to Calton Jail in a hackney carriage. On his way to the condemned cell he repeated several times, 'God is just'. When he entered it and cast his eyes on the bed he exclaimed, 'I suppose you have been prepared for me during the day?' He was answered with, 'Not so, the preparations have only been made since the trial was completed.' Then, as still was the practice for condemned persons, he was secured by iron chains.

Robert Emond was executed on 17 March 1830. 'His struggles were unusually long and violent and it was apparently four or five minutes before the vital spark left him.' Several hundred spectators had come from Haddington and North Berwick to watch the hanging.

On 17 April 1830, a young woman named Margaret Paterson left Edinburgh to visit her parents in Dalkeith. While walking along the road she encountered carters David Dobie and James Thomson who offered her a lift in their cart. A short distance further on, near Gilmerton, the two men assaulted and raped her. So atrocious were her injuries that many newspapers refused to publish the details. Margaret lingered on in agony for a few days before passing away but not before she had given a detailed description of her attackers. The culprits were soon detained and were initially imprisoned in the Lock-up House. As in all cases of rape the trial was held behind closed doors. Although this charge was not proven, her attackers were sentenced to death for murder and robbery. At the end of the proceedings Lord Meadowbank commented:

> It is hardly possible to imagine that persons living in this Christian land could have brought their minds to the Commission of such atrocious crimes. Melancholy it is to think that, had this unprotected female been wandering the world among the most barbarous people she would have been in a state of comparative safety to what she was within three miles of the metropolis of this most civilized country. But such is the fact, that this poor and unhappy woman after having fallen into the hands of these abandoned men was treated in a manner which of necessity was to produce death. She was robbed of the miserable pittance which she had in her possession and this brutality was committed on a person on whom they had the intention of satisfying their still more brutal desires.

Dobie and Thomson were returned to the Lock-up House on the afternoon of 17 August 1830, the day before their execution. Here they spent a sleepless night and shortly after six o'clock the executioner pinioned them. Mr Fisher, deputy governor of the jail, offered them a drink of beer but Thomson refused. Dobie then remarked, 'Oh, I hope our fate will be a warning to that wicked race,' and turned to Governor Rose: 'O, Sir I hope you will protect and comfort my dear wife.' A large crowd watched their execution, among which included a high number of women.

Throughout the nineteenth century, substantial numbers of soldiers were locked up in Calton Prison. In the year September 1845–September 1846, no less than a hundred were detained in it. Many were detained for drinking and brawling in the High Street. Others had been caught trying to desert or had fallen foul of military regulations. While most of the crimes committed by soldiers stationed in Edinburgh were of a minor nature, an exception to this occurred in 1835 when, on 16 May, the 5th Dragoon Guards arrived at Piershill Barracks, located about a mile and a half to the east of Calton Prison.

The following day, Sunday, Private James Bell applied for leave of absence but his superior, Major Moorhead, said that no soldier would be allowed to leave the stables that day. At the evening roll call at seven o'clock that evening James Bell appeared brandishing a pistol. Without warning he opened fire at Major Moorhead who collapsed onto his right knee. James Bell proclaimed to the people now assembled at the scene, 'I shot the tyrant that tyrannized over the troop and me too.' The bullets had struck Major Moorhead in the back and he died from his injuries. The next day James Bell was handed over to the civilian authorities and taken to Calton Prison.

At his trial he pleaded insanity. When confined in Calton Prison, two of the prisoners he shared cells with believed he was not in his right mind. Charles Cameron was in the same cell as James Bell for nearly a month. He testified that the soldier had frequently called for his sword, his horse and then wondered why the officers did not bring them. The Lord Justice Clerk challenged these statements, stating that if the prisoner was insane, it was odd that they had not applied to the governor to have him removed from their cell. While in the army there had been no indication that James Bell had suffered from any form of mental illness. In fact he got on well with his colleagues and was a good soldier. The jury retired and within one minute returned a verdict of guilty. The prisoner was sentenced to death.

On Sunday, 12 July 1835, James Bell was removed from Calton Prison and transferred to the Lock-up House. The following morning, shortly before taking the condemned man to the scaffold, the executioner – John Williams – pinioned his arms. This was the usual practice for all prisoners about to be hanged. The executioner had difficulty in completing this task and astonishingly burst into tears and cried like a child. There was worse to come. As the party approached the scaffold the onlookers heckled the crying executioner. While making the final preparations for the hanging the crowd continued their ridicule. Mr Brown, the Superintendent of Works, intervened, pushing the incompetent executioner aside and making the final adjustments to the rope himself. After it was over stones were thrown at the executioner as he departed. The body of James Bell was cut down and placed in a coffin. A burial service was performed before he was buried within the precincts of Calton Prison.

Domestic violence was rife in the nineteenth century, the root cause, like much crime in Edinburgh, being drink. When brought to the attention of the authorities it did not go unpunished. For example, 'a stout elderly man of a dirty appearance' was placed at the bar for striking and maltreating his wife on 13 October 1837. While under the influence of drink he held his wife by her hair and beat her with a broom until she bled. It was his third appearance in court for assaulting his wife. He was sent to prison for sixty days at the treadmill.

Sometimes a brutal altercation under the influence of drink would have fatal consequences. In a murder committed far from Edinburgh, Charles McEwen was accused of battering his common-law wife to death on a lonely road at Firmouth, Aboyne, in Aberdeenshire in the autumn of 1823. The couple had travelled the country selling tea canisters. At his trial, which took place in Edinburgh, he was found guilty based on circumstantial evidence. Thirty-six-year-old McEwan's memory of the incident was hazy as he had been drinking. After being condemned to death he stated, 'Thank you my Lord – I die innocent – there has not been a Doctor here this day but has perjured himself.' While in Calton Prison, *The Scotsman* reported that:

This wretched man at once ruthless and impenitent, exhibited all the symptoms of a guilty mind by unceasing restliness, moving to and fro the length of his chain with a hurried gait and distraction of his countenance. Lately he had been daily visited by three Catholic clergymen with whom much of his time is consumed and to their exhortations must be ascribed the change in behaviour. He has been more tranquil and social but continues to discover a lamentable insensibility which awaits him. While in a talkative mood he speaks boastingly of his athletic exploits in the Highlands and is familiar with the names of all the English pugilists [boxers]. He expresses great interest in the impending match between Spring and Langan, and a few days after having been shaved, he invited the barber to spar with him, which, of course was declined. Once a week he is visited by a near relation residing in Leith who has attempted in vain to engage him in some suitable conversation. Every attention has been paid to his comfort but he seems to draw his chief temporal solace from a tobacco pipe which he is almost continually smoking. It has been ascertained he is a native of Ireland and his real name is McEoch.

McEwan was executed on 7 April 1824. His death did little to deter domestic violence. Matters in fact went from bad to worse, reaching a head in 1831 when no less than three men suffered capital punishment for murdering their wives. There was widespread shame in Edinburgh with the crimes receiving condemnation in newspapers across the country. James Gow stabbed his wife to death with a shoemaker's knife but at his trial said he was not conscious of committing the act. Three days later, on 14 November, Thomas Beveridge was also convicted of murdering his wife. This was followed on 19 December by James McCourt who was found guilty of kicking his wife – a heavy drinker – to death.

The Lord Justice Clerk commented: 'That men indulging in the immoderate use of spirits should be inflamed by passion and systematically acting on the resolution of imbruing their hands in blood of their own wives, whom they were the last persons they should injure in any way was truly melancholy.' In Thomas Beveridge's case he declared that he frequently came home to breakfast, dinner, and supper and found nothing but a black fire, starving children and a drunken wife. Gow and Beveridge were executed on 2 December 1831, shaking hands on the scaffold just before they were hanged.

In 1835, there was a further case of domestic violence that ended in murder. This time the tables were turned and the murderer was a woman. Elizabeth Banks, who lived in the parish of Borthwick, was accused of poisoning her second husband with arsenic. He was said to have been a brutal man who subjected her to frequent beatings. Immediately after her death sentence she attempted to starve herself to death while in Calton Prison. She did not persist with this and shortly before her death made a full confession to Governor Rose. Unusually, she was not removed to the Lock-up House until the morning of her execution on 3 August 1835 for humane reasons. After almost fainting, Elizabeth Banks managed to walk to the scaffold without assistance.

The next execution in Edinburgh occurred five years later. James Wemyss, an umbrella maker, was found guilty of beating his wife to death with a brickbat and then a stool in a lodging house in Plainstane Close, Edinburgh. After putting her body in bed he made his escape but was caught a few hours later. While in Calton Jail he was assiduously attended by the Revd Sym of Old Greyfriars church and the Revd Hyslop, chaplain of the gaol. They found him lacking in any education. The date of execution was delayed as there was a belief that the death was a result of a drunken brawl rather than an act of deliberate murder. His wife, Sally McRavey, was alleged to have been an alcoholic and the couple were seldom sober. The reprieve was short-lived as, ten days later, James Wemyss mounted the scaffold. However, when the executioner drew the bolt nothing happened. A groan of execration and hisses arose from the crowd. The commotion was increasing when one official realised that the wrong lever had been pulled, ran up onto the scaffold and released it, launching James Wemyss into eternity.

By this time public executions were becoming a fairly rare occurrence in Edinburgh, taking place only every four or five years. Only twenty years previously there had been one or more a year.

Yet another case of domestic violence ended with a walk to the scaffold on 16 August 1850 with the execution of William Bennison, 'a small man with a very peculiar expression of face'. He had poisoned his second wife, Jean Hamilton, by adding a quantity of arsenic to her porridge. Suspicion was aroused when a neighbour's dog died after eating the remainder of her meal. William Bennison's first wife had also died suddenly after vomiting. While in Calton Prison he confessed to the murder of his second wife to the Revd Hay of the Methodist chapel, Leith.

There were some 20,000 spectators at Bennison's execution. The condemned man wore a frock coat, coloured vest and white neckcloth. His last words on the scaffold were: 'The Lord Jesus have mercy upon my soul.' His body was cut down and placed in a coffin for burial in the grounds of Calton Jail.

The next death sentence carried out in Edinburgh was on 25 January 1854. William Cumming had been found guilty of murdering his wife at their home in Leith. In his defence, he related that she fell down stairs while in a state of intoxication and proclaimed his innocence to the end. He added that once he walked all the way from London and numerous times from Glasgow just to visit his wife. When on the scaffold he addressed the onlookers, warning them against the perils of alcohol and that he had been a sailor for forty years, never expecting to meet such an end. At nine o'clock in the morning his body was cut down and removed to Calton Prison, from which it was later removed to its place of internment

The following month Baillie Brown Douglas put forward a motion that:

In the opinion of the Town Council of Edinburgh, public executions as at present carried into effect in the open street, ought to be abolished as very injurious in their influence and tendency and that the council petition both Houses of Parliament to pass such measures as may be necessary to alter the place of execution from the public street to the precincts of the prison where the criminal has been confined.

It would be a further fourteen years before legislation abolishing public executions was passed. During the intervening period there was only one further death sentence carried out in public in the city.

One unexpected consequence of the hanging of William Cumming was the death of the Revd Ferguson in early April. The minister – who believed that Cumming was innocent and had tried to get the death sentence commuted – had caught a severe cold in the Lock-up House while visiting him. The prison governor, Mr Smith, denied responsibility, however, stating that all the windows of the condemned cell were glazed and that there was provision for warm air to be piped into the room.

The last public execution in Edinburgh took place in 1864. On an April evening an intruder attacked Jane Seaton, a nursery maid, in the home of the wealthy grain merchant Robert Tod near Ratho. She managed to flee the scene but was caught nearby and had her throat cut with a razor. The perpetrator of the act, George Bryce, was caught not long after and confined in Calton Prison. He had carried out this horrific attack as he blamed Jane Seaton for poising his relationship with Isabella Brown, who was also a servant in the Tod household. Two doctors who examined Bryce concluded that he was not legally responsible for the crime he had committed due to his 'low mental organisation'. The Home Secretary refused to commute the death sentence and the accused later wrote a confession stating that he was perfectly aware of his actions.

While awaiting execution in Calton Prison, George Bryce conducted himself 'in a most decorous and becoming manner'. The Revd Glover of Greenside church, the Revd Fowler, parish minister of Ratho, and the prison chaplain gave him spiritual comfort. He spent much of his time reading the Bible. Unusually consideration was given to erecting the scaffold on the gatehouse of Calton Prison, a purpose which it had originally been designed for. Objections were raised to this as it was thought that spectators could be endangered by perching themselves on the precipitous rocky crags of Calton Hill. Eventually, as with previous executions, it took place in the High Street at the head of Liberton Wynd.

The procedure differed from previous executions with the condemned man being taken to the cells in the County Building instead of the Lock-up House, which had been deemed as being unfit for purpose in 1855 and had been demolished. Its site was made available for an extension to the Advocates Library.

The scaffold was erected during the night, attracting large crowds. The *Caledonian Mercury* reported that:

> Their behaviour, we regret to state, was most unseemly and disorderly, not at all befitting the solemn and painful occasions. Here and there were ballad singers and itinerant musicians filled the air with discordant sounds, which mingling with the shouts of rough ribaldry, the curses and oaths of the motley multitude gave the scene more of the resemblance of a Donnybrook Fair than that which should have been witnessed on the eve of an execution. The crowd, which number between 12,000 and 15,000, dispersed about eleven. Thousands, however, waited until the workmen commenced to erect the gallows – an operation which commenced at midnight and finished about two ... In fact all night the High Street was like a pandemonium, bacchanalian, revelling and squabbling being the characteristics of the occasion. The feeling throughout was that of hilarity and coarse humour, with a tendency to drunken riot rather than regret or sorrow.
>
> On the day of execution, 21 June 1864, a great number of the female sex surrounded the barricades and we blush to write, there were family parties including children in arms. There were also hundreds of boys with neither parents nor guardians. At one time prostitutes commenced to run races with each other down the pavements when there arose noises which it charitably hoped did not disturb the last slumbers of the unfortunate Bryce as he lay at rest in his cell opposite. Bryce was attended during the night by Mr Rutherford the missionary teacher to the prison of Edinburgh. He took part in the singing of a number of psalms and hymns.

His executioner was Askern of York who was dressed in a black coat and hat that resembled a hedgehog. The use of a short drop left George Bryce struggling for several minutes before he expired.

The previous year a jeweller named James Paterson was murdered in his shop in Frederick Street by Alexander Milne, who undertook work for him. The two men became involved in an argument, which ended with the victim being stabbed in the heart by a double-edged dirk. The culprit was detained almost immediately and after been charged was transported to Calton Prison in a cab. At his trial on 11 February 1863, Milne was found guilty and sentenced to death. The following month his punishment was commuted to penal servitude for life and he was removed from Calton Prison in early April. Capital punishment was not always inevitable for murder.

7

EXECUTIONS IN CALTON PRISON

The grimmest role carried out by Calton Prison was as a place of execution for criminals under sentence of capital punishment. This, however, did not take place until relatively late on in its history. In the mid-nineteenth century there was increasing disquiet about hanging a condemned person in full view of curious onlookers. In a House of Commons debate it was agreed that this form of punishment had fallen into disrepute, 'Through the scandalous scenes which these spectacles were attended, the lawlessness and brutality of the crowd which they brought together and the tendency of the exhibition rather to degrade and harden the minds of the spectators than to produce any ameliorating or deterrent effect.' Legislation was passed on 29 May 1868 proclaiming, 'Judgement of Death [Sentence of Death in Scotland] to be executed on any prisoner sentenced after passing of this Act on any Indictment or Inquisition for murder shall be carried into effect within the Walls of the Prison in which the offender is confined at the time of Execution.' The last public execution in Edinburgh took place in 1864.

Fourteen years went by before the next execution occurred in the city – and this time it occurred privately within the walls of Calton Prison. Frenchman Eugene Chantrelle was the first condemned person to meet his end here. Interestingly, when Calton Prison was built in the early nineteenth century provision was made for the hosting of public executions. A platform was incorporated into the gatehouse facing the public street on which a scaffold could be placed. There was a similar example at Newgate Prison, London. It was assumed that public executions would be transferred from the High Street to the newly opened prison. The *Caledonian Mercury* reported on 10 January 1824 that:

> The change of the place of execution is not yet determined but we understand a model of the apparatus has been directed to be made for the approval of the town council. It is not intended to erect it on the roof of the entrance to Calton Hill Jail but to project a half circular platform connected with the tower on each side of the gate which would be seen a great distance on the road east and west

(Regent Road) without crowding the hill. The better situation would be in front of the gate of the intended debtor's jail. There ample room would be found for the spectators and quite apart from the City. A passage might be made through the courtyard of the Bridewell from the jail to the scaffold.

Expensive new houses, however, had been erected not far from the prison and it appears their owners were less than keen on having public executions not far from their doorsteps. The Lord Provost appears to have had sufficient influence on the magistrates to prevent them moving the place of execution away from the traditional locations in the Old Town.

In the spring of 1878 Eugene Chantrelle was sentenced to death for the murder of his wife, Elizabeth Dyer. He had met her when she was a 15-year-old student at Newington Academy and married her not long after. The unhappy marriage lasted ten years. On 2 January 1878 she was found dead, poisoned with pieces of orange laced with opium. Suspicion fell on Eugene Chantrelle, who had studied medicine. There was some unease in the local press when he was found guilty and sentenced to hang. 'Chantrelle may be guilty but if men [are] to be sentenced to death on evidence of such purely circumstantial nature as that which is to bring him to the scaffold, we must expect that many innocent persons will be put to death in the name of law and justice.' Chantrelle had on one occasion, however, boasted that he could poison his wife without detection by the doctors.

While awaiting his execution in Calton Prison he was watched over in his cell, both night and day, by two experienced warders. To visitors he continued to protest his innocence. Despite his impending doom, however, Chantrelle was in high spirits the night or two before his execution. While in the condemned cell he conversed with the prison doctor and the warders. Chantrelle talked of his time in France and other episodes in his life. The doctor noticed that the condemned man was wearing an expensive gold ring with an embedded diamond. When he enquired about it the condemned man began fiddling with it. Sensing something was wrong, the doctor sprang towards Chantrelle and called on the warders to help. A desperate struggle ensued. Chantrelle fought like a madman and resisted the combined attempts of the warders to hold him down. Eventually he was subdued and the ring removed from his finger. On careful examination the diamond was found to fly back on pressing a tiny spring. It concealed a cavity in which there was enough opium to kill a person. Later the same night Chantrelle confessed that it had been his intention to poison himself rather than be hanged.

The fateful day came on 31 May 1878. Several hundred people had gathered on Calton Hill and some young men had even climbed up chimneystacks in Waterloo Place hoping to catch a glimpse of the proceedings. A screen had been erected at the front of the prison to block the view of the morbidly curious but this was only partly effective.

A few minutes before eight, Eugene Chantrelle was taken to the head warder's room. Here the condemned man sang the 51st Psalm with the chaplain and the warders. Shortly after eight o' clock they all proceeded to the scaffold. First came the prison governor, then the magistrates and halberdiers, the chaplain and the condemned man between two warders, and finally the prison surgeon and others assisting. The scaffold had been erected in a storeroom a little to the east of the main entrance. Due to the low ceiling of the building it was constructed so that Eugene Chantrelle had to stand on a level at the same height as the floor. When the executioner, William Marwood, pulled the lever, the condemned man dropped out of sight, dying without a struggle. 'It is altogether a strange place for a man to be done to death in,' reported the *Dundee Courier*.

A black flag was then flown from one of Calton Prison's towers in accordance with the Capital Punishment Amendment Act of 1868. The body was allowed to hang until the prison surgeon certified life was extinct. Eugene Chantrelle was then stripped of his shoes and lowered into his wooden coffin He was buried within the walls of the prison beside the graves of other criminals who had suffered death at the hands of the hangman in Edinburgh and, as was customary, his coffin was covered with quicklime.

Like most other criminals who ended up inside Calton Prison, it was thought that Eugene Chantrelle was long forgotten. The case was suddenly resurrected in a prominent article in the *Sunday Times* on 18 May 2015, with the heading: 'Calton Jail hanging wrecked my family'. In it Chantrelle's great-grandson claimed that the death of his distant relative had taken a great toll on Eugene Chantrelle's children. His son was sent to London to be educated but killed himself on his twenty-first birthday. Until 1996, the execution had remained a family secret and was not discussed.

From time to time men accused of poaching appeared before the courts of Edinburgh. Most cases concluded with a fine or a short prison sentence. Two poachers, Robert Vickers and William Innes, were, however, condemned to death. On the night of 14 December 1883, gamekeepers John Fortune and James Grosset and rabbit trapper John McDiarmid went out to watch for poachers on Lord Rosebery's estate near Gorebridge, Midlothian.

It was a bright moonlit night. After wandering about for several hours they heard shots coming from the vicinity of Edgehead Reservoir. There they saw well-known poachers Robert Vickers and William Innes on the brow of a hill. Coal miners by trade, both had been drinking heavily earlier that evening. The gamekeepers challenged them to stay still but when both parties were about a dozen yards apart Robert Vickers opened fire.

His shot struck McDiarmid in the arm and shoulder. Grosset dropped down low at that moment just as William Innes opened fire, grazing his back.

A shot from Robert Vickers then hit John Fortune in the abdomen with no less than fifty pellets entering his body. With both his colleagues seriously injured,

James Grosset ran off for assistance. One of the poachers tried shooting him but his gun jammed. John McDiarmid managed to stagger home but bled to death on 8 January. John Fortune had also died from his injuries a few days earlier. Robert Vickers and William Innes had returned home the same morning but sometime that day Innes's gun went off, apparently accidently, while he was working on it. The shot struck him under the jaw, passing out through his cheek. He survived to stand trial in the High Court along with his accomplice. Both were found guilty and on 10 March were sentenced to death.

While awaiting their execution Robert Vickers was kept on an ordinary prison diet but William Innes was given large quantities of milk and meat each day for dinner on account of the poor state of his health due to his gunshot injury.

The day of execution was set for 31 March, some three weeks after the trial. It was to be the first double execution in Edinburgh for fifty years when two carters were condemned to death for murdering a woman. The scaffold was erected outside the East Prison block next to the perimeter wall and enclosed in a wooden building. It was 24ft high and of this 14ft consisted of space underneath the flooring. The platform was 26ft long and in its centre was the drop enclosed on three sides by boarding 3ft high and covered in black cloth. There was a massive crossbeam from which the ropes were hung from iron hooks.

People began to gather outside the prison and by eight o'clock the number had swollen to several thousand. According to *The Scotsman* newspaper:

The greater portion were roughs from the High Street, Canongate and Cowgate. A considerable number mere boys and there were also many women and girls whose aspect indicated a degraded way of life and whose behaviour, like that indeed of the crowd as a whole, was certainly not befitting such an occasion. A short religious service was conducted in the surgeon's room. At its close, James Berry the executioner entered the room dressed in a black suit and satin hat. He then proceeded to pinion Robert Vickers and William Innes.

They were then led to the scaffold a short distance away. As the rope tightened around Vickers' neck he exclaimed in a faltering voice, 'Lord be merciful. God bless my wife and family, Lord remember me.' The bodies hung suspended for the statutory period after which they were placed in coffins along with quicklime. They were then inspected by the prison surgeon and Dr Littlejohn, the police surgeon, who then granted a certificate that life was extinct. The bodies were then immediately interred within the precincts of the prison. Other than the prison officials, doctors and some council staff, five journalists were allowed to watch the execution.

The next execution in Calton Prison took place five years later. This was of Jessie King, the first woman to hang in Scotland since 1862. She was born in Glasgow but moved to Edinburgh where she found employment in a laundry at Causewayside but then took up the practice of 'baby farming'. A woman would adopt and raise illegitimate children in return for a small payment. Jessie King was suspected of murdering at least two young children under her charge. On 18 February 1889 she was found guilty and sentenced to death. This came as a great shock to her as she was only expecting a short sentence. There were, however, attempts to win her a reprieve but they failed.

The scaffold was erected beside the corridor connecting the male and female departments of the prison. It was similar in design to that used previously and in fact incorporated many iron parts from it.

During the two weeks leading up to her execution Jessie King spent much of her time in the company of two Franciscan nuns. At twenty-two minutes to eight on 13 March 1889, a procession was formed in the prison and made its way to her cell. A guard of warders was stationed at her door; the matron was already there. Canon Donlevy then conducted a short service and handed the condemned woman a small crucifix as her arms were pinioned by the executioner. A white cap was then drawn over her head as she was lead to the scaffold with the matron of the prison on one side and the chaplain on the other. Much to the surprise of the reporters who had turned up to witness the execution, they were informed that they were not allowed to do so. The practice of not allowing members of the press to watch the execution of women had recently been introduced in England.

The executioner was James Berry from Bradford, who afterwards stated that he had never seen anyone behave so bravely on the scaffold. When the body was cut down it was found that Jessie King was still clutching the small crucifix in her hand. She was buried in a rough coffin within Calton Prison later the same day. This was the fourth woman Berry had sent to her death. When asked if he had used a new rope, he remarked, 'Oh dear no. I have executed several with that rope. One good rope does a large number.'

It was nearly ten years before the next execution took place inside the walls of Calton Prison. This was despite a petition of 11,000 signatories demanding a reprieve for the condemned man, John Herdman. At the High Court on 21 February 1898, he had been found guilty of assaulting and murdering his common-law wife Jessie Calder in a house in Milne Square off the High Street. The murderer was at the time aged 52 and his victim was a couple of years younger. They had, however, known each other since their youth. Most of the time John Herdman was a subdued character, but drink brought out his brutality.

The day of his execution was 12 March 1898. Some 2,000 people gathered on Calton Hill. John Herdman rose at six o'clock after sleeping five hours and then ate breakfast. At twenty to eight the baillies and other officials entered his cell. Captain Christie, the prison governor, handed Herdman to the magistrates after presenting him with the death warrant. Six journalists were also present. The Revd Mackenzie read the last words of the condemned man:

I, John Herdman, about to pass into the presence of my god, say farewell to all my friends outside. I offer my most sincere thanks to those who interested themselves in the petition for my reprieve. With God I have made my peace and rely on his mercy. I go forward to meet Him. God bless my children.

The executioner was James Billingham, dressed in a tweed suit and wearing a velvet skullcap. Little more than a minute passed between the time John Herdman appeared on the scaffold until he was launched into oblivion. One gentleman remarked to Billingham that he had been very expeditious, to which he remarked, 'It is a pleasure to all concerned.'

On leaving Calton Prison three officials were mistaken for the executioner and his assistants and had to flee the mob in a horse-drawn cab.

In June 1913, the bodies of two young boys aged 4 and 7 were found floating in a pool of water in disused Hopetoun Quarry, West Lothian. It was immediately evident it was no accident as they had been tied together. Suspicion fell on 37-year-old Patrick Higgins whose sons had been missing for some six months. Their mother had died three years previously. At his trial he was convicted of murder with evidence from Sydney Smith who went on to become a famous forensic expert. This was, in fact, his first case.

The accused put forward in his defense that he suffered from epileptic fits and was insane at the time the murders were committed. While in the condemned cell Higgins spent his time reading books and periodicals. He was also visited by his mother and other relatives. The day before his execution he penned a letter addressed to the governor of Calton Prison:

I wish from my heart that you will accept this note from me thanking you for your great kindness to me during my incarceration in the prison. Hoping you will excuse my blunt way of putting it but believe me it is from my heart I say it. I also wish to thank Mr Ross [head warder] for his kindness hoping that you will acquaint him with this note. I would also like to tell him to thank all the officers that I have been under for their kindness and civility – Yours respectfully Patrick Higgins

The condemned man was led to the scaffold in the west block of the building where Herdman had paid the penalty for his crime some fifteen years earlier. A violinist played 'The Lost Chord' in front of a crowd of several thousand gathered on Calton Hill. The executioners were John Ellis of Rochdale and W. Willis from Manchester. The press was excluded from witnessing it. The condemned man 'maintained solid demeanour to the last, and to those whose grim duty it was to witness the melancholy spectacle he seemed to be a man of extraordinary nerve'.

The white cap was pulled over Patrick Higgins' head and the rope adjusted. When all was ready for the fatal moment Canon Stuart recited the fateful words

'Into Thy hands, O Lord I commend thy spirit' whereupon Higgins in a calm voice solemnly replied, 'Lord receive my spirit' and the bolt was drawn. At three minutes past eight the black flag was raised to half-mast over the prison. His body was buried two hours later within Calton Prison. At the time of his conviction Patrick Higgins blamed his downfall on drink.

In 1909, Oscar Slater was condemned to death in an Edinburgh Court for the murder of Miss Gilchrist in Glasgow. His removal to Calton Prison was witnessed by hundreds of onlookers. The prisoner's face was deathly white and as he passed some youngsters they shouted 'cheer up'. As was the case with crimes committed in other parts of Scotland, the condemned person would be returned there for execution. Calton Prison only acted as a place of capital punishment for crimes committed within Edinburgh and the Lothians.

Oscar Slater was transferred to Duke Street Prison, Glasgow, to await his fate. Fortunately for him the death sentence was commuted to penal servitude for life.

Shortly before Calton Prison closed, there were a further two executions. The first was of John Savage in 1923, followed by Philip Murray in the same year. The former lived up to his name by cutting the throat of Mrs Jemima Grierson with a razor in her home at Bridge Street, Leith. She was an alcoholic deserted by her husband. John Savage was a drinker of methylated spirits. The *Edinburgh Evening News* commented:

> The case was altogether sordid and brutal and absolutely devoid so far as the prisoner was concerned of any element which would appeal to the sentiment of the people. It must remain a mystery how anyone could have clung to Savage, as it was alleged one woman did in spite of much rough treatment. Through the greater part of his life he seemed to have repelled most of those who came into contact with him. The social conditions under which he lived, it must be remembered in justice to the man, gave him no help to make way against degrading influences and habits.

As there was still no permanent place of execution in Calton Prison, the well of a stair was used, over which the scaffold was erected. This arrangement had been used on a number of previous occasions. In accordance with instructions from the Home Office, the appliance underwent a thorough examination and testing by the city authorities. The execution of John Savage took place at exactly eight o'clock on 11 June. Around 500 people had gathered outside the prison with a further hundred or so on Calton Hill. No journalists were allowed to watch the proceedings.

The next execution occurred only a few months later on 30 October. Philip Murray, a newspaper vendor, lived off the immoral earnings of Mrs Catherine Donoghue. On the night of 23 June, Donoghue returned to her home in Jamaica Street with William Cree to find Philip Murray the worse for drink and very argumentative. Murray ordered Cree out of the house and a struggle then took place between the two men. Murray struck Cree with an iron and, according to evidence given by Mrs Donoghue, threw him out of a first-floor window, which resulted in his death. The accused denied this, stating that he was winded at the time and unaware of the fate of William Cree. The jury was unconvinced and found him guilty.

The date of execution was set for 30 October 1923. Philip Murray walked firmly and steadily to the scaffold accompanied by Canon Forsyth and a priest. The sentence was carried out at one minute past eight o'clock. The executioner was Ellis from Rochdale who had also hanged John Savage. Also present were the prison governor Major Munro, baillies Sleigh and Couston accompanied by the clerk to the magistrates, Mr Williamson, city architect, Canon Forsyth, Father Bruce, Dr Douglas Kerr, assistant police surgeon, and Dr Harvey, prison doctor. Contrary to the usual practice there was no display of the black flag from a tower to indicate that the sentence had been carried out. This was the first time in Edinburgh that the custom had been departed from.

Not long after the execution of Philip Murray, Calton Prison closed for good. Saughton Prison was now the home of capital punishment. The first execution took place here in 1928 but there was a long gap before the next one. In the early 1950s no less than three people sentenced to death met their end in Saughton Prison. They were, however, the last to do so. The final execution in Scotland took place in 1963 at the now closed Craiginches Prison, Aberdeen.

8

DOWN AND OUT – BEGGARS, TRAMPS AND VAGRANTS

An elderly woman, Matty Geddes, who lived in a small cottage between Barton West Gate and the Old Cramond Bridge, was found dead on the morning of 2 December 1831. She had been murdered with a spade. The suspect was described as a middle-aged man, 5ft 9in in height, heading in the direction of Edinburgh. He was wearing a black hat, a dark green coat and a dark-coloured handkerchief round his neck. Suspicion fell on a vagrant called John Howison who had been begging for money earlier the same day. He was detained and charged for the crime. At his trial he was found guilty and sentenced to death despite pleading insanity.

While confined in Calton Prison he had an extraordinary appetite and even begged food from other prisoners. On leaving for the Lock-up House for his execution he took six rolls with him. Due to his ferocious disposition he was chained to a ring in the wall. Hours before his execution the condemned man made an astonishing confession, claiming that he had murdered no less than eight other people. They included five boys and a girl, most of whom he had dispatched with nothing more than a stick. When these claims were scrutinized there appeared no substance in them. John Howison well may have been insane after all.

Another less serious but still alarming case involving a vagrant was reported in the *Caledonian Mercury* on 18 September 1828:

> An apparition: – the streets for some time past have been much infested by an uncommonly tall, gaunt and ugly African, bare headed and bare footed and altogether as frightful [a] figure as Mumbo Jumbo himself who calls himself Prince John of the Royal Family of Napo.
>
> One evening last week about midnight, as a certain undertaker was going home to the suburbs, along the centre Meadow Walk, he was accosted by the uncouth salutation of 'Hello Massa, how do?' and turning round he glanced the

DOWN AND OUT – BEGGARS, TRAMPS AND VAGRANTS

foresaid African advancing rapidly towards him. Raising a cry of horror that resounded through the Meadows he betook himself to the heels and coming up to three gentlemen threw himself breathless and almost lifeless into their arms. Before he had time to explain the cause of his very strange conduct, the African was close upon them howling and blaspheming at a fearful rate and as soon as became visible to them, the whole party fled in different directions. The undertaker had got but a short way, when he thought proper as the only means of escaping from his persecutor to leap over a hedge, the consequence of was that he fell into a ditch on the other side up to his middle in water. His groans and cries brought the watchman to the spot, by which he was extricated from his perilous situation. The next day the African was caught begging on the High Street.

His 'Royal Highness' was sentenced to thirty days' confinement in the Bridewell.

Throughout the centuries beggars and vagrants were a cause of concern among the more respectable members of society. In 1425 sheriffs were given the power to arrest beggars and keep them in confinement while enquiries were made as to whether they could find employment. If not they would be sent to the King for punishment. Most beggars, tramps and vagrants, however, represented little threat to anyone.

The above two examples were exceptional cases. They did, on the other hand, make up a large portion of the prisoners that were sent to the Bridewell and Calton Prison in the nineteenth century. Some were beggars by choice while others who could not find work were driven to wondering the country in search of work in impoverished circumstances.

When the Bridewell first open in 1795, a notice was placed in the local newspaper warning that idlers, vagabonds and others who led a wandering life were encouraged by householders in Edinburgh who had been harbouring and entertaining them. In future they would be fined 40s for lodging such persons. Beggars and undesirables at this point in time were usually banished from the city limits or held in the Bridewell until this could be arranged. These measures did little to discourage tramps and vagabonds making Edinburgh their destination and the problem persisted throughout the nineteenth century.

The cheapness of steamboat fares was blamed for an influx of Irish beggars to Scotland in 1824. A notorious beggar by the name of Wood was sentenced to sixty days in the Bridewell in 1831 for demanding to see the lady of the house in the New Town and then attempting to force his way in. His wife and children were in court and on hearing the sentence the wife exclaimed, 'God have mercy upon my poor starving bairns.'

Another example of desperation was Margaret Boswell who broke a pane of glass in a police station after she had been turned away from a lodging house. She, however, had her wish granted and received alternative accommodation for thirty days in Calton Prison in June 1844. This was her 139th offence. It was a common accusation against beggars and down-and-outs that they deliberately committed minor offences so that they would be locked up in jail where they would receive food and shelter.

It was recorded that in 1822 a man appeared at the Police Court where he stated he had no employment or friends and earnestly requested the magistrate to send him to the Bridewell for twelve months. It is not known if his request was granted.

On Midsummer's Day in 1890 a census was made of all the vagrants in the cities and counties of Scotland. In Edinburgh there were 591 males, 145 females and 34 children. Twenty-two of them – of whom 11 were Scottish, 6 Irish and 5 English – were confined in Calton Prison or police cells. A similar census was undertaken in subsequent years and the one for 1898 found 558 vagrants in Edinburgh. Of these 42 were in prison, consisting of 20 of whom were Scottish, 15 Irish and 7 English. During the closing years of the nineteenth century, Calton Prison not only had to house beggars and vagrants from the streets of Edinburgh but from both the Borders and Fife which no longer possessed their own prisons. Some 125 offenders were sent to Edinburgh's prison in 1890 from the court at Galashiels, a large number of them being vagrants.

One of the better-known impoverished characters to frequent Calton Prison in the later years of the nineteenth century was Peter Sinclair, dubbed the 'vagrant poet'. In February 1886 he appeared in court on a charge of begging in George Street. He stated: 'I am a poet and many a one stops me on the street and asks for my poetry and that causes the police to think I am begging. I have written many amusing pieces but have never used my small talent for evil purposes.' The magistrate let him go as he promised to behave in future. Unfortunately Peter Sinclair – who the Edinburgh police described as an eccentric – did not keep his word. Two years later he attempted to poison himself in a public house in Manchester. It was also revealed that he had been in asylums in both Edinburgh and Wakefield with 'brain attacks'. The poet was back in court in November 1891 for causing a disturbance in an Edinburgh restaurant as well as for breaking a pane of glass there. On being sentenced, he exclaimed: 'You might have made it more, its nothing at all fourteen days.' His compositions generally got their best audience when he appeared in court, with some rhymes being dedicated to the presiding magistrates. On 2 January 1901 he again appeared in court on a charge of breaking a window in a public house. Peter Sinclair related that on 1 January he had spent 'a happy day' in Calton Prison as he was sober. Bailie Brown stated: 'Don't you think it would be far better then, to give you a few more happy days?' A sentence of sixty days was passed, the 'poet' responding by showing his fine command of the English language. The following year he appeared at the bar 'grotesquely dressed in an elaborately braided white cricketing suit' on a charge of creating a disturbance and collecting a crowd in Shrub Place. Bailie Murray characterised him as a nuisance to society and sent him to Calton Prison for sixty days. Peter Sinclair was last heard of in Berwick in 1906, this time appearing in court wearing only a blanket.

Even in the early years of the twentieth century large numbers of tramps and vagrants were still being admitted into Calton Prison. The 'King of the Gypsies', Charles Faa or Robert Rutherford, was charged with breaking into a refreshment stand in an auction market and stealing a number of items which included bottles of beer and cigarettes. He was sentenced to one year's imprisonment in September 1902. It was stated that he had been driven to commit this crime as he was suffering from a lack of food. In a somewhat similar case William Hughson appeared in court in July 1907 on account of having stolen a quantity of jewellery. The accused stated he once held responsible posts including that of a bookkeeper. He no longer had a job; starvation and destitution had driven him to steal. The sheriff sentenced him to prison for sixty days.

Many, however, were quite content to make their living from begging. An elderly man named Alexander McDonald, who had two wooden legs, was apprehended for going from shop to shop in the High Street asking for money. On being stopped he had nearly £5 on him, the money concealed in a bag attached to his right leg. At his trial the beggar stated he belonged to Edinburgh and was born in Calton Prison. He was sent back to his birthplace for ten days in October 1875. A man called William Stewart was sentenced to twenty days in Calton Prison with hard labour in 1887 for begging. The accused said he could make 5s an hour and defied the sheriff to give him more than sixty days' imprisonment at a time for this offence.

Sometimes beggars operated in groups, as was the case with Charles Thomson, an elderly man who preyed on men going home from work in the West End. In 1903 he appeared in court for 'borrowing a small sum of money' from a university professor. The *Edinburgh Evening News* stated that he indicated his profession by his constant recourse during the case to the unmistakable beggar's salute and the accompanying 'Beg pardon, guv'nor'. On this occasion Charles Thomson escaped lightly with just two days in prison.

By the time Calton Prison closed, the need to beg had been somewhat reduced with the introduction of payments to the unemployed, first in 1911 on a very restricted basis and then more universally in 1920.

9

WOMEN ON THE WRONG SIDE OF THE LAW

A unique distinction of Calton Prison in Victorian times was that on occasions there were more women in its cells than men. In most other Scottish prisons of that era it was usually the opposite way round. Around one third of the prison population in the country in 1844 was women. In early twenty-first-century Britain less than 5 per cent of the prison population was female.

This fact perplexed many interested in penal matters and various explanations were advanced. They included the fact that in mid-nineteenth-century Edinburgh the number of women in a population of 150,000 exceeded that of males by around 15,000. Unlike many industrial towns there was allegedly less work for them as the city possessed no mills. More plausible reasons for why so many women ended up in prison was that in Glasgow persons arrested for minor offences spent the night in a police cell and were then released with a caution. In Edinburgh anyone detained and charged had to go to trial. For most minor offences there was the option of paying a small fine or going to prison for a few days. While men often opted to pay the sum, a larger number of women either refused or did not have the means to pay and ended up behind bars.

Almost all of the female offenders were imprisoned for minor offences. In many cases drink was to blame. In the late 1860s, an average of 12,498 females per year were charged with being drunk and incapable, many of whom ended up in Calton Prison. Women were also often involved in running unlicensed premises known as 'shebeens', some of which were associated with crime. Prostitution was rife in Edinburgh, with numerous brothels in the Old Town. In the late eighteenth century there were at least 117 in the High Street alone. They could also be found in the New Town, particularly in St James Square. There was one in Elder Street that was said to be so wild that no decent person would venture near it at night.

In the nineteenth century the streets thronged with loose women who sold themselves for pennies, which were immediately spent on drink. Some added to their earnings by robbing men on the streets or in the narrow closes. Stolen property could be easily disposed of in the many pawnshops scattered across the city. Records for Calton Prison for the period October 1845 to September 1846 give a breakdown of the professions of the inmates. The most numerous were prostitutes, numbering 573, then labourers, carters and miners with 529, followed by housewives at 417! Even in the Bridewell, there were sometimes more women than men. For example on 23 September 1809 there were twenty-four men and forty women.

Janet Dunbar was sentenced to sixty days' imprisonment in the Bridewell in September 1805 for keeping a disorderly house, riotous conduct and disturbing her neighbours. In the same month another woman was locked up in the Bridewell for sixty days, the first thirty of which she was to be fed on bread and water. Her crime was to keep a house at the foot of Blackfriars Wynd which was frequented by boys and girls and women of the most abandoned character. The following year Margaret Scott and Euphemia Purves were imprisoned in the Bridewell 'for encouraging and enticing very young boys and girls to come to her house where drinking and other disorderly conduct was carried on'. In July 1819, Janet Mitchell, who had recently been fined 10s for purchasing stolen goods, ended up in the Bridewell for sixty days 'for harbouring those wretched females by whom the streets of late been so much infested'. Five girls found in her house received a similar term of imprisonment.

More seriously, on 16 April 1823 Mary McKinnon became one of a small number of women to be executed in Edinburgh in the nineteenth century. She was condemned for murdering a solicitor's clerk in a brothel she kept in South Bridge. When in Calton Prison she initially refused the religious instruction which prisoners facing execution were offered. Later she relented when it became known that her appeal had failed. McKinnon reportedly ate little food and subsisted chiefly on oranges, figs and raisins with the occasional glass of ale. She was removed to the Lock-up House at 4 a.m. on Monday, 14 April. Here on the morning of her execution she had a cold bath and remarked to her jailer that she wished her soul were as pure as her skin. On the scaffold she was seated for part of the time. During her final moments she stood up and waved to the huge crowd seconds before she was hanged. Her last words were, 'Jesus Christ have mercy on my soul.'

Another assault in a 'notorious house' in West Adam Street which nearly resulted in murder took place on 25 May 1829. A man who had gone there got involved in a brawl and was thrown headlong out of the window. After being bled by the police surgeon he was able to give a statement that later led to the arrest of four females at the brothel along with a man.

The following year Mary Jennings, Mary Davidson, Ann McArthur, Sarah McCormick, Helen Muir and Robina Porter were charged with robbing a young man of 27 sovereigns and a watch in a house of ill repute in St James Square. One of the women made an exit from the room with all his clothes. He was then attacked by the others. On making their escape they ran into three policemen who had been attracted to the house by the noise. At their trial, the six women were found guilty and sentenced to seven years' transportation.

In 1863, eight women were detained in connection with the death of William Young who had fallen out of a window in a 'notorious house of ill fame' in Hyndford's Close. After careful investigation it was found to have been an accident. Visitors to this tenement – which was occupied by brothels – were often so drunk that in the dark they mistook its open windows for the door. This was the second such fatality in this close during that year. Three years earlier a man *had* actually been thrown out of one of the windows. Two of the occupants received twelve months in prison for this act.

Women were sometimes involved in other acts of violence, often while under the influence of drink. On 23 November 1827, Margaret Jack assaulted Elizabeth Telfer with a hammer and stool, inflicting life-threatening injuries. For this she was sentenced to six months' imprisonment. Around three years later Margaret McGill was convicted of severely burning Margaret Stoddard with a red-hot iron in a public house at the Canal Basin. She was sent to the Bridewell for six months in April 1830. A 'savage woman' was how the *Edinburgh Evening News* of 6 April 1875 described Janet Ferrier. She had repeatedly struck Philes Brown on the head with a bottle in a house at Echo Bank. This was not the first assault Ferrier had committed. Her punishment was sixty days in Calton Prison with hard labour. A month later Ann Sullivan appeared in court for assaulting her husband and stepdaughter in their house in the Canongate. At the time she was under the influence of drink. Sheriff Hamilton passed a sentence of forty days in prison with hard labour, this having been Sullivan's fifth conviction for assault. In the summer of 1881, a young woman named Mary McDermott assaulted Helen Aitkin, a member of the Salvation Army, as she was leaving a meeting. For this a sentence of thirty days' imprisonment was passed. While under the influence of drink a middle-aged woman named Elizabeth Devon assaulted her husband by striking him on the face and biting him on the arm. In her defence she said that her husband had called her bad names when she asked for some money. The sentence was ten days in Calton Prison in early May 1885.

As Isabella Beatson, an elderly woman of 73 years of age, lay on her bed in a lodging house in the West Bow, Margaret Flannigan approached her and requested a loan of sixpence. When she did not oblige her by giving her the money, Flannigan expressed the hope that she would never rise from that bed. Then she struck Beatson on the head with an earthenware mug. She had to get stitches and was in hospital for six weeks. In late October 1892 her assailant was sent to prison for five months.

For many women, being sent to the Bridewell or Calton Prison became a way of life. While in prison one enterprising female stole some blankets from the chapel and made them into a petticoat in the dayrooms. For this theft she was sent back to prison for a further twenty days in November 1837. A decade or so later an inspector visiting Calton Prison complained that just about every piece of loose property was marked with the word 'jail'.

One of the most habitual offenders was Jane Lovie, a diminutive woman with red hair. In late 1887, at the age of 39, she made her 303rd appearance in the Police Court. During her life she had been sentenced to sixty days' imprisonment about a dozen times, undergone terms of thirty days over twenty times and countless periods of imprisonment ranging from twenty days to twenty-four hours. The police were, however, fond of her and testified that 'Little Jeanie' was a character of unimpeachable honesty. When offered the option of a fine, which she was apparently able to pay, she preferred to go to Calton Prison instead. Over a period of seventeen years it was calculated that she had spent ten of them in prison. Most of the offences were for being drunk and disorderly. On one occasion Jane Lovie was arrested for attempting to commit suicide by throwing herself off the George IV Bridge. Later, she stated that she had had no intention of jumping – she only wanted to get a bed in Calton Prison. It was 'no bad bed' there and while locked up she had the opportunity to make some money to enable her to buy more drink. Whenever 'Little Jeanie' earned some money she would rush to the nearest public house and spend it. She tried avoiding being in prison at New Year so she could participate in the festivities.

There were many other similar cases of women who notched up numerous offences while under the influence of alcohol. Alice Taylor appeared in the Burgh Court in May 1874 for stealing an article of clothing in Jones' lodging house in the Grassmarket. At one time or another she had appeared in all the courts in Edinburgh for numerous offences. She stated at her trial that 'drink was at the bottom of it all'. Her sentence on this occasion was twenty days' imprisonment. An elderly woman, Margaret Park, better known as 'Burn the Bible', appeared in court in early August 1874, charged with creating a disturbance in Catherine Street. At the Police Court, it was recounted that most of the previous twenty years of her life had been spent in Calton Prison. Another old woman well known to the police was Georgiana Madden who was found guilty of making a disturbance on the North Bridge during June 1885. She was sent to prison for twenty-one days, already having over a hundred convictions. Women condemned to sentences of penal servitude did not serve them in Edinburgh but were sent to Perth Prison. In the 1880s, when Calton Prison was undergoing reconstruction, many female offenders, sometimes with their infant children, were dispatched there. After its enlargement, Calton Prison also received female offenders from the Scottish Borders. Mary Hardie of Hawick was sentenced to twenty-one days for creating a disturbance that lasted all day in her neighbourhood. Already having notched up twenty-four convictions, when sentenced to a further term of imprisonment, Hardie exclaimed amid great laughter, 'That'll be the Calton then'.

A number of female prisoners were transferred from Glasgow to Calton Prison from Glasgow in July 1893 due to a shortage of cells in that city. In March 1905, a woman named Elizabeth Igo was charged with being drunk and disorderly in Rose Street. She already had a long list of convictions and was sentenced to sixty days in Calton Prison. On hearing this she exclaimed, 'That won't make me any better, you should give me six years while you're at it.' This remark would be true of very many of the women sentenced to short terms in Calton Prison.

Women could also end up in prison in the nineteenth century for a wide variety of other offences. Catherine MacFarlane was brought to Edinburgh from Dumbarton Prison in December 1821 to complete the final four months of her eighteen-month sentence. Her offence was to conceal her pregnancy.

A female wanted by the police for impersonating a man was detained in Greenock and later transferred to Edinburgh. During 1871 she had worked as a labourer in the vicinity of Kirknewton. So masculine was she in appearance that no one suspected her of belonging to the fairer sex. Eventually she 'married' a young woman from Ireland but a quarrel took place and her partner informed the police of her true gender.

Women were frequently involved in pickpocketing on Edinburgh's streets or other minor thefts. Margaret Henderson and Elizabeth Campbell were charged with stealing a few shillings from a clerk in Bread Street on 23 January 1879. The former was sent to jail for twelve months with hard labour and the latter got two months. Mary McDonald, a known thief, stole two tumblers for flowers from a grave in Calton Cemetery. For this crime she was sent to prison for five days in May 1888. Another incorrigible criminal, Margaret Flynn, stole a flowerpot from the door of a shop in George Street on 20 January 1890. The sheriff passed a nine-month prison sentence on her.

Some women were driven to commit crimes out of desperation. Ann McKenzie was found guilty of stealing 10½lbs of beef from a butcher in Nicolson Street. She had three previous convictions for similar offences and was sentenced to eight months in the Bridewell in April 1838. Around the same time, Elizabeth Auld was sent there for six months for having stolen a quantity of bread from a meal dealer in Horse Wynd, Leith. Jean Aitkin, 'a wretched looking creature, advanced in life', received a term of twelve months in the Bridewell. She had stolen a wooden stoup in December 1838, having three previous convictions of theft.

In August 1874 a woman named Easter was charged with stealing potatoes from Dean Bridge Gardens. One evening her two children were caught carrying potatoes off in a pitcher. When questioned both the boy and girl stated that their mother had sent them to get potatoes for their supper. Their mother was sentenced to ten days' imprisonment. One wonders what became of them.

10

BOYS AND GIRLS IN TROUBLE

When the Bridewell and Calton Prison were built there was no age restriction on the criminals that could be placed in them.

The young age of some of their inmates was, however, a major concern of those who administered such institutions. By the mid-nineteenth century active steps had been taken to establish industrial schools for boys and girls charged with criminal offences. Calton Prison, however, still received young prisoners in late Victorian times, sometimes as an interim measure until they were sent to a reform school. Borstals did not come into existence in Britain until 1902.

When the Bridewell was opened in the late eighteenth century, many young criminals were incarcerated within it. In April 1798, the magistrates sentenced two boys to twelve months' imprisonment here for stealing bottles. They also found the purchasers of the stolen property liable for the full value to their owners. The *Caledonian Mercury* commented: 'There is no crime so frequent amongst servants and children attended with greater injury to their morals than this, occasioned chiefly from the ready market for the sale of them.'

Four boys who were apprentices were caught stealing melons, pears and other fruit from a 'gentleman's garden'. Two of them were apprehended the following day and sent to the Bridewell in August 1801. They were to be detained here for fourteen days where they were to be 'kept at hard work'. Three years later James Scoular, John Dun, William Dun, John Dow, John Crook and John MacKay, all young boys from the Calton area, were caught in the act of vandalizing one of the trees on the green. They were about to be sent to the Bridewell for three months but their relatives intervened and they were let off with a fine and a caution.

Janet Mason, described as a very young girl, was committed to the Bridewell for stealing clothes from a house in Thistle Street towards the end of 1806. This was the third time she had been caught stealing, so the judge ordered her to be confined in a solitary cell and fed on bread and water.

Even in the early nineteenth century, it was realised that imprisoning young offenders was not a satisfactory course of action. The Committee on Boys met in the Bridewell and attempted to find employment for them on release. They also took charge of those who had no friends or relatives. In September 1814, they reported some examples of their work:

1. Two boys confined for theft, bound to a relation and doing well.
2. Boy confined for theft, sent to Campletown to learn a trade but he remained there only a short time.
3. Two boys confined for theft, bound for four years to learn weaving at Rutherwell and were behaving well.
4. One boy confined for theft bound to Mr Gowdie but behaved so ill, that he again is confined in the Bridewell.

More unusually, the committee members found a boy from America in the Bridewell. He had run away from his friends but they were able to reunite him with some of his relatives who lived in Britain.

One enterprising boy, aged around 15, had spent time in the Bridewell for insinuating himself into respectable households in the country under the pretence that he was a son or member of an upper-class family from Edinburgh. He was last heard of in Dublin in 1819 but may not have remained there long as the police sent their counterparts there a warning about him.

The same year, two boys who were apprentices in a printing office stole the sheets of printed text for books and sold it as waste paper. For this they received sixty days' solitary confinement in the Bridewell and to be fed on bread and water. A publican who repeatedly furnished them with drink, probably paid for by the purchasers of the stolen property, was fined £5. The *Caledonian Mercury* reported on 3 April 1819:

> The magistrates, we are happy to find, are determined to punish with the utmost rigour all who keep public or tippling houses open for the reception of young boys who being in general incapable of resisting the temptations held out to them and foreseeing the consequences of vicious conduct, are often inveigled into these houses and an inlet is opened to the commission of crime.

The threat of confinement in the Bridewell proved little deterrent to some. The sheriff substitute in the Police Office sentenced two 'young lads', James Vaughan and Alexander Millar, to sixty days' solitary confinement in the Bridewell and to be fed on bread and water for stealing. Before leaving the police office Vaughan contrived to steal a pair of shoes and Millar a hat from the other prisoners who were confined in the same room as them. For this second crime they were brought before the magistrate a few days later and were sentenced to a further sixty days in the Bridewell, to commence after the expiry of the first sentence.

The following year, in early 1820, a young boy, David Donaldson, was sentenced to thirty days' solitary confinement in the Bridewell and to be fed on bread and water for stealing a pair of shoes from a shop in Broughton Street. The father of the child stated that 'all attempts to reclaim his son had been ineffectual, he denying all knowledge or belief in the Gospel and refusing to attend church'.

A list of commitments to the Bridewell submitted to the police commissioners of individuals of 15 years old or younger, from Whitsunday 1820 to 1821, amounted to 128 in number, being about one ninth of the total. Some of them had been committed three or four times in the course of the year. One girl, in the course of her short life, had been returned to the Bridewell no less than twenty times. Another, a boy aged 13, had been confined there nineteen times and several others had notched up at least ten visits for periods of between thirty and sixty days. The age of the youngest was 7 years old, who was sentenced to thirty days for begging. The report concluded that:

> ... boys and girls are sent to the Bridewell without any effect whatever being produced and accustomed as they are to it, they spend half their time in this confinement without any improvement, nay what is infinitely more to be lamented, it is but too certain that it is there the seeds of wickedness and profligacy germinate and that they leave the Bridewell more hardened in vice and more initiated into the means their vicious habits into practice.

Although it recommended some other form of punishment should be found for children inclined to commit crimes, the conclusions of this report seemed to have been generally ignored. It was not until the late 1840s that a serious attempt was made to reduce the number of young persons being imprisoned.

A boy whose term of confinement had just expired 'discovered an invincible propensity to thieving by stealing', and just before he was about to be released he committed a further crime by stealing a shirt and pantaloons that were about to be washed and removed them to his cell. In March 1823 the Police Court sentenced him to a further thirty days' confinement.

The *Caledonian Mercury* on 10 April related:

> ... an extraordinary example was presented on Tuesday of early maturity in crime. Two children of 6 years in age were charged with having been found in a commercial stair on the previous night, under suspicious circumstances, one of them being asked what he was, replied with most cool effrontery that he was a labourer! The truth is both are most expert and habitual thieves and that they already distinguished themselves by a number of feats and daring. The father of one of them was liberated from the Bridewell only upon Monday.

In some cases the parents actively encouraged their children to commit crimes. In late July 1824, a young girl was charged with passing counterfeit coins with her father aiding and abetting her. She had gone into a shop in the High Street upon the pretence of purchasing a small quantity of London Roasted Corn Coffee.

The half-crown she tendered for it was refused as it appeared to be a forgery and the girl was detained a short time later. Her father's house was searched and in it were found items for making coins. The girl had been before the court on numerous occasions on the same charge. On this occasion she was sent to the Bridewell for sixty days. Her father on the other hand was acquitted! The *Caledonian Mercury* reported that, 'These wretches are well known in the Police Court by the name of Miller's Gang.'

At a meeting of the Fire and Police Committee of the council in December 1825, it was suggested that a House of Refuge be established for young offenders. This suggestion met with unexpected opposition. The Lord Advocate in a most forcible speech said that such an institution would be nothing less than a juvenile bridewell:

> Either the delinquent was hardened or he was not. To send a hardened individual to a House of Refuge by his own choice where no coercion could be exercised over him, in place of sending him to the Bridewell where the law took its course, would not, by anyone who thought on the subject, be considered an improvement on the system.

It was decided to spend the available funds on fire fighting purposes instead.

In July of the same year two boys named Grant and Gunn entered a house of a dealer in old clothes in the Cowgate. They dressed in clothes which they took a liking to but were detained almost immediately. Grant appeared in court in a borrowed jacket and a rug that was formed into a kilt. They were both sentenced to sixty days in the Bridewell. Gunn's father appeared in the witness box and begged that his son be placed in solitary confinement.

A few months earlier, a boy called Gilbert Macrae appeared in court on no less than six charges of stealing books from public libraries. He was awarded one month in the Bridewell for each charge. A dealer in old books by the name of Chisholm who purchased several of the volumes 'under suspicious circumstances' escaped with a fine of 2 guineas.

Edinburgh was plagued by a host of young pickpockets and thieves in 1826. Many were banished from the county by the courts but were soon back on the streets of the city. One summer's evening a gentleman had his watch stolen by a well-dressed woman on South Bridge. He managed to apprehend her, however, and, much to the astonishment of the police, the culprit turned out to be a boy called McLeod dressed in women's clothing. The thief was already well known to them.

Watches were a favourite target of criminals of all ages, being small and often valuable. Some boys who sold firewood to a woman, owner of a small shop in St Andrew's Street, took the opportunity to steal her watch. They sold it on to a broker in Libberton Wynd. All were later traced by the police. At the beginning of 1828 the two boys who stole the timepiece were sentenced to sixty days in the Bridewell, as was the broker and his wife.

In February 1830, Robert Alexander, 15 years old, pleaded guilty to a charge of stealing an umbrella from a shop in Princes Street. Already having a reputation for being a thief, he was sentenced to four months in the Bridewell.

At the same time, a 9-year-old boy who was the leader of a juvenile gang and known as the 'Captain', was sentenced to four months' imprisonment in the Bridewell for robbing a spirit dealer's till in the Cowgate. During his term he was to undertake hard labour. The sheriff condemned the conduct of his parents as this was the third child from the same family to be punished for theft. The eldest of these was only 11 years old and was currently in the Bridewell serving a sentence of eighteen months.

In September 1832, the local newspaper, the *Caledonian Mercury*, questioned the point of sending young offenders to Calton Jail. It alleged that the greater number of robberies that took place in Edinburgh were actually planned in there:

> … juvenile delinquents instead of being confined by themselves, excluded from all communication with those who have become experienced proficient in the commission of crime, are it seems huddled with old offenders, by whom they are tutored in the arts of depredation and instructed in the various modes by which the usual safeguards of property may be overcome.
>
> The consequence is that many or rather most of those who are reclaimable subjects when first sent to prison, by the time their period of durance expired are confirmed beyond the redemption of crime and prepared to enter a course which must inevitably terminate in death or in deportation to the colonies.

The newspaper went on to state that if the prison continued to allow youth offenders to be influenced by the exploits of the experienced criminals the best course of action for the safety of the citizens of Edinburgh would be to raze Calton Prison!

Reform was coming but it was still over a decade away. William Vere, Donald Mackenzie, John Allan Peebles and William Berry, all boys no older than 7 and Peebles who was about 5, appeared in court in March 1833 on five different charges of housebreaking. The father of Berry appeared alongside them accused of resetting the stolen items. He had incited his own son to commit the robberies. Lord Gillies stated he had never come across such an unfortunate case before. He could not condemn sufficiently enough at conduct of the boy's father who was sentenced to fourteen years' transportation. The boys were sent to the Bridewell for fourteen months.

Children were often the victims of crime themselves. Peter and George Watson received twelve months in the Bridewell for the offence of 'child stripping'.

They had removed the clothes of a youngster in a common stair probably for no other reason than that they wanted to steal them. In late Georgian Edinburgh three 'little boys' – William Dickson, Hugh Grant and Patrick Cavenagh – were placed before the bar in February 1835 for stealing some metal tablespoons from a shop in the Cowgate. Dickson and Grant were punished by a term of seven years' transportation. Cavanagh – who pleaded guilty unlike his two accomplices and was the youngest of the three – received a sentence of twelve months' imprisonment and hard labour in the Bridewell.

At the beginning of the year 1838 it was reported that there was an unusually large number of prisoners in Calton Prison, including 136 males and 83 females. A considerable number of them were under 20 years old while several were under the age of 14.

In the 1847 Twelfth Parliamentary Report on Prisons in Great Britain the inspector was still of the opinion: 'that every person, however young, who is convicted of an offence betokening bad habits, should at once be sent to prison for such a period as will afford a fair chance of his reformation.' He was, however, opposed to short sentences as the young criminal became immune to punishment if he was frequently sent to prison. Mr Smith, the governor of Calton Prison, supported this conclusion, as did the governor of Dundee Prison. The *Morayshire Advertiser* commented on this prison report on 3 September 1847:

> Such are the appalling evils arising from frequent and short periods of imprisonment and as these principally occur in our police courts, it were well that some means were adopted to remedy the state of matters thus impending, instead of effecting the reformation of offenders. The abolition of the system of short imprisonment for petty offences is, therefore, loudly called for, if it is wished to stem the torrent of juvenile delinquency which intends so much to increase. But short imprisonments are not the only evil complained of as increasing crime. In some cases imprisonment is inflicted for which remonstrance was only necessary.

A widely published example of the excessive recourse to imprisoning child offenders was the case of a 12-year-old boy who was committed to the Lock-up House on 10 March 1846, charged with playing a game of marbles to the annoyance of the public. He was released the following day on an order from the sheriff. In the three years ending November 1845, 240 juveniles under 10 years of age had been committed to Calton Prison. A prison inspector reported that among the prisoners in 1847 was a 7-year-old child who had been committed for stealing clothes from another child.

The Lord Provost of Edinburgh visited the prison and made the following entry in the inspection book:

21st August, 1847, visited the prison this day and looked into every cell. Found the whole clean and in good order. It is melancholy to see the number of boys from nine years old and upwards and I cannot stop questioning the propriety of sending many of them to prison for petty offences and for instance, D.S., a boy of 11 years of age, imprisoned on the first time for beating another boy and taking from him an ounce of gingerbread and another boy for stealing rabbits. But if the statement of the boys J.H. and W.C. about ten or twelve years of age be true, and I have no reason to doubt it, I think the punishment inflicted on them is most disproportionate for pulling some beans at the top of a field near Newhaven, an offence of which, when I was a boy I was more than once guilty and if the same judgement had been metered out to me, I might have been ruined for life (signed) Robert Black, Lord Provost.

The Inspector of Prisons, Mr Hill, commented further on such cases, stating that such a system of justice 'is not measured out to the children of the rich and suspicion is likely to arise on the impartiality of the administration of the law'. He concluded that, 'If such acts, as those which have been mentioned was in all cases visited with equal severity, the halls of many of our great public schools would probably soon be thinned!'

From around this time onwards the number of juveniles committed to Calton Prison began to drop dramatically, thanks to the efforts of Mr Smith, its governor. Many offenders were sent to ragged or industrial schools as an alternative. They were established in 1847 and were followed by reformatories a decade or so later. In 1851 Mr Smith stated that for every five children under 14 committed to his prison six years previously, there was now only one. This, however, did not altogether bring an end to children being locked up in the cells of Calton Prison. The Reformatory Act of 1866 obliged magistrates to send children to prison prior to sending them to a reformatory. It was not until 1893 that this practice came to an end.

In November 1873, 12-year-old John Dobbie was sent to Calton Prison for twenty days for stealing eight files and four irons from a cellar in Leith.

Six years later, two live rabbits were stolen from premises in Salisbury Square by three boys, Hugh Liddle, Patrick Monks and James Nicol. Monks and Nicol were fined £1 each with the alternative of going to prison for three days. Liddle's mother, who was present at the trial, stated that she had lost control of her son, who was sentenced to ten days in Calton Prison and afterwards to be confined in a reformatory for five years.

For another minor theft committed in 1882, four boys – John Flynn, James McGregor, John Thomson and Walter Anderson – found themselves in the Sheriff Court. Their crime was stealing gooseberries and blackcurrants from an occupied house. Flynn, McGregor and Thomson had been convicted of a similar offence around ten days previously and were sentenced to five days' imprisonment, while Anderson was sentenced to three days.

A boy named Andrew Crawford, aged 12, appeared in the Sheriff Criminal Court in June 1889 charged with entering a house in the Cowgate and stealing £55 from a drawer. As this was his second appearance in court he was sent to Calton Prison for five days to be followed by five years in a reformatory.

A month later three girls appeared in the Police Court charged with the theft of goods, principally boots on display outside shops. They were ordered to be detained for ten days in Calton Prison and afterwards to be sent to a reform school.

John McLean, 12 years of age, was arrested for snatching a purse out of the hands of a 10-year-old girl in the Canongate. The sheriff ordered him to receive six strikes from a birch rod or, if unable to stand the punishment, to go to prison for six days.

In the closing years of the century perhaps the most notorious juvenile to end up in Calton Prison was Alan Ferguson, aged 16, the son of a former Postmaster-General. He was a student at the exclusive Glenalmond School, Perthshire. On 15 October 1893, Alan set fire to the prefects' room, which then engulfed three masters' rooms and twelve bedrooms. Immediately preceding this act of arson, he had attended a Sunday morning service in which the Bible story about Daniel being thrown into a fiery furnace was mentioned. At this point Ferguson remarked to a companion that, 'He thought he would set fire to this place.' A few days earlier he sustained an injury while playing football and had been behaving erratically. The case received widespread publicity. The young fire-raiser was found guilty and sentenced to twelve months' imprisonment. Just under a week after the conclusion of the trial Alan Ferguson was removed from Calton Prison to Perth Prison where he was to serve out his sentence.

Waterloo Place, close to Calton Prison, and the area around Register House had long been a gathering place for local youths, much to the chagrin of the general public. Seven members of a gang, aged between 13–17 years, who had caused much trouble in the locus, found themselves in court on 4 March 1898. Witnesses had visited the homes of the boys and in one case the parents were living apart and could not be traced. Another boy, the ringleader, was illegitimate and his father was an alcoholic living in a one-roomed house with a woman of bad repute. His mother had died some time ago after sustaining serious burns while drunk. A third boy's parents were travelling show people and he had run away from them. To make a living he sold newspapers and slept in toilets at night. The worst case was that of a boy called Lonie whose parents were inveterate shebeeners. He was well known to the police and already had seven convictions. The sheriff remarked that all seven gang members seemed to be 'very bad boys and a nuisance to everyone'. Three of the accused were sent to prison for seven days, one for three days, two for two days and the last one to eight stokes with a birch rod.

With the establishment of borstals to separate juveniles from adult criminals, by the beginning of the twentieth century few young people ended up within the walls of Calton Prison. According to the authorities in both Edinburgh and

Glasgow there was an epidemic of crime among the young attributed to so many fathers being away on military service. This continued into 1919 and Lord Johnston proposed that offenders should be birched, as a term of imprisonment was the first step to a criminal career.

11

THE LONG ARM OF THE LAW

With Edinburgh being a large and important city, some criminals who had committed serious offences in other parts of Britain fled here hoping to avoid detection. Perhaps the most notable of these was Maria Manning, who was originally a native of Switzerland. She was living in impoverished circumstances with her husband Frederick Manning in Bermondsey, London, in 1849 when they befriended Patrick O'Connor, a wealthy moneylender. They were, however, scheming all the time to grasp his wealth. Inviting him round to their house, the couple shot their victim and hit him on the head with a hammer. Frederick Manning thereafter fled to Jersey while Maria Manning headed north to Edinburgh. While here, she tried to cash some railway bonds which were stolen from Patrick O'Connor. It was an unfortunate mistake as details of the stolen property had been circulated by the London Police. She was soon arrested at a lodging house in Haddington Place while reading details of the murder in *The Times*!

Maria Manning was detained briefly overnight in Calton Prison where she spent a restless night and pleaded that she was too ill to be removed. Permission was given for her to have 'strong stimulants as brandy and other spirits which she had been accustomed and the deprivation of which was believed to be the occasion of her illness'. After breakfast Maria Manning had recovered enough to travel back to London with a police escort. At their trial both Maria Manning and her husband Fredrick were found guilty and sentenced to death. The sentence was carried out in front of Horsemonger Lane Gaol on 13 November 1849. Among the huge crowd of onlookers was the novelist Charles Dickens. It was the first execution of a husband and wife in England since 1700.

It was not only high-profile criminals seeking sanctuary in Edinburgh who ran the risk of discovery. Sarah Stevenson, alias Catherine Campbell, who had escaped from the convict prison in Cork, Ireland, was apprehended in October 1860 while being treated in the Royal Infirmary. A burglar and horse thief, she was removed to Calton Prison once she had recovered to await her return back to Ireland.

A more unusual case was that involving James Carlin, an engineer, who was detained on a warrant for the murder of a native at Kimberley, South Africa, in March 1885. The victim was beaten to death by a number of white men who were involved in the illicit purchase of diamonds. After much legal haggling, James Carlin left Calton Prison for South Africa on 3 August in the company of two detectives. In the event, the capital charge broke down and the accused was sentenced to a short term of imprisonment on a minor charge.

In November 1898, Lord Lovat's niece, a tall good-looking blonde, arrived in Edinburgh. She immediately hired horse and carriage and embarked on a shopping spree, filling her lodgings with goods from drapers, jewellers and wine merchants. Acting upon information from a warehouse company, detectives followed her movements. When apprehended, the woman only had 9*d* on her. Further inquiries were made and it was found that she was not in fact related to Lord Lovat or the Rothschild family as claimed. 'The Lovat Adventuress', as the newspapers dubbed Catherine Lovat Fraser, received twenty days in Calton Prison for fraud to the value of £20. On further investigation it was found that this imposter had committed similar frauds in numerous towns including Brighton, Bournemouth and Hastings. When she stayed in Surrey, it was said that 'the visitor was very free in the distribution of favors among tradesmen but more reserved in parting with money for their payment'. Those that were owed money eventually besieged her lodgings. At this point Catherine decided to flee to Edinburgh. When she was released from Calton Prison her troubles were far from over as she was re-arrested and taken to London. At her trial in Bow Street Court it was disclosed that Catherine Fraser was the daughter of a Welsh Methodist minister. Her sentence this time was seventeen months in prison with hard labour.

12

TRANSPORTATION

Banishment from the City of Edinburgh for minor crimes and public nuisances was still used as a form of punishment in the early nineteenth century. It was not abolished until 1830. A more drastic form of expulsion, however, was introduced in this epoch, which saw criminals transported to the British colonies. From 1678 onwards a number of the religious dissidents known as the Covenanters were removed to the plantations of the East Indies and Virginia. The Privy Council continued to sentence relatively small numbers of people to transportation 'beyond the seas' in the eighteenth century. With the loss of America after the War of Independence prisoners were sent instead to Australia from 1786 onwards.

At the beginning of the nineteenth century, transportation as a form of punishment for Edinburgh's common criminals was almost unknown. After the end of the Napoleonic Wars the situation began to change and in the 1820s and 1830s large numbers of persons all of ages who fell foul of the law found themselves on ships bound for overseas destinations. This form of punishment was popular with those that administered the prisons as it reduced the number of persons confined in them and hence the amount of money that had to be spent on maintaining them.

Up until 1840, convicts from all over southern Scotland were marshalled at Calton Jail. Here they would be held until a ship was available to take them to Millbank on the River Thames. Those sentenced to transportation were not sent directly to their destination. Part of the punishment was to spend some time confined in a convict prison in Britain. They would be held for three months before it was decided where to send them. Initially many were held on old naval vessels known as hulks on the River Thames. There was, however, an outcry about the squalid conditions on board and in time they were phased out of use. Millbank Prison eventually replaced them.

On 14 November 1818, the following prisoners are recorded as having arrived at Calton Jail from Glasgow for the purpose of being transported:

James Boyd	housebreaking and theft	sentenced to death but commuted to transportation for life.
James Martin	housebreaking	seven years' transportation.
Robert Stevenson	forgery	seven years' transportation.
David Meffen	theft	seven years' transportation.
Thomas Wilson	housebreaking and theft	seven years' transportation.
John Thomson	theft	seven years' transportation.
Peter Wilson	forgery	seven years' transportation.
Wilson Cameron (from Paisley)	housebreaking and theft	seven years' transportation.
James Miller (from Ayr)	housebreaking and theft	fourteen years' transportation.
John Young	housebreaking	seven years' transportation.
Alexander Gilmour	forgery	seven years' transportation.

The following year, James Ross was found guilty of stealing a number of silver plates from a house in York Place, Edinburgh. For this he was sentenced to seven years' transportation. At the same time, John Morrison received a sentence of fourteen years' transportation for committing a number of thefts including the stealing of a pocketbook containing £6 from a servant.

In the early part of the nineteenth century, those sentenced to transportation were sometimes also publicly whipped before they were imprisoned. Brothers David and William Beatson were found guilty of stabbing several individuals on New Year's Day, 1822. After they were sentenced to fourteen years' transportation, they were removed from the Lock-up House on 18 August 1822 and fastened to the end of a cart. They were taken to the top of Castlehill where their punishment commenced. The executioner whipped them down the Royal Mile, escorted by mounted and foot soldiers. They stopped at certain points on route where six lashes were administered to them before moving on. On reaching the Netherbow the punishment was halted. Coats were thrown over the two prisoners who were then conveyed to Calton Jail to await transportation.

Not all convicts awaited their transportation passively. *The Scotsman* newspaper on 24 January 1824 reported on one such disturbance but it does seem to have been exceptional:

> On Thursday last, (22 January) twenty two of these felons were sent from Calton Jail on board one of the Leith smacks for London. As a collective body they are, by Governor Young and his turnkeys, considered the most hardened and

mischievous set that have ever been within the walls of the jail. Some weeks ago they formed a resolution to murder one of the turnkeys and affect their escape. The deadly weapon was a table knife made sharp in the point and the back.

Fortunately the plot was discovered and the weapon was taken from them, at the same time a large hole was made in the wall leading to the common sewer and by that passage an attempt has been made to affect their escape.

This being discovered, it became necessary for Governor Young to order the ringleaders to be ironed, this was resisted by the felons and immediate death was threatened to the man who first dared approach them in a hostile manner. Governor Young then politely requested the assistance of Mr Hutchinson, Mr Light and Mr Steers, debtor prisoners and Mr Hay who cheerfully complied.

The additional force changed the state of matters and the convicts, instead of attacking, secured themselves behind the wooden and inner door of their cells.

Exertions were then made to break open the doors and had that been effected, give and take would have been the order of the day but Governor Young very prudently drew off his party and waited the orders of the magistrates before he would proceed further. The convicts, however, had seen enough to satisfy them that neither their imprecations nor their threats had any effect upon the party attacking and they capitulated to the turnkeys and submitted to be ironed by them and the smiths, on condition that they were not to be attacked by those gentlemen who armed with sticks had come to the assistance of the governor. This was agreed to and a number of them were ironed. Some days before they were removed from jail they broke down the stair leading to the courtyard and with the iron rails of the stair they endeavored to injure everything within their reach in particular the locks on the iron doors of their cells.

The *Caledonian Mercury* made the following observation about the above disturbances in their columns:

> It is a curious fact, that those men or rather lads, who have kept the jail in such a state of alarm for some time past were all convicted before the High Court of Justiciary here and that the convicts from other places have never, since their arrival, occasioned any apprehension or uneasiness. The keepers, indeed, have remarked that they dreaded more the desperate characters of some of these fellows belonging to their own city than forty others which they had under their charge at one time from the west country [of Scotland].

Charles McGee was after a long investigation convicted in February 1825 of housebreaking. He had stolen perfume and two portable writing desks, a perfume from a house, as well as breaking into a store belonging to John Allan, cabinet maker, in Cowan's Close, Crosscauseway. The punishment was transportation for the whole period of his natural life.

Women were not exempt from transportation either. Margaret Ferguson and Janet Bain were charged with robbing Daniel Robertson of his watch on the South Bridge on 20 April 1826. He stopped for two minutes to talk to the women during which time he lost his watch. On missing it, he turned back and made his loss known to a warden. The two women were overtaken in Niddrie Street and detained. Margaret Ferguson was found guilty at her trial and, aggravated by a previous conviction for theft, was sentenced to be transported for fourteen years. She had previously been convicted at Inverness Sheriff Court and was punished by seven years' transportation. This, however, was commuted to confinement in Millbank Prison from which she was discharged after two years.

Often convicts' journeys ended here. Many of those that arrived from Scotland were found to be in such a poor state of health that they were ordered back to their native country. In 1851 an inquiry was instituted in London into the death of David Sinclair, aged 14, a prisoner in Millbank Prison. When he died he was in a very emaciated state. The boy had been admitted to Calton Prison on 24 December 1850 under sentence of seven years' transportation for theft before being moved to Millbank Prison. He was transferred to the prison infirmary on 6 January 1851 in a very poor state. Four days later he died. Mr William Helps, the resident surgeon, stated that he saw the deceased on his arrival at the prison. Sinclair was very emancipated and pale but according to the surgeon it was not unusual to see prisoners from Scotland in such a condition.

It was stated that several other prisoners who arrived from Calton Prison with the deceased were in a debilitated state. Those that came from Scotland were said to be in a worse state than those from any other part of the country. Mr Helps attributed this to the diet in Scotch jails, where the inmates were only fed oatmeal gruel and porridge but no meat.

In July 1826, Charles Quin, a boy of 15, was accused of breaking into the house of Graham Bell, advocate, in Broughton Road and stealing two salt spoons. He was found guilty of theft but not of housebreaking. The sentence was transportation for life as he had a reputation for being a thief. A few weeks previously Charles Quin's younger brother had been sentenced to fourteen years' transportation.

Around the same time Robert Hall pleaded guilty to stealing a cart saddle and harness from a house in Ladyfield Place. He was sentenced to transportation for fourteen years. In fact this was not the first time he had been sentenced to transportation. He had been caught stealing articles from the house of Bishop Sandford in 1815 and was dispatched to Botany Bay, Australia. When he was arrested he had only been back in Scotland for a few days after serving his sentence! This, however, was not an isolated case: many of the convicts came home to Edinburgh from the penal colonies and returned to their life of crime.

On 20 January 1829, twenty-nine convicts from Glasgow were lodged in Calton Jail to await transportation. The following year in early August, twenty-two male convicts were taken in the 'new caravan' from the prison by Easter Road to Leith for the hulks on the Thames.

Over the next decade there was a constant stream of Edinburgh offenders sent overseas often for trivial offences. John Bell pleaded guilty to stealing a shawl and received a sentence of seven years' transportation for this. Around the same time, in May 1830, William Simpson was found guilty of two acts of pickpocketing and received the same punishment. The following year John Fraser, a painter, stole a number of hens from a house in High School Yards. For this he was sentenced to seven years' transportation. Edward Campbell stole a bonnet and received a similar sentence, as he was 'repute a thief'.

Alexander Napier, Thomas Robertson and George Kinnear helped themselves to 20s from a till. The oldest was 19 years old and the youngest 14. They all were condemned to fourteen years' transportation.

Robert McPherson broken into a house in the parish of Southwick and Mary Munro reset the stolen property. He received a fourteen-year term and she a seven-year term.

In July 1833, Isobel Chapel was accused of stealing a pair of trousers from a house in the Old Flesh Market, Leith. In court she pleaded guilty and was sentenced to seven years' transportation.

A more unusual case took place in the same year. William Cusine, who was sitting as a spectator in the Police Court, walked off with a hat belonging to a young man, leaving his own 'shocking bad hat' in its place. At the end of proceedings, the owner informed police officers of his loss of property. They immediately recognised the 'old hat' as belonging to Cusine, who had previous convictions. For this misappropriation, he was punished with seven years' transportation.

At the beginning of 1833, George MacQueen was accused of stealing a pair of boots from a shop in Leith Street and James MacQueen and Margaret Thomson of selling them. In court the two MacQueens pleaded not guilty and the female prisoner guilty. All three, however, were found guilty. The thief received seven years' transportation while James MacQueen and Margaret Thomson each got a year's imprisonment in the Bridewell. At this, James MacQueen remarked that he would rather have had the same sentence as his brother George!

Isabel Campbell was arrested for stealing a pair of tongs and a copper teakettle from Isabella Gordon. Having previous convictions, she was sentenced to transportation for seven years.

In January 1835, three notorious thieves, (1) James Ross alias Haldane alias Graham ; (2) Edwards (first name unknown) alias Adam Dunlop alias Edward Graham alias Minigall alias Edward McMinigall alias McMunigall, and (3) David Stewart alias Smith were found guilty of entering the shop of George Leggat in Candlemaker Row by breaking a pane of glass and stealing a number of whips. They were all sentenced to fourteen years' transportation.

Later in the year on 26 May between twenty and thirty female convicts were conveyed from Calton Jail to Leith. Here they embarked on the smack *Venus* bound for the hulks in the River Thames.

The following year a man called Arthur, a druggist, was put to the bar at the Court of Justiciary charged with setting fire to his shop by applying a lighted match to a quantity of gunpowder and turpentine with the intention of destroying his stock for the purpose of defrauding his insurance company. He was found guilty and sentenced to transportation for life. 'The prisoner is a young man about 23 years of age of respectable appearance. He manifested the utmost coolness during the trial and heard the sentence without any peculiar emotion.'

At the end of March 1844, thirty-four convicts arrived at Granton to embark on the appropriately named ship *The Royal Adelaide* for Millbank Prison. Twenty-four of them were from the west of Scotland and ten from Calton Jail.

In a space of ten days in June 1847, no fewer than ninety-nine male convicts set sail from Granton to Millbank Prison. Thirty went on the vessel *Victoria*, thirty-nine on the *Royal William* and thirty in 'the Leith steamship'. Fifty-seven convicts were from Calton Prison and the remainder from prisons in Glasgow and the west of Scotland. Of those sent from Calton Prison, thirty-nine belonged to the county of Edinburgh, eight to Stirling, three to Jedburgh, two to Dumfries, four to Elgin and one to Inverness.

Around this time the effectiveness of transportation as a form of punishment was beginning to be called into question. Some thought that it would be better to retain the convicts in Britain and have them put to work on construction projects in this country. Others questioned if transportation was really a form of punishment at all. Its administration was now divided into four stages, with the intention of moving the offender away from criminal tendencies and corrupting influences:

1. Separate confinement in the local prison.
2. Compulsory labour in England within such a moderate distance from home as shall be consistent with exact supervision.
3. Deportation to a distant colony.
4. Partial restraint in the colony.

During the last few weeks of December 1849, no fewer than sixty-three convicts under sentence of transportation were removed from Calton Prison bound for Millbank and Wakefield prisons. Forty of that number belonged to Edinburgh and the remainder to other counties whence they had been brought to the city for trial or en route for transportation. Even after they left there was still a large number of other convicts in Calton Prison awaiting orders for their removal.

A fire at Parkhurst Prison on the Isle of Wight, a convict depot notably for boys, led to overcrowding at Millbank and Wakefield. With little accommodation available at them, there were no less than sixty male convicts in Calton Prison in mid-September 1850 awaiting to be transported south. To rectify the situation, it was decided to remove as many of them as possible to Perth Prison along with convicts held at Aberdeen and Glasgow.

In early 1854 Lord Palmerston notified the Prison Board that no prisoner under sentence of transportation be kept in the local prison unless in cases where they suffered from contagious diseases. This instruction allowed for the removal of six male invalids from Calton Prison.

One of the higher-profile cases of transportation took place as this form of punishment was nearing its end. It involved the former Lord Provost of Leith, Robert Philip, who was placed before the bar of the High Court charged with lewd, indecent and libidinous practices towards two 10- and 12-year-old girls in his office at Old Church Wharf on 26 September 1855. At the age of 65 he was found guilty and sentenced to fifteen years' transport. Around the same time a 17-year-old member of the Edinburgh County Militia, James Samuel, received a similar term of punishment for assault and libidinous practices on a 6-year-old girl.

In 1853 the Penal Servitude Act had been passed, substituting sentences of four years' penal servitude for the existing ones of seven years' transportation. A second Act was passed in 1857 making the sentences of penal servitude correspond exactly to the previous sentence of transportation. The last convict ship sailed for Western Australia in 1867, but a decade before Tasmania had refused to accept any further criminals from Britain. This was the case for Bermuda and Gibraltar as well. Those now sentenced in Edinburgh courts to penal servitude still had to travel to English jails after spending their first year of confinement in Perth Prison. Scotland did not have a prison for convicts until the opening of Peterhead in 1888.

13

THE RAILWAY

On 27 January 1874, the early morning passenger train from Edinburgh was heading north to Perth. As it approached Bo'ness Junction at 7.23 a.m., a mineral train entered the main line to reach a siding. As the passenger train was running about eight minutes late it was assumed by railway staff that the line was clear. The locomotives from both trains collided head-on underneath a large stone bridge, part of which collapsed on the wreckage.

The engine driver of the mineral train escaped unhurt. Fate was less kind to those on board the passenger train. Its locomotive was dashed to pieces with the driver dying instantaneously. The first carriage was third class and was 'smashed to atoms'. It contained a large complement of passengers, all of whom perished at the scene. Beyond it was a second-class carriage in which several persons died with others seriously injured. In all some fifteen persons died. Seven of the injured passengers, however, later resumed their journey to Perth. Their appearance on the platform with bandaged heads, lame legs and in some instances bleeding wounds was pitiable. They included a convict named Francis Murphy who was being taken from Calton Jail to the general prison at Perth. His face was marked with blood and he walked with difficulty from the railway carriage to the cab. An officer from Edinburgh in charge of Murphy, named James Grey, also received cuts to the head and other injuries. A second Edinburgh officer who was also escorting the prisoner, John Law, was far more seriously injured, sustaining a deep wound to one of his legs, and could not continue the journey to Perth.

The construction of the railways in the mid-nineteenth century had a dramatic impact on life in Scotland, including crime and punishment. Prisoners could now be easily transported between prisons or brought from remote parts of the country for trial in Edinburgh. At the beginning of Queen Victoria's reign there were nearly sixty prisons in Scotland but by the early twentieth century the number had fallen to less than a third of this number. Railways not only enabled the prison authorities to administer their jails more efficiently, they also opened up new opportunities for those bent on crime. Criminals could now travel around the country to commit robbery and theft. Indeed the railways themselves, with their passengers and freight, offered new temptations for the dishonest.

High-profile prisoners were often a major public attraction and moving them by train represented problems for the prison authorities. One such case was Dr Pritchard who was accused of murdering his wife and mother-in-law by poisoning them at their home in Glasgow. On the morning of 26 June 1865, he was removed from North Prison by cab to be taken to Edinburgh for trial.

The vehicle had no sooner entered the railway station in Dundas Street than the long beard and well-known features of Dr Pritchard were recognised by some bystanders. News spread like wildfire and passengers surged in his direction so that they could see this notorious character with their own eyes.

Dr Pritchard and his escort of two officers to whom he was handcuffed took refuge in the stationmaster's office. A crowd now gathered round it and refused to disperse. The stationmaster gave instructions to the engine driver to blow the train's whistle as if it were about to depart but was to remain stationary. This ploy worked well as the passengers immediately clambered aboard their train. As soon as all the carriage doors were locked Dr Pritchard was led out of the office and placed in a carriage reserved for him. When he arrived in Edinburgh considerable numbers had gathered at the railway station to await his arrival. The prisoner was driven to Calton Prison in a cab.

At his trial Dr Pritchard was found guilty of murder and sentenced to death. This punishment was carried out in Glasgow, the accused having the distinction of being the last person to be publicly executed in the city.

Many of the prisoners transported on the railway had been accused of offences of a minor nature and no special arrangements were made for their movement. On at least one occasion this lack of special facilities was a source of complaint. In the summer of 1902, John Gilmour at a committee meeting of the Fife County Council raised the subject of the conveyance of prisoners to destinations outside the county. He complained that there was no arrangement by the North British Railway to provide extra accommodation when prisoners were being taken to prisons in Dundee and Edinburgh. This very often resulted in two or three men, handcuffed and in a very dirty and disreputable state, being shoved into a third-class carriage. Very many of the prisoners sent from Fife to Calton Prison were tramps or vagrants. It was pointed out that it was unfair for the other passengers on the train to rub shoulders with such characters. Gilmour stated that disease might be spread by these filthy men coming into contact with the other travellers. Some were covered in vermin and on one occasion a passenger who came across three prisoners in a compartment was heard to remark, 'There is more in that carriage than God knows about.' An additional complaint was that the prisoners were then removed to Calton Prison in ordinary cabs. It was against the grain of the cabmen to take these fares but they were obliged to do so. Chief Constable Bremner added that the prisoners would not walk from the station to the prison.

In 1911 there was a convict van attached to passenger trains for removing criminals from Calton Prison to Peterhead Prison. Released prisoners posed a different problem. At a meeting of the Edinburgh Town Council in the spring of 1888, concern was expressed by the Lord Provost that out of about 700 prisoners brought to Calton Prison from the country during the previous year, 230 had decided to remain here instead of returning home. This swelling of the ranks of the criminal classes could represent a threat to law and order in Edinburgh. It was also believed that the number was greatly underestimated. The offenders who resided in other parts of Scotland were usually taken to Waverley Station at the end of the sentence and put on a train to where they came from. Many, it was thought, probably tore up their railway tickets once purchased for them and disappeared back on to the capital's streets. Others decanted from the train when it made its first stop.

Once inside the imitation fortress walls of Calton Prison, escape would be almost impossible. In a number of instances prisoners tried to make their break for freedom en route there.

At the beginning of 1864 a prisoner guarded by a police officer boarded a train at Perth bound for Edinburgh. The prisoner was handcuffed and safely secured in the carriage. As the train neared its destination it passed through Scotland Street Station. On emerging from Scotland Road Tunnel, it was found the prisoner had suddenly vanished. The police officer got off the train and proceeded back down the tunnel where, in the middle, he found the prisoner's cap where the fugitive must have leaped out of the carriage. At the nearby station, the police officer ascertained that a man with blood on his face was seen by railway officials to emerge from Scotland Road Tunnel shortly after the train had passed through it. There was, however, no trace of the prisoner, who had disappeared onto the streets of Edinburgh.

Ten years later, on 23 June 1874, a much more violent escape attempt was made by two prisoners who were being moved from Greenock Prison to Edinburgh to be tried in the High Court. James Howieson and John McGinley, alias Ferguson, who had been arrested on charges of housebreaking and theft, were escorted by prison warder Daniel McAllister and Mr Clarke, governor of Greenock Prison. Nothing unusual occurred on the first part of the journey but shortly after the train had passed Bellside one of the prisoners managed to slip his handcuffs. He then drew a knife, which he had concealed in his clothes, and made a murderous attack on his escorts, seriously injuring the prison warder.

Having disabled their guards, the prisoners then jumped out of the train, which was travelling at a speed of around 40mph. The alarm was not raised until the train stopped at West Calder. The police at Shotts were informed and a locomotive commandeered to search for the prisoners. The fugitives were found hiding in a moss, close to Benhar, next to the railway line. One of them had injured his leg and had difficulty walking. By the afternoon of the same day they had been safely locked up in Calton Prison.

In late May 1907, a respectably dressed middle-aged man was standing on the platform of Thornton Junction Railway Station. He was being taken to Calton Prison by a policeman after receiving a sentence at Buckhaven Police Court. Suddenly he bolted away from his guard and ran along the platform. He then pulled out a knife and drew it across his throat. The policeman caught his arm after the first thrust, which had not inflicted much damage. The unfortunate man was attended to by a doctor who happened to be at the station and was able to continue his journey to Calton Prison.

Escape bids were occasionally made when prisoners arrived at Waverley Station. One such incident took place on 17 May 1909. Among the passengers that arrived on that date were eight prisoners escorted by four members of the Fife Police. A young man who had received a fourteen-day sentence for assaulting the police in Dunfermline slipped the handcuffs which linked him to another delinquent and ran off. He did not get far as he was caught by a police officer at the foot of Cockburn Street. In due course he was taken to Calton Prison to serve his sentence.

Waverley Station itself attracted may thieves who would prey on the travelling public. Those that were caught would end up in Calton Prison a short distance away.

A robbery of a far more serious nature took place in early February 1869 when £800 was stolen from mailbags on a train making its way from Carlisle to Edinburgh. Five days after the theft John Thomson, a stoker employed by the Caledonian Railway, was apprehended on a charge of stealing a bank letter that contained notes belonging to various banks. He was caught when he attempted to pass one of the notes at Waverley Station as payment for a first-class ticket to Glasgow. On giving change the booking clerk compared the note's number with those that had been stolen. He alerted a policeman, who followed Thomson to the platform, apprehending him when he boarded the train. On searching his lodgings all the missing money was found. John Thomson stated in his defense that he had found the money in Dalry sidings. After a trial at the High Court this dishonest railway worker received a sentence of seven years' penal servitude.

He was not the only railway worker to end up behind the walls of Calton Prison after a high-profile trial. There was concern that the large number of workers, or navvies as they were known, employed in the construction of the railway network could be a catalyst for crime and disorder. Frederic Hill, Inspector of Prisons for Scotland, writing in the Twelfth Report for Prisons, 1847, stated that most of their fears were not realised and often the construction work on the railways passed off without any serious trouble. Mr Vere, the resident sheriff at Lanark, said that he was astonished at the general good conduct of the railway labourers and that in proportion to their number, he thought there were fewer offences committed by them than at most ironworks in the district.

There was, however, a major disturbance in January 1848 when a large number of navvies were laid off by the Caledonian Railway on completion of work in the vicinity of West Calder. Most of them were Irish, although there were a small number of Scots and English. The Irish numbered around 1,000 and they lived in a temporary village of huts at Cobbinshaw, which they were instructed to evacuate. The inhabitants of West Calder village situated around 1.5 miles away were not on good terms with their new neighbours and planned to demolish the makeshift settlement themselves. With rumours of the impending destruction of their accommodation around 600 Irish labourers pre-empted the situation and armed themselves with pikes, sticks and even guns. They descended on West Calder and threatened to burn it to the ground. The villagers, reinforced by around twelve county constables and Scots navvies, fought a pitched battle at the entrance to the village. Despite being outnumbered by about two to one, the Irish were routed by the residents and fled.

However, they threatened to return. Early the following day fifty men of the 3rd Dragoon Guards left Piershill Barracks, Edinburgh, for Mid-Calder where they remained ready for action. Police meanwhile were engaged in apprehending the principal characters involved in the riot. They succeeded in capturing three of the ringleaders who, along with a man captured with a gun in his possession, were locked up in Calton Prison by the end of the day.

When the prison was first built the valley below it was occupied by houses and Trinity College, Kirk. In the late 1840s they were swept away and no less than three railway stations were built in their place. In time they were amalgamated to become Waverley Station. Prisoners incarcerated in south-facing cells were able to look down on this new mode of transport, which gave the population new freedom of movement, and be taunted by the fact that they were going nowhere.

In 1845 a railway tunnel 400 yards in length was completed under Calton Hill a short distance to the east of where the prison stood. Nine years later on 7 December 1854 it was the scene of a serious collision between two trains.

A goods train was having difficulty negotiating the gradient in the tunnel as it made its way towards Waverley Station. A passenger train close behind on the same line ran into the back of it. The impact broke the coupling chain and several carriages rolled down the tunnel and into a third locomotive on the track behind it. The guard's van was smashed to pieces and the carriage next to it was seriously damaged. One elderly man died at the scene of the accident and around twelve other passengers were seriously injured. The engine driver, stoker and guard of the goods train, along with several other railway officials, were apprehended by the authorities. At the subsequent trial Mr Rowbotham, the general manager, and Mr Petre, locomotive superintendent of the North British Railway, were acquitted of the charge of culpable homicide. William Macintosh, telegraph and signal operator, was found guilty of allowing three trains to pass each other in quick succession and sentenced to three years in prison. James Jeffrey, signal operator, received an eighteen-month prison sentence for failing to show a danger signal. They would be imprisoned in Calton Prison a short distance away from the scene of the accident.

Four years after this trial, Alexander Robertson, an engine driver in employment with the North British Railway Company, appeared before the High Court on a charge of culpable homicide and neglect of duty. On 20 October 1858, he was driving a special goods train from Edinburgh to Galashiels when it ran into the back of a cattle train at Heriot. The guard's van was wrecked, with one man being killed and another seriously injured. Robertson said the night was foggy but that he was aware of the cattle train in front of him. He was found guilty but leniency was recommended and he received a prison sentence of six months.

Fortunately there appear to have been few accidents over the next half century in which railway workers ended up in the confines of Calton Prison for neglect of duty. Isabella Hislop appeared on 4 July 1881 before the City Police Court charged with robbing a fellow passenger of an albert chain and a pair of gloves from a fellow passenger when the train was passing through Calton Tunnel. For this crime she was sentenced to thirty days in prison.

Shortly before midnight on 27 December 1906, the Scotch Express steamed out of King's Cross Station bound for Aberdeen. It was driven by 60-year-old George Gourlay, one of the North British Railway Company's longest-serving drivers. So experienced was he that he had been given the honour of operating Royal Trains. On its final stage of the journey the weather conditions deteriorated. On reaching Arbroath it could go no further as the track ahead was blocked with snow. Here it was decided to make up a train from several stranded ones and take the passengers back to Dundee. The huge express engine was nominated to haul the coaches but was so large it could not be accommodated onto the turntable. Hence it had to be driven backwards with its tender at the front. By now it was snowing heavily and the light was fading fast. Only one line was in operation due to a derailment of some goods wagons. The southbound train had not travelled very far when it ploughed into a local passenger train that was halted at Elliott Junction. It derailed and fell onto its side, whilst its carriages were smashed into matchwood by the powerful express locomotive.

George Gourlay managed to clamber out of the cab but his young fireman was trapped under the tender and passed away in hospital. Some twenty people died, most of whom were passengers on board the local train. To everyone's surprise George Gourlay was taken into custody by the police and charged with driving a train in a reckless manner and while intoxicated.

At his trial Gourlay said that the signalman at Arbroath had said that the block system was not working and that he was on his own when he proceeded south. The passenger train he was driving never exceeded 17/18mph. As for drink, it was stated that George Gourlay was offered a drink of whisky after the crash.

Other railwaymen testified to the unsatisfactory working of Elliott Junction on previous occasions. The jury, however, found Gourlay guilty of manslaughter and he was sentenced to five months in Calton Prison. He was accorded exceptional treatment, being confined in a cell with both a fire and a light. Meals could be obtained from outside the prison and books and periodicals were supplied.

Even so there was a great public outcry over the imprisonment of George Gourlay. A petition with 25,000 signatures was raised in no time and his sentence was questioned in the House of Commons. After serving three months in Calton Prison, the engine driver was released on 12 June 1907. A crowd gathered in anticipation at the prison gates. Their wait was in vain as instead of letting him out at the usual time of 8 a.m., he was freed at 5.20 a.m. A placard bearing the words 'Right Hearty Welcome' greeted the veteran driver when he got within sight of his home.

Two years later there was a malicious attempt to derail a train. In early February 1909, the Dundee to Edinburgh express smashed into a railway sleeper placed on the track. George Wright later surrendered to the police and confessed to the crime. He stated it was instigated with a friend whose brother had been employed by the railway and had lost an arm in an accident but did not receive any compensation. For this act of folly George Wright was sentenced to five months in prison. The sheriff stated:

> … he had heard of a good many mad things taking place in Fife where madness was not very uncommon. But anything as mad and as wicked and as utterly senseless and devilish as this he had never known of in Fife. If he were to send the accused to Edinburgh to be sentenced he would be holding by implication that the sentencing of fools and idiots was work only fit to be done in Edinburgh. He thought it was possible to do justice with some mercy to fools and idiots in Fife!

14

SAILORS IN DEEP WATER

Sailors imprisoned in the north-facing cells were able to look out onto Calton Hill and see the Nelson Monument on its summit towering above them. It was built to commemorate Admiral Lord Nelson and his victory over the French at the Battle of Trafalgar in 1805. Built in the shape of an upturned telescope, it would remind those mariners who had ended up on the wrong side of the law that they had not lived up to the 'Nelson spirit'.

Henry Moody, a sailor, was sentenced to two months' imprisonment in the Bridewell in 1801 for throwing a bottle onto the stage of a theatre from the upper gallery. Five years later Thomas Briggett, alias White, was committed to the Bridewell for breaking into a garden on Leith Walk and stealing fruit. Not content with this he also destroyed the trees. His incarceration was short-lived as it was discovered that he had formerly belonged to the Royal Navy and 'he was speedily transferred to his former situation'.

The most sensational case involving sailors imprisoned in Calton Prison occurred early in its history. On 19 May 1821, the schooner *Jane* set sail from Gibraltar for Brazil with a crew of seven under the command of Captain Thomas Johnstone. The cargo consisted of olives, silk and, more unusually, thirty-eight barrels containing Spanish dollars. The latter proved too much of a temptation for some of the crew who planned to do away with the captain so that they could get their hands on this valuable cargo. On the night of 7 June, the first mate, Peter Heaman, shot the captain in the head while he was asleep in his bed. James Paterson rushed to help his captain but Peter Heaman brutally assaulted him with his musket. The captain managed to get to the deck, holding his hand to his head. He cried out, 'What is this?' whereupon Francois Gautiez and the mate attacked him and knocked him insensible before throwing him overboard along with the body of James Paterson. They then intimidated the other crew members into swearing an oath on the Bible to never disclose what they had witnessed. Peter Heaman was now the only crew member who could steer the ship and stated it was their intention to make for the Orkney Islands. The weather, however, compelled them to steer towards the Isle of Lewis. Here they decided to drill holes in the *Jane* and scuttle her. The vessel, however, was driven ashore before it sunk. On reaching the shore they divided up the Spanish dollars with each receiving around 6,300 coins.

Roderick McIver, surveyor of customs at Stornoway, had got word that there was a smuggling vessel anchored in the area. He set out to investigate and came across Heaman, who said he was the mate of the brig *Betsy* of New York, which had been lost off Barra Head. He stated that he had quarrelled with the captain who had gone off in a separate rowing boat making for Liverpool. The rest of the crew had taken another boat and attempted to reach the mainland but had been driven ashore at the place where he had found them.

Mr Iver searched some of the chests and to his surprise found Spanish dollars in them. While alone, the cabin boy who had witnessed the murder of Captain Johnstone and James Paterson told him the true facts. The crew were detained by Mr Iver and his staff and were sent to Edinburgh where they were imprisoned in Calton Prison. Peter Heaman, from Sweden, and Francois Gautiez, a French national, were charged with piracy and murder. The other crew members, including two Scots, were considered to have been acting under the fear of losing their own lives.

The trial took place on 25 and 27 November before the judge, Admiral Sir John Connel. Gabriel Surenne, a French teacher, acted as interpreter.

The jury found the prisoners guilty and they were sentenced to be executed on the sands of Leith within the tidemarks. This location was chosen instead of the usual venue for capital punishment in the High Street as it was the tradition to hang pirates on the seashore.

On 9 January 1822, between 8 a.m. and 9 a.m., the magistrates proceeded in carriages to Calton Jail, where a detachment of 3rd Dragoon Guards had arrived. At about 9.30 a.m. the great gate of the prison was thrown open. A procession which would have done visiting royalty proud made its way through it. First came a detachment of cavalry followed by a large number of policemen, then the City Officers bearing their halberds. Next came three carriages: in the first were the bailies of the city, in the second two attendants for the magistrates and the Revd Wallace, a Roman Catholic clergyman, and in the third were the Revd John Campbell, one of the ministers of the city, and the Revd Porteous, chaplain of the jail. Then followed a cart with a seat on which the condemned men sat. This was surrounded by police. The end of the procession was brought up by a party of dragoons. A huge crowd said to have been between 40,000 and 50,000 in number had gathered on Leith sands to witness the execution. Peter Heaman confessed his guilt on the scaffold and warned all to avoid his fate. He then shook hands with Francois Gautiez before being launched into eternity. This was the first and last time anyone was executed in Scotland in the nineteenth century for piracy.

There were, however, other sailors who committed murder and ended up behind the walls of Calton Prison. In early 1821 Thomas Steel, the mate of the ship *Harmony*, was tried before the High Court on a charge of murdering Charles MacPhail, a sailor on that ship. He was sentenced to nine months' imprisonment. While being transferred back to the west coast of Scotland from Calton Prison to serve his sentence, Steel attempted to escape. It took a considerable effort to recapture him, as he was a stout athletic man. The remainder of the journey was completed with the prisoner clamped in irons.

A Greek sailor named Mayatos appeared at the High Court in Edinburgh charged with the murder of a seaman named Campbell and severely wounding another called Williams. This crime took place on board the British ship *Pontiac* when it was some 700 miles off Callao on 13 October 1863.

Two doctors appeared as witnesses and testified that they had examined the prisoner and were of the opinion that he was insane, believing the two men he had attacked were bribed to kill him. The court ordered that Mayatos be confined in Calton Prison 'till her Majesty's Pleasure be known'.

On 14 March 1881, David Rintoul and John Shewan forced open a door with a chisel to a common stair in Elm Row. They were discovered by a policeman, Constable George Low, who asked them to account for their proceedings. The two men lashed out, hitting Low on the head with an iron bar and stabbing him over fourteen times. He died shortly afterwards.

They were captured soon after and taken to Calton Prison where they remained for three months until their trial in the High Court. Both the accused were seamen on board HMS *Vigilant*, a fishing cutter berthed at Granton. Shewan's father had been a captain of a vessel with a Turkish crew and the dagger used to murder the policeman originally belonged to him. John Shewan, aged 17, was sentenced to fifteen years' penal servitude while David Rintoul, aged 20, got off lightly, receiving a term of eighteen months' imprisonment.

A murder committed much further away ended up with the culprit also being detained in Calton Prison. A fatal quarrel took place on board a ship in Almeria Harbour, Spain. Albert Strickland, aged 45, was involved in an argument with Albert Battison and wounded him. He died in hospital on 14 January 1913. When the vessel arrived at Leith, the assailant was arrested and taken to Calton Prison. He was later transferred to London to stand trial in Bow Street Police Court.

Sailors also ended up in Calton Prison for many other reasons other than murder. On Monday, 17 June 1850 the steamship *Orion* left Liverpool with a full complement of passengers, many of them women, bound for Glasgow. At about a quarter to two on the following morning it struck a rock. Water came rushing in. The lifeboats were launched but were so overcrowded that they were immediately swamped. Two, however, managed to make it ashore. Others managed to swim to safety. They did not have far to go as the *Orion* had sunk within 150 yards of the coast and close to Port Patrick Lighthouse. Of the 212 passengers and crew of thirty-eight, around forty-one were drowned. There were many schoolboys on board returning from English schools for vacation. 'One little fellow about ten years of age who had been clinging to a box was offered assistance by his tutor but refused it and told him to try and help the ladies. He survived.' Numerous small boats went to the assistance of the drowning passengers. The loss of the *Orion*, a modern vessel, shocked the British public, and even more so as it occurred on a night when the visibility was good and the sea was calm. Witnesses said it was so close to the coast that they thought it was attempting to enter Portpatrick Habour. The death toll, however, would have been much higher were it not for the fact that the *Orion* had three masts. Many of the passengers managed to climb up them until they were rescued.

Captain Thomas Henderson, First Mate George Langlands and Second Mate John Williams were charged with culpable homicide and reckless negligence. They were taken to Edinburgh to await trial in the High Court. This commenced at the end of August and continued into early September. The captain alleged he had gone below deck to take a rest, leaving the vessel in charge of a competent officer. The second mate stated he had steered the vessel to the best of his judgement and that the accident had arisen from the deficient state of the ship's compasses or other machinery and that he therefore was not liable. It was stated in their defence that the *Orion* was built out of iron, which could have an adverse influence on compasses. John Williams confessed he had not the slightest idea the ship was in danger until he saw land directly ahead, by which time it was too late to avoid it. Apparently the view from the wheelhouse was restricted and it was difficult to see what was ahead.

While the first mate was released without charge, the captain was found guilty and was sentenced to eighteen months' imprisonment. The second mate received a sentence of seven years' transportation. Neither had passed any examinations for their posts. A contemporary newspaper reported on the fate of the two men:

> The prisoners were taken to the Calton Gaol in a hackney coach between seven and eight o'clock on Saturday evening (7 September). They arrived sometime before the van which conveyed the convicts who were tried the same day at the High Court. Williams appeared in extreme dejection and submitted in perfect silence to the usual operation of exchanging his own cloths for the prison dress which consists of a coarse suit of dark grey cloth, jacket, trousers, vest and canvas shoes. His conduct since his incarceration has been exceedingly exemplary.
>
> He has given an account of his feeling on becoming aware of the perilous course of the 'Orion' and immediately succeeding the wreck. He states he had not the slightest idea of danger till the land was seen right ahead when he instantly became aware of the impossibility of escaping it. Nevertheless, he immediately

went to the wheel and endeavored to give another direction to the vessel but the fruitlessness of all effects to prevent the approaching catastrophe he saw at a glance and the agony of his mental suffering at that moment and ever since has been of the most intense description. He fully admits to giving an erroneous course to the steersman, although how he should have done so is a mystery even to himself.

Captain Henderson has not conducted himself in so becoming manner as the inferior officer. He displays more impatience and moroseness than vexation to his sentence or loss of reputation. The surgeon of the Calton Goal, has we are informed, signed the medical certification necessary to the removal of Captain Henderson to the Central Prison at Perth where he will undergo the remainder of his sentence.

A few days later his transfer took place.

The following year a number of sailors appeared in court charged under the new Mercantile Marine Act, the first case of its kind in Scotland. Seventeen seamen from the ship *Herefordshire*, which had recently arrived at Leith having transported the 79th Regiment from Quebec, were accused of willful disobedience to the lawful commands of the officers. They refused to weigh anchor and put the ship in a condition to sail on her voyage from Quebec. This refusal to perform their duties continued until the ship arrived at Leith on 30 August 1851. The sheriff stated he wished to punish the sailors so as to give a warning to others. Sixteen of the men were sentenced to eight weeks in Calton Prison with hard labour. The boy among them got six weeks' imprisonment.

In March 1873, four seamen who were crew on the brig *Maggie* appeared at the Edinburgh Sheriff Court for disobeying orders. The vessel had left South Shields for Salerno but four days into the voyage it sought shelter in the Firth of Forth due to adverse weather. Daniel Evans, William Hanridge, John Ouncer and George Arthur refused to proceed any further, arguing that the brig was overloaded, undermanned and that the forecastle was leaky. For refusing to proceed to sea they were sentenced to four weeks' imprisonment in Calton Prison. A few days later, however, the matter of unseaworthy cargo ships was raised in the House of Commons, the *Maggie* being cited as one such example. It was stated that the Board of Trade had no power to stop it from sailing unless they received a complaint from the MP who brought the matter to the attention of Parliament. They stated that they would further investigate the matter.

It was only two years later that a similar case was brought before the Edinburgh Sheriff Court. Nine able-seamen refused to proceed to sea from Leith in their ship, alleging it was taking on too much water for them to reach its destination of Point De Gale in Sri Lanka. The captain said it had left North Shields in perfect condition but on its way to Leith had grounded in the Firth of Forth. The damage, however, had been made good. Sheriff Hamilton thought the sailors' complaints were of a trivial nature and sentenced them to one month's imprisonment with hard labour in Calton Prison.

James Thompson, a ship's fireman, ended up in Edinburgh Sheriff Court for disobeying orders from the captain of the *Nerano* berthed at Leith. When the vessel was anchored in Chesapeake Bay, off Baltimore, USA, he was instructed to wipe down the engines along with four other firemen. He refused, as he was not feeling well. The sheriff sentenced him to seven days in prison. Few other inmates in Calton Prison have ever been punished for a misdemeanor committed so far from Edinburgh. The other four firemen had deserted before his ship arrived at Leith.

A far more serious attempt to avoid going to sea was made by Soren Odin Morthen, second mate, and Leon Philemon, crew members of the American brigantine *John Swan*. They had drilled holes in the side of the ship in an effort to scuttle her. Soren Morthen had previously offered a doctor £2 to state he was unfit to go to sea. In May 1879, Morthen was sentenced to sixty days in prison and Philemon to thirty days.

One of Calton Prison's more exotic inmates was Ali Abdul. Himself a seaman, he arrived as a stowaway on board the *Ammon*, a grain ship from Adelaide, Australia, towards the end of 1919. The court imposed a short sentence on him so arrangements could be made to return him home to Egypt where he had boarded the *Ammon* in an attempt to find work.

Like soldiers, sailors were sometimes detained in Calton Prison for desertion or failure to report for duty. Joseph Leith, a trawler fisherman, was charged with failing to report to Castlehill Barracks, Aberdeen, on 7 September 1916. In his defense, he stated that he had been discharged from the Royal Navy in 1899. Since the beginning of the First World War he had participated in minesweeping operations on board trawlers. He was the only one left of the crew of a vessel that had been blown up. In March, Leith came ashore at Aberdeen on sick leave. Later in the year he was on patrol in the south where he came ashore without permission. For this he received twenty-eight days in Calton Prison. The sheriff dropped the charge against him as the former sailor could not have received his call-up papers as he had been in prison.

Throughout the nineteenth century there were a number of cases involving 'sailors' turning up in Edinburgh who turned out to be not all they seemed. In 1824 a young man from England was apprehended under suspicious circumstances. According to the *Caledonian Mercury*:

> ... he told an implausible story of having come from Berwick in search of a pilot. Unfortunately for him he was found to have made a trip to Leith in July last when he represented himself as the captain or son of the captain of a schooner then lying at lock 16, on the Forth and Clyde Canal, and obtained in consequence lodging and thirty days' board with some small sums of money, till his father on the schooner arrived.

For this deception he was sent to the Bridewell where he was to experience the treadmill.

Two men dressed as sailors presented the following document which bore the Royal Arms and was written in a 'beautiful and distinct hand' to Mr Thomson of the Royal Exchange in the hope of receiving charity:

Port of Montrose, 6th Dec, 1837 –
These are to certify that the bearers hereof, Alexander Jamieson, chief mate, James Duncan, William Frazer and Thomas Robinson, late seamen belonging to the ship 'Galena' of Stockton-upon-Tees, which vessel, being on her homeward bound passage from Demerara, laden with a general cargo consigned to the Port of Bristol, unfortunately mismasted and foundered at sea on the night of 2d instant. The crew consisted of fourteen in number including master and mate and two female passengers, all of whom perished, with the exception of the above mentioned and passengers who took to the ship's boats and after being exposed in that perilous situation for twenty seven hours, they were most providentially descried by the crew of the schooner Betsey. William Brown, master, who most humanely bore down towards their assistance, took them on board and landed them at this port in a situation of distress. William Brown, master of the schooner, Betsy came before us, two of her majesty's justices of the peace and satisfied us in every particular as to the truth of the preceding statement, therefore in consideration of their distress and present necessity, we grant them this our certificate and passport (signed) Robert Millar J.P., James Walker, J.P.

When the two 'sailors' were examined in court by a captain, it was found that their story was full of discrepancies. For this deception they were sentenced to sixty days in the Bridewell. The magistrate added that he hoped they would experience the treadmill while they were there.

The same year James Taylor, a notorious character who had just been released from the Bridewell, was detained for presenting a letter to several Edinburgh citizens falsely stating that he had been a passenger on the ship *Rose of London*. It had foundered at sea and had lost property to the amount of several hundred pounds and he claimed to be utterly ruined.

Pretending to be a sailor in distress appears to have been a popular form of fraud which continued into the next century. Englishman Albert Collinson obtained board and lodgings to the value of 2s 6d by stating that he was a naval seaman who had been discharged from the service after being wounded in the second Battle of Graspan. The Sheriff Summary Court in December 1901 sentenced him to seven days in Calton Prison. He had committed similar deceptions across the country including at Bodmin, Exeter, Liverpool and Greenwich.

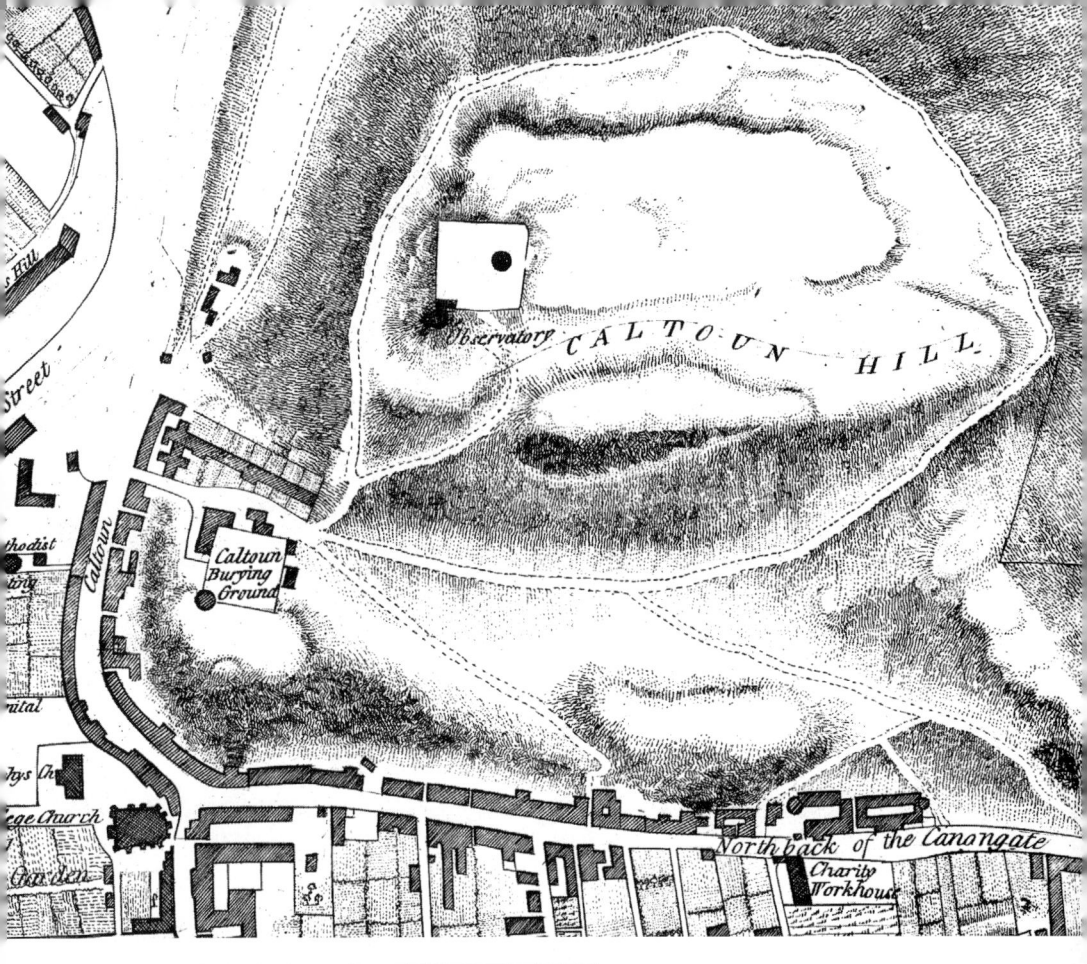

1   A section of a map of Edinburgh by John Ainslie which depicts Calton Hill in 1780 – a time when few buildings had been constructed on its upper slopes. (Map Collections/National Libraries of Scotland)

2   The entrance to the old prison of Edinburgh in the Tolbooth. Note the jailer carrying a large key. There is also a soldier on guard duty. The Victorian era saw the introduction of professionally trained prison staff that replaced the traditional turnkeys and gaolers. When the building was demolished in 1817, the novelist Sir Walter Scott acquired the oak door with padlock and keys which he used in his garden at Abbotsford House. (Edinburgh City Libraries. Licensor www.scran.ac.uk)

3   The Tolbooth in the High Street next to St Giles Catheral which served as Edinburgh's main jail until the opening of Calton Prison in 1817. (City of Edinburgh Council-Edinburgh Libraries www.capitalcollections.org.uk)

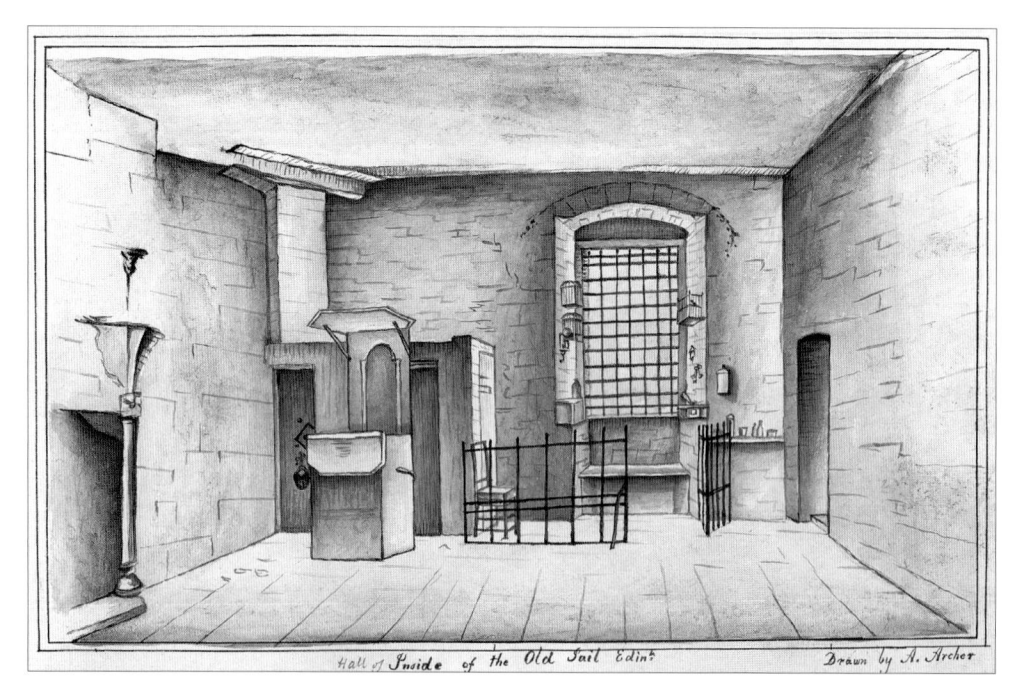

4   A drawing of the hall in Edinburgh's Tolbooth by Alexander Archer, 1817. On the left is the door to the condemned cell and on the opposite side is the door to the scaffold. A pulpit can also be seen in the left corner. (Edinburgh City Libraries. Licensor www.scran.ac.uk)

5   This computer-generated image depicts one of Robert Adam's designs for Edinburgh's Bridewell. While a building similar to that in the centre of the picture was constructed, the two wings which were to house the lunatic asylum and debtors' prison never progressed beyond the planning stage. (Sandy Kinghorn. Licensor www.scran.ac.uk)

6   The Bridewell stands in a rural setting, *c*.1807. Regent Road has yet to be built along the southern slope of Calton Hill. In the background is Arthur's Seat. Originally there were plans to enclose the Bridewell with a many-sided perimeter wall inside of the rectangular one visible in the picture. It would have been further fortified by an external walkway with an elaborate wooden palisade to protect the Bridewell from an external attack. (RCAHMS. Licensor www.scran.ac.uk)

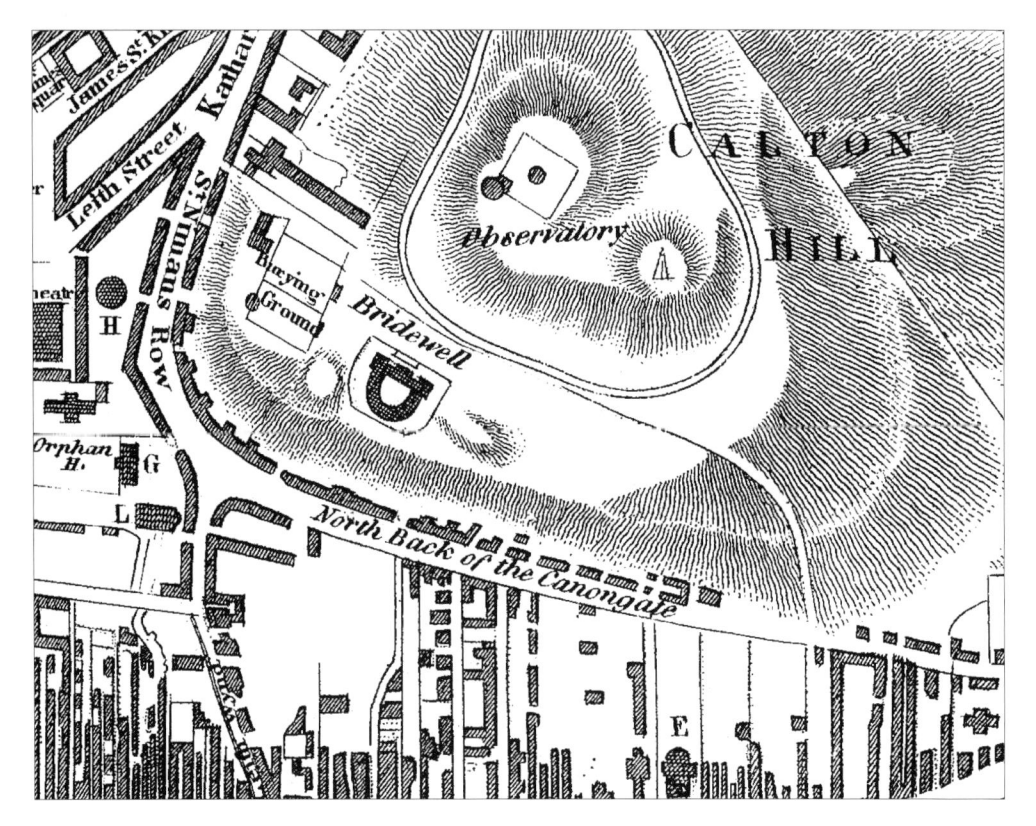

7   The Bridewell stands relatively isolated and inaccessible on the southern slope of Calton Hill on the Post Office map of Edinburgh, 1807. (Map Collections, National Library of Scotland)

8   A view of the east end of the Bridewell, erected in 1796. The architect was Robert Adam. In the background is the Governor's House for Calton Prison which was designed by Archibald Elliot. In the foreground two men are working in a saw pit in which board lengths are being cut from a square piece of timber. (Edinburgh City Libraries. Licensor www.scran.ac.uk)

9 The north side of the Bridewell viewed from the upper slopes of Calton Hill in the early nineteenth century. This building, which was inspired by the architecture of Scottish castles, was demolished around 1881 when Calton Prison was modernised. (City of Edinburgh Council – Edinburgh Libraries, www.capitalcollections.org.uk)

10 A painting of Calton Prison in 1824 by John Gendall not long after it was completed. It is viewed from the summit of Calton Hill looking towards Edinburgh Castle. (City of Edinburgh Council – Edinburgh Libraries, www.capitalcollections.org.uk)

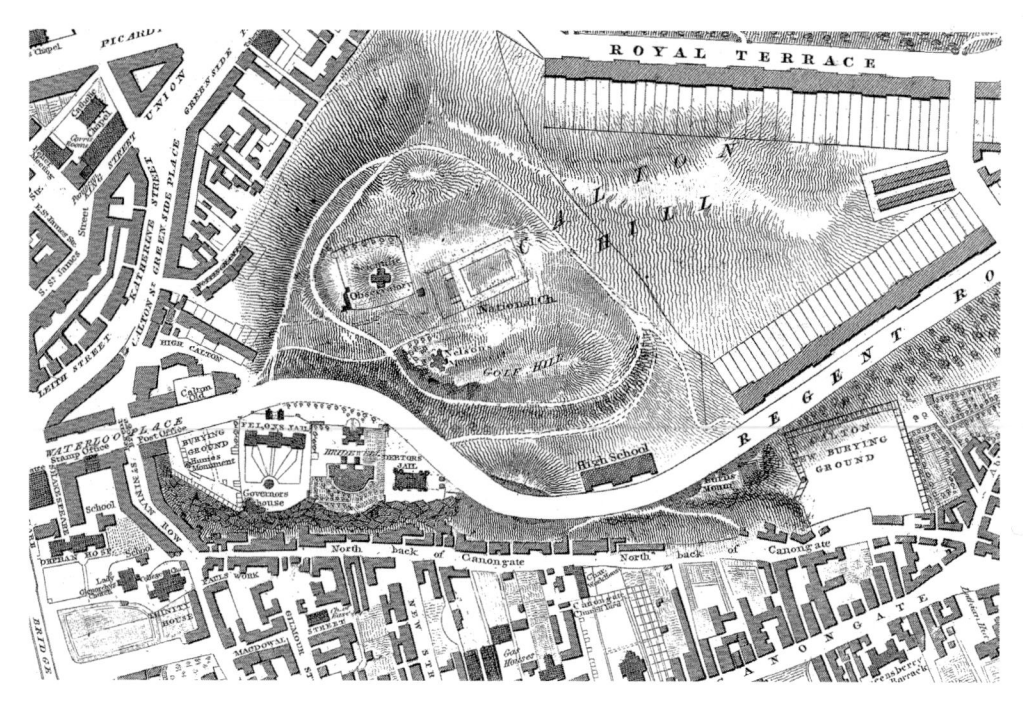

11   This map of Edinburgh by John Wood in 1823 shows the new Calton Prison next to the Bridewell. A debtors' prison occupies a site immediately to the east of them. It was in fact never built, although the east wing of Calton Prison was erected on the site in the mid-1840s. (Map Collections, National Library of Scotland)

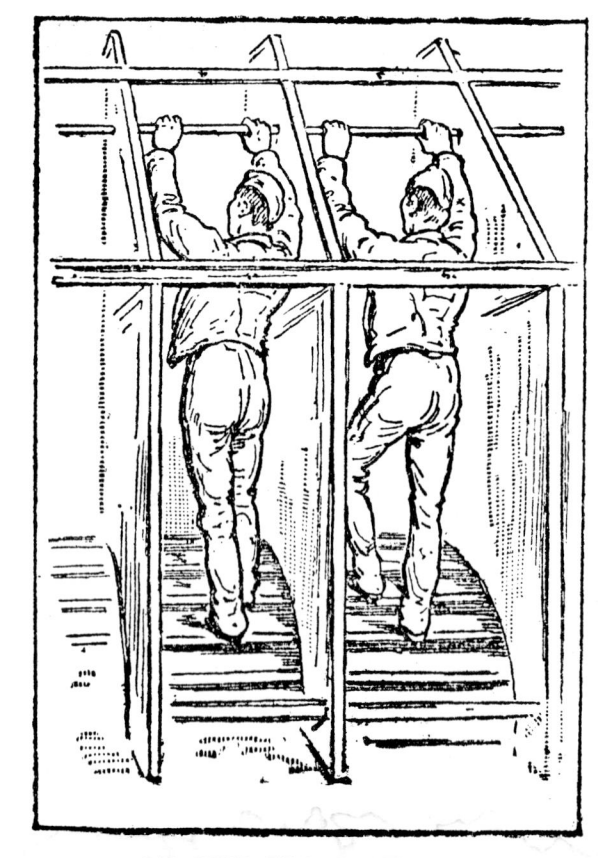

12   Prisoners at hard labour on the treadwheel in an English prison. Both the Bridewell and Calton Prison had treadwheels but this form of punishment fell out of favour with the prison authorities and had been abolished by the late 1840s. (Photolibra)

ON THE TREADWHEEL.

13 A portrait of William Burke as he appeared in court in 1829. He was Calton Prison's most notorious inmate, being responsible for no less than sixteen murders for the purpose of supplying bodies for medical research. (Scottish National Portrait Gallery. Licensor www.scran.ac.uk)

WILLIAM BURKE.

as he appeared at the Bar,
taken in Court.

14 Calton Hill and the North Bridge viewed from the top of the Mound. On top of the hill is the Nelson Monument and further down the slope is Calton Prison. From an engraving by Thomas Shepherd, 1829. (City of Edinburgh Council – Edinburgh Libraries www.capitalcollections.org.uk)

15   A picture of the recently opened Calton Prison in 1829 by Thomas Shepherd. It depicts the north side with Regent Road next to its boundary wall. The Gatehouse had four small apartments, used variously as an office, for the turnkey in charge of the gate, as a sleeping apartment for the turnkey, and by the cook. (City of Edinburgh Council – Edinburgh Libraries www.capitalcollections.org.uk)

16   A public execution in the High Street in the early nineteenth century. St Giles Cathedral is visible in the background but the Tolbooth which served as the prison has been demolished, dating the picture to some time after 1817. The site today is next to the road junction between the High Street and the George IV Bridge. (City of Edinburgh Council – Edinburgh Libraries www.capitalcollections.org.uk)

17 A prison hulk at Deptford on the River Thames. These old ships were used for the confinement of prisoners waiting to be transport to Australia and other penal colonies. Prisoners were used as labour in the naval dockyards. (Photolibra)

18 Perhaps the earliest photograph of Calton Prison taken by the well-known photographer David Octavius Hill in the late 1840s. The building on the left is the Bridewell and to its right is the original Calton Prison completed in 1817. (Special Collections, Glasgow University Library. Licensor www.scran.ac.uk)

19 The Canongate Tolbooth in the Royal Mile in 1866. It contained a jail and in the first half of the nineteenth century was used to house civil prisoners when there was a shortage of accommodation in Calton Prison. (City of Edinburgh Council – Edinburgh Libraries www.capitalcollections.org.uk)

20 View of Calton Hill and Calton Prison looking over the railway tracks and coal wagons at the eastern entrance to Waverley Station in the mid- to late nineteenth century. (RCAHMS. Licensor www.scran.ac.uk)

21 A prisoner working a crank handle in an English prison. It was also the favoured form of physical punishment in Calton Prison. (Photolibra)

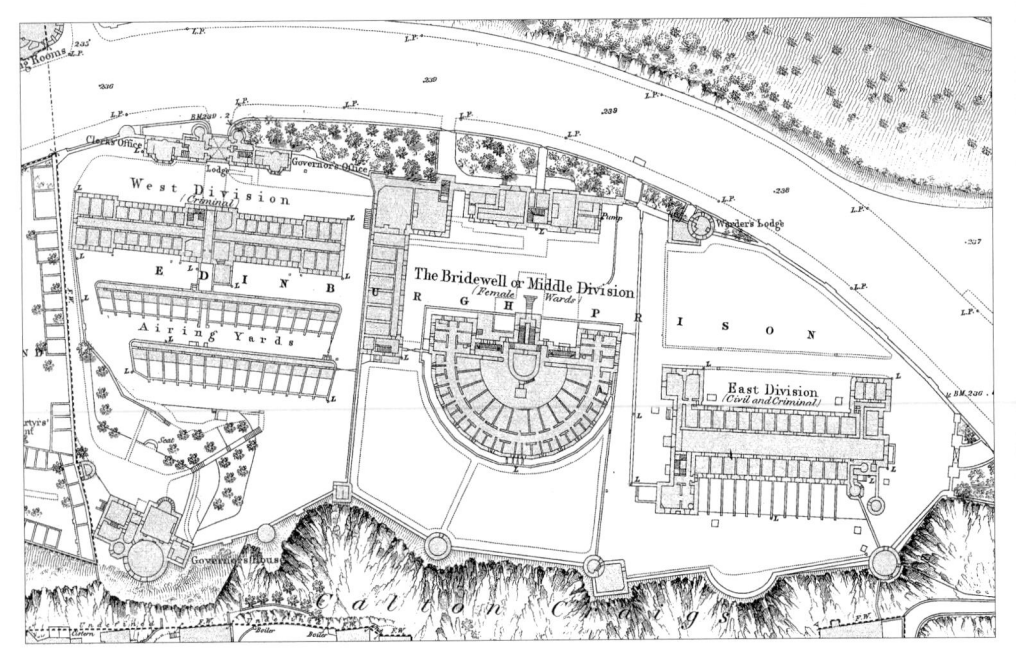

22 A plan of Calton Prison from the Ordnance Survey large-scale map of Edinburgh, *c.* 1850. Interestingly Ordnance Survey maps in the latter part of the nineteenth century just depict a blank area with no buildings, presumably for security reasons. (Map Collections, National Library of Scotland)

23 A plan of Calton Prison in 1887 depicting its final layout. (RCAHMS. Licensor www.scran.ac.uk)

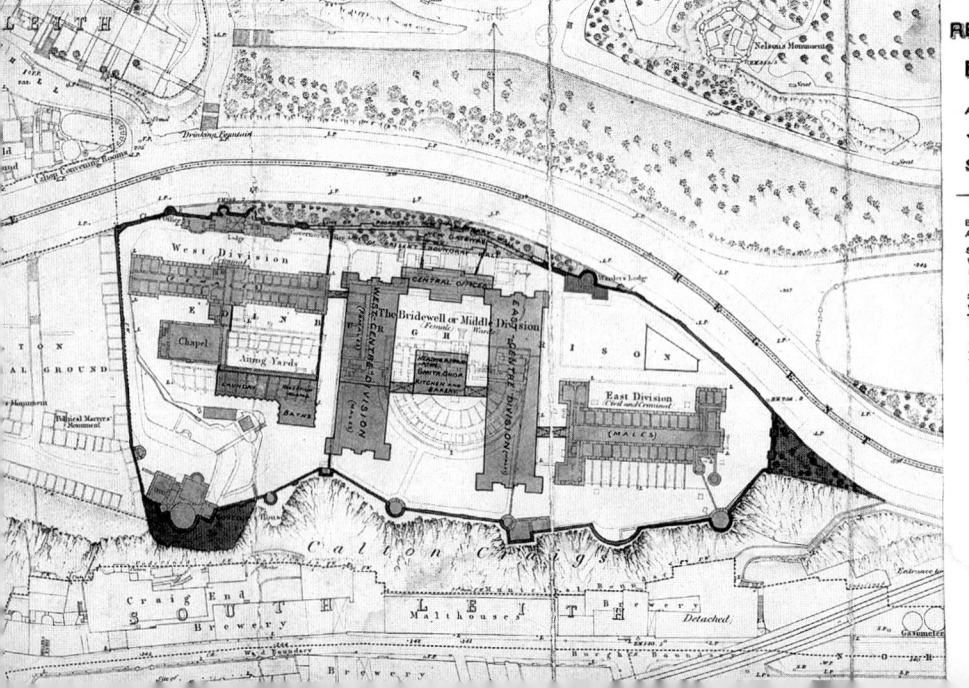

24   Workmen employed in the reconstruction of Calton Prison 1881–88. (RCAHMS. Licensor www.scran.ac.uk)

25   The northern front of Calton Prison facing onto Regent Road in the early twentieth century. (Francis Chrystal/RCAHMS. Licensor www.scran.ac.uk)

CALTON JAIL. EDINBURGH. EAST FRONT. 335.

26 Above: The east gate of Calton Prison on Regent Road. This part of the prison was constructed in the mid-1840s. The site was originally set aside for a debtors' prison. (RCAHMS. Licensor www.scran.ac.uk)

27 Calton Prison viewed from Calton Hill. The East Wing features prominently in the picture, which is thought to have been taken between 1862 and 1873. (Jan Weijers via Peter Stubbs)

28 A bird's-eye view of Calton Prison in 1902 with the Nelson Monument in the top left corner of the photograph. The Calton burial ground is visible in front of the prison. (City of Edinburgh Council – Edinburgh Libraries www.capitalcollections.org.uk)

29 Calton Prison viewed from Calton Hill in 1892. (City of Edinburgh Council – Edinburgh Libraries www.capitalcollections.org.uk)

30 The Governor's House, the only surviving building of Calton Prison, seen from the old burial ground, Waterloo Place. (Malcolm Fife)

31 St Andrews House viewed from the Old Town. This large government office stands on the site of Calton Prison. (Malcolm Fife)

15

THE CRIMINALLY INSANE

Robert Fergusson was an esteemed Edinburgh poet in the late eighteenth century. His works even inspired Robert Burns who was a contemporary. Over time his writings became more and more melancholy. In the summer of 1774 he fell down a flight of stairs and became seriously ill. As a consequence of this he suffered from depression and religious melancholia. Eventually it was decided to place Fergusson in the Edinburgh Bedlam, part of the Edinburgh Charity Workhouse. He was transported there in a sedan chair but when he realised where he was going 'he set up a halloo of helpless misery and shouted hideously'. Once there he was placed in a stone cell with a bed of straw. His condition continued to deteriorate until he died two months later in October 1774.

Nearly fifty years later, conditions were much the same. A printed statement entitled 'The Charity Workhouse and City Bedlam' stated: 'Twenty cells, on the ground floor, are damp and where the patients in winter must suffer severely from the cold. Part of these, attached to the old City Wall, have no fireplaces or means of heating them.'

Relatives were often left to look after next of kin suffering from mental illness. Meanwhile those that had committed a crime or who were a threat to their fellow citizens were flung into jail. Here they mingled with other prisoners, which was not a satisfactory state of affairs as they could intimidate and upset them.

Dr Andrew Duncan, who treated Robert Fergusson while he was in the Edinburgh Bedlam, was moved to set up a 'Lunatic Asylum' where the inmates could receive enlightened and humane treatment. Now known as the Royal Edinburgh Hospital, it opened at Morningside in 1813, initially for patients whose families could afford to pay. According to returns made by ministers in different parishes in Scotland there were 4,650 lunatics in Scotland in 1818. Of these 636 were maintained solely by their parishes and 1,513 partly by their parishes. In addition to this total there were a further 183 'lunatics and idiots' in the Edinburgh Bedlam and the Glasgow Asylum. An extension for the Edinburgh Lunatic Asylum was opened in 1842 for poor patients and for taking over the care of the city's Bedlam inmates in 1844. In 2015, the Bedlam Theatre, Forrest Road, stands close to its site.

The Prisons (Scotland) Act of 1839 stated that provision should be made for criminal lunatics. The general prison at Perth opened in 1842 and had accommodation for a small number of 'insane' persons. Four years later the old part of the prison was adapted for this purpose. The extension of facilities was in part due to demands from the managers of chartered asylums to be relieved of the care of the criminally insane. By 1855 there was accommodation for thirty-five males and thirteen females. Little treatment was offered to those confined in its gloomy stone cells, with the emphasis being on security.

Throughout the nineteenth century criminally insane men and women ended up with the walls of Calton Prison. In many cases it was only for the duration of their trial or whilst deciding what the best course of action was for treatment.

At the end of May 1819, John MacFarlane was put to the bar at the High Court of Edinburgh. A month before he had appeared at Perth Circuit Court charged with the crime of sheep stealing. As it could not be decided whether or not he was insane, the matter was referred to the High Court to ascertain whether he was fit to be brought to a criminal trial. His appearance here excited general astonishment, being dressed like a common beggar and sporting a long bushy beard. The *Caledonian Mercury* on 3 June 1819 stated, 'His appearance was not ferocious, but exhibited more of idiocy than insanity and was frequently softened by a vacant smile when he looked around.'

The Revd Mr Porteous, chaplain at Calton Jail, testified before the court that he found the prisoner always in the same state and believed this came from the weakness of his intellect. Asked if he ever read the Bible, MacFarlane stated that he could not see, having lost his sight when shot at while employed in illicit distillation. When questioned as to what he had done with his proceeds from the stolen sheep, the accused said he fell in with lewd women in Dundee and lost it! Mr Sibbald, governor of Calton Jail, testified that he had paid particular attention to this prisoner since he was placed under his charge. MacFarlane regularly asked for his Tommy, a name used for a penny loaf in Perth Jail, and paid the appropriate sum for it. Lord Justice Clerk then asked the prisoner if he thought stealing was a crime. He replied, 'Surely when they put me in jail for it.' When questioned as to how long he had been confined in Calton Jail, he stated five or six weeks. On being told that if he remained in it he should be shaved, he replied it would weaken him and added, 'Samson lost his strength when he was shaved.' The court came to the conclusion that John MacFarlane, in his present state of mind, was not fit to stand trial. He would be brought up at some future time. Mr Sibbald was directed to continue his attention to him. The Lord Justice Clerk further remarked that if the prisoner's deficiency of intellect appeared confirmed, he should be confined for life, as he was not fit to be at large.

A much more serious case of insanity took place in a private asylum situated to the west of Edinburgh in December 1824. One of its inmates, whose behaviour was causing concern, was attended to by two of the staff. When one of them left the room, the inmate seized a knife and plunged it into the side of his attendant. He then stood motionless before his victim as if nothing had happened. The inmate was transferred to Calton Prison, with his case remitted to the Court of Judiciary. The injured attendant died the following day from his injuries.

Seven years later, in November 1831, George Waters appeared at the High Court of Edinburgh on the charge of murdering his son. Two months earlier, while out for a walk in Inverleith Park, he stabbed his child with a fork and then threw his body into a ditch. The child was discovered a short time later. The accused was known by his workmates as 'daft Geordie Waters'. The explanation for his unstable mind was attributed to the deaths of his two other children in addition to his brother and sister. The court found him guilty but insane. He was sentenced to be confined in Calton Jail all the days of his life or until his friends could arrange for him to be housed in an asylum. At this time there were still no special prison facilities in Scotland for those who had committed serious crimes while their minds were unbalanced.

Euphemia Pryde, the wife of a collier at Edgehead Windmill, near Dalkeith, appeared in court in June 1838, charged with murdering her child. She had thrown the 12-month-old child 20ft out of a window. Dr Spittal and other witnesses stated that Pryde, aged about 40 and 'of lank and rather swarthy appearance', was unfit to stand trial. She had suffered from epileptic fits all her life and more recently from depression. It was decided that on this evidence there would be no further legal proceedings and that in the meantime the unfortunate woman would be remanded in Calton Jail and kept in confinement during the pleasure of the court.

On Saturday, 18 June 1842, Alexander Robertson, jailer of Dunbar Gaol, was attacked in Dunbar High Street. The assailant was Eugene Ernest Augustus Whelps who claimed he was the Prince of Osnaburg and the son of the Duke of York. The High Court in Edinburgh found him guilty of stabbing and cutting an officer of the law who was attempting to take him into custody for riotous behaviour. A sentence of six months in Haddington Prison was handed out to him.

By the mid-nineteenth century, the general prison at Perth was accepting the criminally insane from all over Scotland. None the less all was not well in Edinburgh. At a Law Committee Meeting of the City Parochial Board, it was suggested that the government should take responsibility for this category of criminals. Mr Stott stated that prisoners who became insane while in Perth Prison were sent to Calton Prison three or four days before the expiry of their sentence so Perth ratepayers would not have to support them. Some thirteen had been transferred between 1852 and 1856, none of whom had any previous connection with Edinburgh.

Treatment of those referred to as lunatics was still far from satisfactory in this city. The local newspaper, the *Caledonian Mercury*, printed a letter on 20 March 1858 in which Dr James Alexander requested a rigorous investigation into the treatment of two mentally ill persons.

The first involved William Kennedy who was detained by the police as a lunatic. After appearing in court on two consecutive days the police surgeon certified him as 'a furious lunatic' and sent him to Calton Prison. He was detained here before being sent to Morningside Asylum with a broken arm and dislocated shoulder. In the second case a pensioner who had committed a minor misdemeanor was sentenced to a short period of imprisonment. When he was due for release the City Inspector of the Poor was informed that he was of unsound mind and sent him to the City Workhouse. The old man died here a few days later. On examination it was discovered that he had a fracture to his ribs. While in Calton Prison he had been put under the charge of two other prisoners instead of having a prison warden assigned to him. The Edinburgh Prison Board carried out an internal inquiry into the above cases at the instigation of Dr Alexander but blame was not attributed to anyone. The editorial in the *Caledonian Mercury* wrote a scathing criticism in which they complained that two serious assaults had taken place in the prison, one of which resulted in a death and was culpable homicide. It was stated that there should have been a public inquiry into the matter but an order from the Crown Office prevented any further investigation.

The Prison Report of 1862 related that there were two recorded cases of insanity within Calton Prison. A prisoner was committed for trial for killing a fellow patient in an asylum. The other was a woman who was sentenced to sixty days' imprisonment. She became insane in prison and was committed to an asylum. This was not an uncommon occurrence and similar cases happened at regular intervals over the next few decades.

Two high-profile murders were committed by assailants who were deemed to be insane in mid-nineteenth-century Edinburgh. The first took place at Juniper Green, then a hamlet some 5 miles south-west of the city. On Monday, 18 March 1850, a police constable was called at the house of Dr Wilson after his servant raised the alarm. There they found a dreadful scene: lying on the floor was the lifeless body of Dr Wilson with his 'head beaten almost to jelly' by a pair of tongs. The body of his mother aged about 85 was then discovered in the passageway. The previous evening a man called Peter Pearson, who was in his forties, had called on the doctor to obtain his medicine. He had spent nearly three years in Morningside Asylum, being released in 1846. The servant girl said he was acting strangely and was too terrified to stay in the house overnight. When she raised the alarm the following morning, the police constable discovered the murderer lying naked in Dr Wilson's bed. He exclaimed, 'Here I am quite clean you see. You are all searching for the Kingdom of Heaven – but I will thrust you all down to Hell.' A coach took the powerfully built murderer, who was over 6ft tall, to Calton Prison to await trial. When brought before the High Court, Dr Spittal, who had examined him while in confinement, stated that Pearson was 'in a depressed and melancholy state'. It was decided that he was insane and therefore unfit to plead. From Calton Prison the murderer was transferred to the general prison at Perth. Peter Pearson lingered on here until 1865, when another senseless outrage was committed in Edinburgh.

A young man, John Hunter, lived with his parents and sister at Dalrymple Crescent, The Grange, a district of large villas favoured by businessmen. On a Thursday morning shortly after eleven o'clock his neighbours discovered a horrific scene. Mrs Hunter and her daughter were lying dead in a pool of blood on the pavement in front of their house. They had attempted to escape from John, who had attacked them with an iron bar. He was detained a short time later and locked up in Calton Prison. The double murder received widespread publicity the length and breadth of Britain thanks to the electric telegraph, which was used to relay the details to regional newspapers.

At the trial, James Simpson, surgeon of Calton Prison, said that from the moment he set eyes on John Hunter he thought he was deranged. 'His insanity takes the idea he is a mighty man such as those in the Old Testament but he is superior to them all. He labours under the impression that his strength is enormous and that he is under the influence of spirits and can do wonderful things.' Dr Littlejohn also examined him while in Calton Prison and thought his insanity could be attributed to a form of dementia. John Hunter told him the Holy Spirit dwelt inside him, enabling him to perform feats of great strength. He also spoke of his long hair as proof of his strength. It was decided that the trial should proceed no further due to the accused's state of mind. John Hunter was sent back to Calton Prison under the order that he be detained at Her Majesty's Pleasure.

It was not only those residents of Edinburgh who committed murder while their minds were unbalanced who ended up within the walls of Calton Prison. On 12 July 1869, David Henderson appeared before the High Court on a charge of murdering his 8-month-old daughter in his home at Wick. It was decided that the accused was not fit to stand trial at that time after a statement from a doctor who had examined him. He was ordered to be detained in Calton Prison until there was some possible improvement in his condition.

On a less serious note a thief named George Nisbet appeared before the Sheriff Court in January 1890. The prison medical officer and another doctor both stated he was of unsound mind. When the accused was admitted to Calton Prison he seemed normal, but the following morning he refused to speak and had not uttered a word since. Dr Littlejohn characterised his insanity as 'obstinate taciturnity'. George Nisbet was accordingly sent back to jail.

In 1902, King Edward VII inherited the throne from Queen Victoria, who had died the previous year. Professor Ivison MacAdam, dressed in his colonel's uniform, was carrying out some last-minute chemistry experiments in Surgeons Hall before travelling to London for the Coronation. While Professor Ivison MacAdam was talking to his brother, Dr Stevenson MacAdam, a university porter, Daniel McClinton, entered the laboratory brandishing a rifle and without warning shot the professor dead. He told the victim's brother that he would not shoot him if he did not interfere. At that point James Forbes, a student, came to see what was happening. McClinton shot and killed him, proclaiming, 'this is another of the same lot'. He then handed over his rifle to Dr MacAdam.

Sir Henry Littlejohn, the police surgeon, examined Daniel McClinton, who was locked in Calton Prison awaiting trial. The prisoner told him that he would 'swing for this' but would do it again. According to the surgeon there was little wrong with him. 'He was an old soldier who had a hard life.' This was not the conclusion of Dr John Batty Tuke, a specialist in insanity cases. He had seen the accused in Calton Prison where McClinton stated that the professor had paid Freemasons and Orangemen to spy on him. Dr Tuke was of the opinion he was insane. The Lord Justice General did not accept this and the jury found Daniel McClinton guilty of culpable homicide and he was sentenced to penal servitude for life.

This was not the only murder trial that took place in court during that week. There were, in fact, no less than four, including that of Colin Murray Brown, a trainee minister who had beaten his elderly landlady to death in early August 1902. In his case there was no question of his insanity. Prior to his court appearance he had been held in Morningside Asylum. His trial was little more than a formality and he was ordered to be detained at His Majesty's Pleasure.

As 1905 drew to a close, the residents of North Richmond Street were startled by the brutal murder of a young woman, Elizabeth Tavendale. George Gordon, who lived with Elizabeth, was detained for cutting her throat. At his trial, Gordon stated he was insane when he committed the crime. Dr Henry Hay, the prison doctor, stated he had been under his observation and that there was nothing to suggest that George Gordon was not responsible for his actions. What, however, astonished him was the callousness of the prisoner. Dr Littlejohn had also examined the accused shortly after he had arrived at Calton Prison on the day of the murder. His opinion was that George Gordon 'was of a low type mentally and physically – commonly called a hooligan'. On his first night in prison he had told Thomas MacDonald, a warder, that Elizabeth Tavendale had come home and called him filthy names and as a result he had lost his temper.

At the conclusion of the trial, George Gordon was found guilty and sentenced to twelve years' penal servitude. The motivation for his actions was that the deceased had been having an affair with a soldier.

The following year a woman who had drowned her two infant children in the River Tweed was detained for twelve days in Melrose Asylum. She was then removed to Calton Prison by order of the sheriff. At her trial she pleaded guilty to culpable homicide and was sentenced to six months' imprisonment. This incident prompted Dr Carlyle Johnstone, superintendent of Melrose Asylum, to make a complaint against 'criminal lunatics' being detained in public asylums. He argued that:

... a protest must be raised against what appears to be a growing tendency to make use of asylums as convenient houses of detention for dangerous criminals. The modern asylum is essentially a hospital, its arrangements are not designed to meet the requirements of a jail and in so far as its conditions are made to resemble those of a prison, its efficiency as a hospital must suffer, it is most unfair that respectable members of the community sent to the institution for medical treatment should be forced into association with malefactors and murderers. The presence of such persons on the wards is keenly resented by the patients.

Such a complaint could not be made concerning John O'Neil. Described as a tall gawky-looking man, he was seen behaving oddly at Tolcross on 22 March 1909. He suddenly seized Francis Dennis, a 6-year-old boy, and threw him down some stairs leading to a public lavatory. The unfortunate child landed headfirst and was killed. John O'Neil was detained by a member of the public and on the way to the police station sang songs. He said that at the time his mind was confused and that he believed blood was flowing in the streets and shots were being fired. In addition, his brother was in a procession with his head off and his arms torn from his body. After being detained in Calton Prison for nearly two months, John O'Neil was tried in the High Court on 10 May. Dr Littlejohn, now a professor, attributed the accused's condition as acute mania brought on by him coming from a quiet place in Ireland to a large city! Although found guilty, it was stated that he was insane at the time of the crime. Lord Gutherie pronounced an order of confinement in Perth Prison. After that there were few other insane criminals confined in Calton Prison who had committed crimes that would be noteworthy of the newspaper headlines until it closed seventeen years later.

16

HEAVENLY MATTERS

In the first half of the nineteenth century, few taxes in Edinburgh were more unpopular than the Annuity Tax. The Church of Scotland was the recipient of the money raised, which did little for its popularity among the middle class on which the main burden fell. A long struggle was waged against this imposition, which at one time was 6 per cent of the rents of houses and shops within the city. The tax roused such deep resentment that many citizens refused to pay and their possessions were confiscated and sold. Public resistance eventually made it difficult to seize goods so the authorities changed their tactics and imprisoned those that refused to pay.

During December 1850, officers with a warrant went to the house of a non-payer at an early hour in the morning, entered his bedroom and took him off to Calton Prison without time to wash or shave. He did not remain there long as his business partner paid the outstanding sum. A Mr Todd, on the other hand, spent seven weeks in the Lock-up House for his defiance. In 1855 78-year-old Mrs Pringle, a grocer, was 'carried off to jail' for refusing to pay the tax.

One of the few accounts of life in Calton Prison, 'A Week in Jail', was penned by William Brown in 1859. A man 6ft 6in tall arrived at his shop one morning. He was a sheriff's officer for the purpose of apprehending him in prison for the non-payment of the Annuity Tax. On his arrival, 'There stood the gate-keeper young Samson, six feet nine inches high and proportionately broad, whose gigantic stature strikes a poor prisoner with awe the moment he plants his foot on prison soil.'

At a small office near the gatehouse, the deputy governor offered William Brown another opportunity to pay the tax. He refused and was dispatched to a cell in a building for debtors:

> Having passed through all the courts, we reached the foot of a very long narrow winding stair, which puts one in mind of the stairs of some high steeple or tall monument. A massive gate had to be opened before reaching it which, being unlocked, I had just crossed the threshold when I was left alone to climb the narrow ascent without a guide. I found two gates at the top of the stair and a

warder waiting to open them, that I might enter into my new lodgings. After I had walked a few minutes up and down the passages, the warder pointed out to me my allotted cell, No.92, a small square room, 12 feet by 9 feet, the walls and roof of which were as white as snow. The floor was stone. An iron bed, one chair, and a small table, comprised the furniture ... After surveying it, I had a walk along the passages, which were very long and narrow, 189 feet by 3 feet 3 inches. The cells were entered from one side of the passages and all were numbered.

Later that day, William Brown related that:

I had just retired to my cell when a deputation from the prisoners arrived, with an invitation to come to the kitchen, where they said I would be warmer and more cheery. I consented and found them all happy, some debating, some cooking, and some playing draughts. One of them, a man of seventeen stones weight was very merry ... He seemed to have a new tune for every move he or his antagonist made at the game. All appeared to be on good terms and striving together to make a prison a palace. An elder of the established Church, a singularly inoffensive old man, told me that he had never, during his long life, seen such a display of love and Grace as he had witnessed in that prison. [It should be noted that debtors were classed as civil prisoners as opposed to criminal prisoners and were granted far more liberties than them. For instance they did not have to undertake prison work.] ... I was told that I would not see my wife or any of my friends, till eleven o'clock the following day, between that hour and one o'clock, being the only time visitors are permitted to see prisoners, the only exception being in favour of an agent.

The gas was turned off in the evenings, which prevented William Brown reading the books he had brought with him.

I was awoke about six in the morning by ... an unusual and unearthly sound, resembling the rattle of distant thunder, only that the peals were shorter and more continuous. It could not be thunder for the sound seemed to come from subterraneous depths, nor the presage of an approaching earthquake, for happily such tremors don't visit the Calton. What then could this dismal, growling, groaning, thunder, earthquake-like noise be? I lay meditating for some minutes before the truth dawned on my mind – it was the sounds arising from the unlocking of the cell doors of the criminal department in the flats below and in all directions, north, south, east and west. It was an hour after this that my own cell door was unlocked. I arose and after making my bed and sorting my little room, took half an hour's airing in the cages which were entered from an opening in the passage opposite my cell. In the facility afforded for a morning walk, without the trouble of going far to get it, the prison surpasses the most of our city dwellings and it would be well if builders and others interested in the welfare of the community before proceeding with the erection of new tenements, would visit and inspect the cages of Calton Prison.

After dispatching my first Annuity Tax breakfast, I repaired to the cages for an airing and a chat with my new companions and with a view to gather further information regarding the outs and ins of prison discipline. I found most of the debtors there playing at marbles with all the sprightliness and gaiety of boyhood.

While William Brown was in Calton Prison, there was a demonstration against the Annuity Tax:

About half an hour before the time of the meeting, a great number had gathered on the walk of Calton Hill, immediately below Nelson's Monument. Seeing them look towards the prison, I put a handkerchief out of a broken pane, which was observed and responded to with such hearty and lively manifestations as roused the fears of the jail kings, who were in terror, notwithstanding the strength of their castle, that it might be successfully stormed by such an overwhelming, warm hearted and patriotic multitude as were now assembled on Mars Hill. A message was sent up from one of our kings to our warder, to cause the flag immediately be taken in, which order was instantly obeyed. We were not permitted to show our colours again. However, I had an occasional peep out at the broken pane, which was only a few inches long and broad and even this seemed to keep the powers in awe, for the under governor made his appearance and shut us out of the room – the only one that looked out towards the hill.

Momentum was gathering against the Annuity Tax and shortly after William Brown was released the rate of payment was reduced and in 1870 it was abolished.

Church ministers played a large part in the life of Calton Prison. They often visited it to provide comfort and advice to its inmates. Occasionally, they found themselves imprisoned within its walls. The Revd D. Craig appeared before the Sheriff Court in June 1831 charged with twenty-one acts of theft, all of which concerned the theft of books. They were all found in his house and no attempt had been made to sell them. The court, however, thought the best course of action was for him to be removed from the country and the Revd D. Craig was sentenced to 'transportation beyond the seas for fourteen years'.

In 1886, the Revd Leys received one month's imprisonment for contempt of court. Having looked after his two grandchildren for six years, he refused to return them to his son when requested because his son wished to place them in a Roman Catholic institution. The son, however, later dropped the demand for possession of his children so his father could be freed from Calton Prison.

In 1902, Richard Whytock, a well-known street preacher, received a sentence of three months in Calton Prison for assaulting his six children as well as failing to feed them. In the same year the Revd McDonald of the United Free Church persisted in preaching in Coatbridge church when he had been dismissed for being incompetent. He continued to defy the ban and eventually received one month's imprisonment, much to the disgust of many members of his congregation. On his release, the Revd McDonald stated he had been treated very well. He was confined in a commodious cell, the same in which Herdman, the last man hanged in Edinburgh (until that time) was placed in temporarily just before he was taken to the scaffold. The two small windows high up in the wall, of course barred, looked towards the south and the cell was cheerily enough lighted as prison apartments go. He never got outside his own room and the only exercise he took was in what he called 'the cage', a little place with a grating above. The furnishing of the cell consisted of a table, two chairs – one for the use of visitors – and an ordinary iron bedstead. The Revd McDonald also had a fire in the room, which would doubtless be needed to keep up the temperature of the old stone walls and floor.

17

POLITICAL UNREST

When Calton Prison opened, the French Revolution was only twenty years old. The government was concerned that an uprising may take place in Britain. These fears were given substance in 1820 when the 'Radical Rebellion' broke out in April. An economic downturn had caused unrest among factory workers, particularly weavers, which was centred on Glasgow, with a strike with widespread support taking place at the beginning of the month. An offshoot of the disturbances took place not far from Stirling in what became known as the Battle of Bonnymuir.

Fourteen dissidents captured during this confrontation were transported down the River Forth from Stirling to Newhaven by steamboat. They were then taken by coaches to Calton Prison with an escort of soldiers. One of them, Andrew Hardie, gave a declaration while imprisoned here declaring that he had left Glasgow on the night of 4 April to join a party of radicals who were assembling at Gadshill. He had heard several times in the course of the evening that there was to be a general rising of the people in the country and that England was all in arms. Armed with a musket but no ammunition he met forty other rebels at Gadshill. They then went on to Condorrat where they were joined by a party led by John Baird. A hussar who they encountered was handed a copy of 'The Address to the People of Great Britain' and allowed then to flee. The Carron Ironworks was the target of the rebels, who were now all armed with muskets and pikes. Unfortunately for them, hussars and foot soldiers from Stirlingshire Yeomanry intercepted them before they could reach it. However, they decided to make a stand and fight back. Some of the rebels were seriously wounded but not before the commander of the hussars had his horse shot from beneath him.

The prisoners were removed to Edinburgh Castle after about a week in Calton Prison. Some time later they were taken to Stirling to be tried before a special court, such was the fear of the government of public unrest. Three ringleaders, including Andrew Hardie and John Baird, were sentenced to death for high treason. Eighteen others were transported.

Throughout the nineteenth century there were outbreaks of industrial unrest. Three colliers who attempted to form a union amongst their fellow workers on the Estate of Wallyford in 1818 were brought before the magistrates in Edinburgh who decided to place them in Calton Prison.

The most notorious trial to take place in the city involving a labour dispute was that of the Glasgow Cotton Spinners at the end of 1837. The weaving industry was suffering a serious downturn and the mill owners attempted to push through wage cuts. The workers responded by striking in August. Violence broke out and a strikebreaker was shot. The authorities responded by arresting the leaders of the union on charges which included attempting to set fire to houses and factories, assaulting blacklegs [those who refused to strike], conspiracy to keep wages up and disturbances at Oakbank factory.

On Tuesday, 14 November, the five prisoners were conveyed without warning from the Glasgow bridewell to Edinburgh Prison, chained in iron manacles, to await trail. This led someone to write to the *London Dispatch* complaining, 'The working classes of this Kingdom have again been insulted and deeply injured by the further cruel treatment of the cotton spinners.' There was widespread sympathy for the accused with demonstrations being staged across the country in support of them. Only three of the less serious charges against them were proved. Nonetheless, they were sentenced to seven years' transportation. The union leaders, however, got no further than the hulks at Woolwich where they spent three years before being pardoned.

There were further outbreaks of industrial unrest with miners often at the forefront throughout the remainder of the nineteenth century. In April 1864 there was a strike of street sweepers in Edinburgh. Four persons were sent to Calton Prison for three days for 'annoying' men who were employed by the Inspector of Cleansing to do their work.

In 1848, there was a wave of unrest across Europe with revolutions in France, Germany and Italy. On 7 March the evening peace in Edinburgh was disturbed:

> … by a riotous mob which consisted chiefly of young blackguards, well-known thieves, a sprinkling of navvies and accompanied as common in such cases by numbers of loose women and neglected children. There was nothing political in the riot which commenced about half past eight o'clock. About that hour a band led by one or two men who were armed with formidable sticks and who appeared to belong to the mechanic class, took up positions in Princes Street, the crowd was composed of several hundred persons. They proceeded westwards smashing every lamp in the way. They also vented their anger on some windows.
>
> They walked up the Mound and down the High Street, smashing windows including those of the new police office.

Constables walked down the High Street four abreast in an effort to disperse the crowd. Cavalry from Piershill Barracks came to their assistance and members of the public were sworn in as special constables. Around forty persons were brought to court for participating in these disturbances. A small number received sixty days in prison, three youths got forty days, four were sentenced to thirty days, four to twenty and three for ten days.

During the First World War a number of political dissidents who were thought to represent a threat to the war effort were locked up in Calton Prison. They included William Gallacher who was a leading trade unionist and opposed to Britain's involvement in the conflict. The final straw for the government was an article he wrote for the Clyde Workers Committee journal, *The Worker*. Along with its editor John Muir, they were found guilty of sedition and locked up in Calton Prison, away from their sympathizers on Clydeside. William Gallacher wrote that:

> It was by far the worst prison in Scotland, cold, silent and repellent. Its discipline was extremely harsh and the diet atrocious. There was no 'association' labour. Most of the prisoners worked in their cells at mat-making and similar occupations.
>
> The one hour's exercise in the morning was the sole opportunity we had [of] seeing each other, when desperate attempts were made to exchange a whisper or two.
>
> For breakfast, we had thick porridge and sour milk. For dinner, soup and a piece of dried bread, and for supper, thick porridge and sour milk.
>
> Unfortunately, poor health, prison confinement but mainly the whispered suggestions of a semi-crazed member of our movement, which had preyed on his mind, had seriously affected McDougall, so that he began to have illusions of persecution. One Sunday morning, after we had been in about six weeks, we were seated in a chapel awaiting the chaplain's entrance. As he came in and approached the pulpit, McDougall stood up and shouted, 'Sir, I want you to write to my father. The warders are talking at my door at night to drive me insane.' Two warders led him back to his cell. Later that day he had a terrible nervous attack. It was a heartbreaking experience to have to sit in one's cell and listen to him, without being able to do anything to help. Of course, no one had been talking at his door at night. The warders all went home after the prisoners had gone to bed, except for the officer at the gatehouse. And only a watchman in rubber-soled sneakers made the rounds at night. It was not possible to talk in any part of the hall without the sound of being heard in every cell.
>
> To illustrate this Maxton occupied the next cell to mine. At 'Nine o'clock bell' bed time, I made it a practice to tap the verse of the 'Red Flag' on the wall, while Maxton contributed the chorus, after which I gave an alleged rendering of 'Hip, Hip, Hurrah!' After a month of these daily tapping obbligatos, a prisoner on an upper tier complained about the noise, and Maxton was removed to another cell.

The day after his breakdown, McDougall was transferred to Perth for special care. Following this affair, questions were asked in the Commons regarding conditions in Calton Gaol. It was decided, therefore, that certain officials, together with a representative of organised labour, should pay a visit to the prison.

In February 1917 William Gallacher was released from Calton Prison. Two and a half years later he was back for 'instigating and inciting large crowds to form part of a riotous mob' at Glasgow while campaigning for a forty-hour working week. This time he was sentenced to three months along with Emanuel Shinwell who got five months. Both men went on to become well-known Members of Parliament, William Gallacher representing the Communist Party and Emanuel Shinwell the Labour Party. Arthur Woodburn, who was also imprisoned in 1916 in Calton Prison, rose to become the Secretary of State for Scotland shortly after the end of the Second World War. It is said that he salvaged some stones from the building when it was demolished to construct a path in his garden. He had, however, little affection for the former prison, describing it as 'the poorhouse of all prisons with the cold chill of a grim fortress'. Not everyone, however, was of this opinion. James Maxton, who was a conscientious objector and organised strikes during the First World War, was sentenced to a year around the same time as Arthur Woodburn. While in Calton Prison he was employed as a joiner and remarked that the place was 'very comfortable' and found life 'enjoyable' with him being given access to good books.

Even once the conflict was over the government felt threatened enough to charge Captain James White DSO for making seditious speeches at an unemployment demonstration at the East Meadows in 1921. When in the witness box he made a long speech in which he stated that he had begun the struggle thirteen years ago when he gave up his commission in the army, convinced by the writings of Tolstoy that the (British) Imperial Army only existed to maintain in a condition of unstable equilibrium a society founded on a system of rapacious greed. Sheriff Orr was less than impressed and sentenced him to two months in Calton Prison. Mrs Laing who presided over the meeting was sentenced to three weeks.

18

CROFTERS IN REBELLION

In the latter part of the nineteenth century and the early years of the twentieth century there was simmering unrest in the western Highlands. Much of it centred on land ownership, with large tracts in the hands of a few wealthy individuals while smallholders had to scrape a living from a few acres. Few persons could have been more alien to Calton Prison than the crofters. Many had never been to a big city before and some only spoke Gaelic.

The first challenge to the landlords came in 1874 when an attempt was made to evict a number of crofters from the island of Bernera. They had rioted after some of their grazing land had been annexed for a shooting estate. Three of the crofters singled out for their resistance were found not guilty when brought to trial. Up until then the smallholders had no protection in law against eviction. Now emboldened by the sudden turn around in events there were further moves to oppose tyrannical estate owners. This resulted in what was referred to as the Crofters War, which started in 1882. It opened with the Battle of the Braes and unrest spread to Glendale on the Isle of Skye. Here the crofters had been informed by the landlord that they could not collect firewood from the seashore or even cut rushes in place of it. They also had their grazing land taken away.

Police action against them proved ineffective and eventually a number of crofters went onboard the Royal Navy gunboat HMS *Jackal* to conduct negotiations. The outcome of this was that five of the crofters agreed to stand trial. In the end, in February 1883, three of the crofters – Donald McLeod, John Morrison and John MacPherson – travelled south to appear before the Court of Session in Edinburgh. The outcome was not what they had expected. The men were sentenced to two months' imprisonment in Calton Prison. Back on Skye the verdict 'on the Glendale Crofters has been received with great surprise and sorrow. The people now freely state that they will carry on the agitation to the bitter end and will never surrender until their grievances are redressed.' They became known as the Glendale Martyrs.

According to *The Scotsman* newspaper on 17 March 1883, the three crofters were 'being treated not as ordinary offenders but as misdemeanants and are detained in the civil prison. They are not obliged to do any work and are allowed to see their friends and to peruse the newspapers or any book they may desire to have while the privilege of providing their own food is accorded to them.'

The crofters were released at 8 a.m. on 15 May where they were met by a crowd of around a hundred sympathizers along with two pipers in Highland costume.

Later in the same year there was a riot at Strome Ferry close to the Isle of Skye. The inhabitants of the village were incensed that the two steamers should attempt to land large consignments of fish here to be transported by the Highland Railway on a Sunday. Ten men were arrested for rioting and swearing in Gaelic. At the end of July 1883, they found themselves in front of the High Court in Edinburgh. In their defence it was stated that the old Scottish laws regarding the sanctity of the Sabbath was still in force. The working of cargoes on this day grievously upset those with strong religious convictions. Despite this, the ten men were found guilty of rioting and mobbing and received a sentence of four months' imprisonment. The Lord Justice Clerk added that 'the sentence that I shall pronounce, though it may seem lenient, it is by no means nominal. Very few men who have once been soiled by the atmosphere within prison walls are ever able to take up altogether the life they left behind.'

In fact they only spent fifty-six days in prison before being released on 21 September 1883. Prison officials provided them with a railway pass home and 5s each.

The small island of Calavay was at the centre of another land dispute. A number of crofters had taken possession of part of it and planted potatoes on ground that did not belong to them in defiance of an interdict against them. Five of those involved agreed to go of their own accord to stand trial in the Court of Session in Edinburgh. In their defence it was stated that 'the men were without education' and did not realise the consequences of their actions. They, however, received a token sentence of one month in Calton Prison. The Highland Land Law paid for them to be supplied with special meals while they were there. On their release the crofters stated that they were grateful for the kind treatment they had received from the prison staff.

In 1886 the Crofters Act was passed to address their grievances. However it did not put an end to the disturbances. At the end of that year six crofters were imprisoned for mobbing and rioting at Bornesketaig on the Isle of Skye. On 15 December they were confined in Calton Prison for three months. When they were released they were met at the gate of the prison by Mr Smith and Mr Blackburn, members of the Edinburgh Trades Council, and taken for breakfast in the Buchanan Hotel.

There was a further outbreak of trouble in early January 1888. It was the climax of the long-running Crofters War. Landlords were dividing up their estates into large farms and in the process marginalizing the smallholders and depriving them of places where they could graze their livestock. On Christmas Day 1887, a meeting of landless crofters was held on the Island of Lewis and it was decided that the tenant of Aignish Farm was to be warned that he should leave the property and take his livestock with him. Dykes began to be pulled down on New Year's Eve. The day of reckoning was 9 January 1888.

As dawn broke, around 1,000 protesters arrived at the farm. The authorities had anticipated trouble and had already dispatched soldiers from the Royal Scots. There was also a party of thirty-six marines from HMS *Seahorse*, which had been visiting Stornoway at the time. Some of the crofters were detained by them and attempts were made to rescue them by their colleagues. Stones and missiles were thrown. The marines had to drive them back at bayonet point. It was only due to the presence of the local sheriff that events were prevented from spiraling totally out of control. Even so, many of the crofters were badly wounded, as was the commander of the Royal Scots and several policemen. Armed with a revolver, Mr Ross, the deputy fiscal, attempted to detain one of the ringleaders but was seriously injured in the face. The crofters succeeded in driving the cattle off Aignish Farm and towards their own township.

On 13 January thirteen of those detained for rioting were taken aboard HMS *Jackal* and taken to Edinburgh for trial. According to some sources, several were outside of the locus where most of the trouble took place.

They were not the only crofters who found themselves before the court. On the mainland opposite the Isle of Skye at Clashmore, Assynt, the subfactor of the estate had been assaulted on 15 December 1887. The crofters then drove their own cattle onto its fields.

They were all tried in the High Court and sentenced on 3 February 1888. Of the twelve Aignish prisoners, seven were sent to Calton Prison for twelve months. Two who were proved to have taken a prominent part in the proceedings were sentenced to fifteen months' imprisonment and the remaining three in regard to whom the attempted rescue of prisoners and assault of police and military were found not proven were sent to jail for nine months. A man who had been caught in the act of destroying the farm fencing received a sentence of six months. One of the Crown witnesses who had never been off the Island of Lewis, on being brought to Edinburgh appeared to have lost his mind and he began howling like a dog. He was transferred to an asylum. Further crofters involved in the Aignish disturbances were brought to trial during the following months. Of three Clashmore prisoners convicted, a man named Hugh Matheson was sent to Calton Prison for six months and two women for nine months each. 'There was some little sensation in court when the sentence on the women was intimated,' stated the *Southern Reporter* on 9 February 1888. In July a man arrived in Edinburgh and turned himself in to the authorities proclaiming that it was he who had attacked the factor while dressed as a woman and not Hugh Matheson. In early August all three of the Clashmore prisoners were released from Calton Prison.

There had been further embarrassment for the authorities earlier in the year. A woman under the name of Mrs Gordon Baillie came to Edinburgh on 14 February 1888 to plead the cause of the crofters and especially of the two Clashmore women languishing in Calton Prison. She succeeded in obtaining an audience with the prison commissioners who gave her permission to visit the two female prisoners on 17 February. Mrs Gordon Baillie told her friends that she was really the Countess of Moray; an irregularity in the marriage of one of her ancestors deprived her of the title. She claimed that she owned estates in Skye as well as 75,000 acres in Australia, which she wished to utilize for the benefit of the crofters. On 19 February Mrs Gordon Baillie left Edinburgh abruptly. Edinburgh Police succeeded in tracing her history back to 1869, which revealed she lived in Dundee with her mother who was a washerwoman.

Professor Blacket, who had dined with the imposter, stated: 'I verily believe she would have deceived the Devil himself.' By July 1888 Mrs Gordon Baillie appeared before the court of Westminster with her husband on charges of fraud.

There was another outbreak of unrest in the Hebrides in the early twentieth century. In 1908, two fishermen of the island of Barra squatted on the adjacent island of Vatersay. In spite of an interdict against them they remained in possession of part of the island. They were brought to Edinburgh on 1 June 1908 to appear in the Court of Session and answer a charge of defying the law. Their fare to the city was in fact paid by the owner of Vatersay, Lady Cathcart, so they could account for their actions. The two men stated that they urgently needed land for their allotments and had offered to pay rent for the land they had requisitioned. They were sentenced to two months in Calton Prison but were released after six weeks. The government put forward a proposal for dividing the farm on Vattersay, which Lady Cathcart agreed to do.

Eleven Lewis crofters ended up in Calton Prison for trespassing onto Reef Farm at Uig. They were sentenced to six weeks' imprisonment in the spring of 1914 but were released after two. The squatters stated that they made their living mostly by fishing and required a little land to eke out an existence. There was land in abundance on Lewis, which was used to graze sheep. The temptation to trespass was great. The Secretary of State for Scotland agreed to open an inquiry into the crofters' grievances and the matter was debated in the House of Commons. On leaving prison they stated that they were pleased with the kindness shown to them by all the officials from the governor downwards. While serving their sentences they were told that they could change from their prison garb into their ordinary cloths. As they had travelled to Edinburgh in their best Sunday clothes they unanimously decided not to ruin them by wearing them in Calton Prison!

After the end of the First World War there was a further outbreak of unrest on Skye and on Uist. Six Skye crofters who were ex-servicemen ended up in Calton Prison in late May 1923 for contempt of court. There was widespread public support for the men and the matter was raised in the House of Commons. This resulted in them being released early in June 1923. At the time a further group of crofters were due to appear before the Court of Session for also taking possession of land on the Isle of Skye. These events gave an impetus for the government to address the grievances of the crofters, which eventually put an end to the activities of the 'land raiders'. Reform was further helped as Ramsay McDonald, who was the son of a farm labourer, became prime minister in the following year.

19

IRISH TERRORISTS

Shortly after ten o'clock on the night of 20 January 1883 a large explosion resounded across the south of Glasgow. Streetlights suddenly went out, and a woman holding a baby jumped out of a window in alarm. The local inhabitants came out onto the streets and saw flames leaping out of a 160ft-tall gasholder at the Tradestown Gas Works, which then suddenly collapsed. When it exploded the fire made a hole at the foot of a bed in a nearby house and then passed right through the front windows and the door, cracking its walls and bringing down the plaster of the roof. Other houses in Muirhouse Lane were also damaged. Eleven people were hurt by the blast, including a father and son who were severely injured. Fortunately, when it exploded the gasholder was only a quarter full.

The same night a shed belonging to the Caledonian Railway Company was totally destroyed. A few hours later a group of young men discovered a box on a viaduct used by the Forth-Clyde Canal. Thinking there may be a body inside, they opened the lid and it exploded. Despite all of them being blown to the ground and burned they all managed to make their way to the local police station.

Suspecting that the gasholder explosion was no accident, an expert from the Home Office was sent to examine it. He concluded that the detonation had been caused by dynamite. Suspicion immediately fell on Irish nationalists campaigning for Home Rule. At that time all of Ireland was under British Rule. It was not until later in the year that ten men were arrested on suspicion of causing the explosions.

On 14 December 1883 they were brought to Edinburgh for trial. Unusually they did not go to Calton Prison but were immediately taken to cells underneath the courtroom and locked up there. There was great concern that a rescue attempt may be made by sympathizers. Letters had been sent threatening to blow up Parliament House or bring down enough of Calton Prison to enable the accused to stage an escape. The buildings and surrounding streets were patrolled by police armed with revolvers and soldiers from the Gordon Highlanders. At the trial of the 'Glasgow Dynamitards' it was disclosed that they were members of the Ribbon Society, an offshoot of the Fenian Brotherhood. The Lord Advocate, J. Balfour, caused a sensation in court when he stated that if the canal aqueduct had been blown up as planned, thousands of people in the lower-lying part of Glasgow may have been drowned. All the accused were found guilty. Terence McDermott, Thomas Devany, Peter Callaghan, Henry McCann and James McCullagh were sentenced to penal servitude for life. The remaining five, James Donelly, James Kelly, Patrick McCabe, Patrick Dunn and Denis Casey, each received seven years' penal servitude on the grounds that they were not aware of the extent of the operations of the Ribbon Society.

At the conclusion of the trial the ten men were transferred to Calton Prison. They were manacled and grouped in two companies of five each. Mounted policemen and constables in cabs escorted them there. Their stay here was shortlived. The ten men were removed from Calton Prison on 27 December 1883 with the utmost secrecy. At about nine o'clock in the morning the prisoners, all manacled, were placed in the prison van and driven to St Margaret's Station, which hitherto had most exclusively been used by the Royal Family on their visits to Holyrood Palace. So not as to attract attention the men wore their own clothes and the warders who guarded them were not in uniform. They all boarded a third-class carriage which was then coupled to a special locomotive that took it to Waverley Station. It was then attached to the *Flying Scotsman* to take them south accompanied by Captain Christie, the prison governor, and Major Dudgeon. James Donelly died of consumption in Chatham Convict Prison in 1887. By 1901 all the other 'Dynamitards' had been set free.

There were attempts to perpetrate other bomb outrages in Britain in the years after 1883. Two years later there was a plot to blow up the House of Commons and the Tower of London. In 1890, there was another attack on a gasholder in Glasgow but no one was arrested for this.

Shortly after the end of the First World War, Ireland descended into armed conflict with those opposing British rule taking up arms against the government and its soldiers. The last year of the Irish War of Independence in 1921 saw a number of sympathizers for the Irish Nationalist cause in Calton Prison awaiting trial. In March, sixteen alleged Sinn Feiners including one woman were tried for transporting weapons. Sergeant Denholm of the Alloa police testified to chasing, on the night of 4 December, a motorcar containing two of the accused. The police car eventually managed to overtake it and stopped. The men in the other car then drew to a halt some distance behind it and threw bags containing gelignite, a rifle and a pistol over a hedge. Fuse wire and 404 detonators were also discovered at the scene. Nine of those on trial were found guilty and received prison terms varying from five years' penal servitude to twelve months' imprisonment.

On information received, the police raided a house at South Bridge on 16 July which was 'being frequented by undesirable people'. In it they found three men and three women thought to be involved in organising Irish Nationalist activities in Edinburgh. The three women were released but the men each received sentences of three months in Calton Prison.

In early August, Sean O'Doherty, James Devaney, James Kimmet and Lena MacDonald appeared in court charged with attempting to transport rifles and a revolver from Dundee to Glasgow. Two of the men received a sentence of three years' penal servitude while the third got eighteen months. On leaving court Sean O'Doherty shouted out triumphantly, 'God Save Ireland'.

The same day as the above trial concluded on 8 August, a further twelve Irish sympathizers appeared on a far more serious charge of conspiracy and murder. Earlier in the year a senior Irish Republication officer, Frank Carty, had been arrested. On 4 May he was being transported from the Central Office Court, Glasgow, to Duke Street Prison when the vehicle was ambushed in an attempt to set him free. A gun battle broke out in Cathedral Square. Inspector Robert Johnston was killed in the first volley of shots and Detective George Stirton was wounded as he and another detective returned fire. The prison van, however, drove on and arrived at Duke Street Prison riddled with bullet holes. The police responded by arresting a large number of suspects, of whom thirteen were sent to Edinburgh for trial, although one was later released. Each evening at the end of the proceedings large numbers of curious onlookers lined the streets hoping to catch a glimpse of the suspects being taken back to Calton Prison. The trial concluded with the charges of conspiracy and murder against six of the accused being not proven and the remaining six were found not guilty. All were then released.

Not all explosions were the handiwork of terrorists. In what was called the 'Infernal Machine Outrages', tempting parcels arrived at the respective residences of William McDonald and Mrs Barrow on 15 February 1882. When opened at the former's house the package exploded, wrecking the house and injuring the five occupants. Mrs Barrow's package was opened by her brother. It too detonated, injuring three persons. All the injured subsequently recovered although Alexander McDonald, William's father, was almost blind for nine weeks.

Suspicion fell on Charles Costello who had repeatedly made threats against both persons. He had been previously convicted of annoying Mrs Barrow and fined. Costello was arrested the same night as the explosions and held in Calton Prison to await trial. The jury found him guilty and he was sentenced to twenty years' penal servitude. As the accused had also made threats against the Lord Justice Clerk, he was banned from returning to Scotland at the end of his sentence. This, however, did not deter him and he was rearrested at Colinton seventeen years later. While in Chatham Prison he attempted to escape by digging a tunnel. He was released after serving sixteen and a half years. Shortly after his detention, Charles Costello was dispatched to Peterhead Prison to serve the remainder of his sentence.

20

SUFFRAGETTES

The tube filled up my breathing space, I couldn't breathe. The young man began pouring in liquid food. I heard the noises I was making of choking and suffocation – uncouth noises human beings are not intended to make and which might be made by a vivisected dog. Still he kept on pouring.

This was probably the closest Calton Prison, resembling a medieval fortress, came to inflicting torture within its walls. It is an account by Ethel Moorhead of being force-fed. In February 1914, she became the first suffragette to suffer this in Scotland.

Towards the end of the Victorian era there was a move among upper- and middle-class women to participate in politics. Ethel Moorhead was born in the 1870s and studied art in Paris where she was talented enough to have several exhibitions. In 1910 she joined the Women's Social and Political Union. Her first recorded act of dissent took place the following year when she threw a rock at MP Winston Churchill at a political meeting in Dundee. In 1912 she smashed a glass case in the Wallace Monument. In addition she also threw a stone at a car that she thought was carrying the Chancellor of the Exchequer, Lloyd George.

At that time suffragettes' tactics were becoming ever more extreme and now involved fire-raising. Ethel Moorhead was caught in possession of fire-lighting implements in Glasgow in 1913. Her punishment was eight months' imprisonment in Duke Street Prison where she went on hunger strike. This led to her early release but it was on condition that she reported back there, which she failed to do and went on the run for several months. When she was recaptured at Peebles she found herself locked up in Calton Prison.

Suffragettes were also force-fed in Perth Prison, where the methods employed were even more brutal. Ethel Moorhead contracted double pneumonia after being force-fed, a consequence of food getting struck in her lungs as a result of this treatment. At a meeting of the National Political League held at the foot of Leith Walk on 24 February 1914, Mr Wilson McLaren stated that he 'had just learned that force-feeding was now in operation in Calton Hill Prison. He could not find words strong enough to express his disgust and indignation at such a thing being tolerated in Edinburgh.' The prison doctor had actually refused to administer force-feeding to Ethel Moorhead and two outside doctors were employed instead. Mr Barnes, a Glasgow MP, raised the matter of allegations of the ill treatment of Ethel Moorhead in the House of Commons.

Mr McKinnon Wood, the Scottish Secretary, stated the following in the government's defence:

> Miss Ethel Moorhead, alias Margaret Morrison, alias Mary Humphries, alias Edith Johnstone, alias Mrs Marshall, was under sentence of eight months' imprisonment for breaking into a house with intent to set fire to it, this being her fourth conviction. During the past few months there had been a number of cases of arson in Scotland, the last being the burning of the ancient church of Whitekirk in Haddingtonshire. In one case that of Aberuchill Castle, Perthshire there were several servants in the castle at the time of the fire, who were, he was informed rescued with great difficulty. [A recent investigation has concluded that the fire at Whitekirk Church was probably accidental.]

While Ethel Moorhead was on hunger strike half a dozen of her supporters gathered on Calton Hill and attempted to send encouragement to her by megaphone. They chose a time late one evening when there would be little traffic passing the prison below. Messages such as 'No surrender', 'Keep the flag flying' and 'Your friends outside are thinking of you' were broadcast. Proceedings were brought to an end with the arrival of a policeman.

Ethel Moorhead, however, was not the first suffragette to end up in Calton Prison. When Sir Edward Grey, the Foreign Secretary, visited Leith in early December 1909, Edith Hudson and Elsie Brown from Leicester caused a disturbance which included breaking a window in a post office. They were given the option of paying a fine or spending two weeks in prison. The two suffragettes plumped for the latter punishment on the grounds that if they paid the fine it would be an admission that they had done wrong. When Miss Brown arrived at Calton Prison she refused to change her cloths for the garments handed to her. She stated that she was then forcibly stripped and dressed in a degraded costume marked with broad arrows and worn by common criminals. Both women, however, were released after an anonymous person paid their fine — against their wishes.

An attempt was made to burn down the grandstand at Kelso Racecourse — seen as a bastion of male pleasure — in spring 1913. Arabella Scott, Edith Hudson and Elizabeth Thomson were charged for this act of arson, as was Donald McEwan. Scott, Hudson and McEwan were sentenced to nine months in Calton Prison with Thomson receiving a term of three months. After only five days Elizabeth

Thomson was released under the Prisoners Act, nicknamed the 'Cat and Mouse Act'. This allowed for prisoners on hunger strike to be set free on licence when their health was threatened. Once they had recovered they had to return to their confinement.

The following day Arabella Scott was also allowed home. At a meeting of support for them by the Women's Social and Political Union it was revealed that the prisoners had been allowed to wear their own clothes in Calton Prison but were not allowed see friends, to receive letters or read newspapers. A spokesman stated that 'it was disgraceful that political prisoners should be so treated and it was for every member of the Union to keep worrying the Secretary for Scotland and Members of Parliament for Scotland until these women were treated as political prisoners.'

In early May 1914, Arabella Scott was rearrested at Brighton and conveyed back to Calton Prison in connection with the attempted fire at Kelso Grandstand. She immediately went on hunger strike again and was released from captivity a few days later. Her sister visited her in prison and Arabella Scott was obliged to take a few sips of water so that she could speak to her. Once free she immediately went to England to lend her support in the Ipswich by-election. As she had failed to return to Calton Prison on her own accord she was detained in London on 18 June and returned to Scotland, fighting all the way back. Arabella Scott was locked up in Perth Prison where she was force-fed. On her release on 26 July 1914, she said 'the only effect had been to strengthen her principals'.

From an early age Elizabeth Watson was an enthusiastic supporter of the movement for votes for women. She learned to play the bagpipes at the age of 7 and used her musical talent in support of the cause. While still a young girl Elizabeth Watson gave prisoners at Waverley Station who were returning to Holloway Prison a musical send off. She also stood on Calton Hill and played the bagpipes to suffragettes locked up in the prison. At the age of 14 she became the only female member of the Highland Pipers Society.

In 1918 Parliament gave women over 30 who were householders the vote.

21

FOUL DEEDS IN THE HIGHLANDS

In Victorian times there were a number of high-profile crimes committed in the Scottish Highlands that reached national headlines. The culprits were brought to Calton Prison to have their fate decided by the High Court.

On 19 June 1877, Alexander McDougall was transferred from Inverary Jail to Calton Prison by Inspector Fraser from Dunoon to stand trial in the High Court. A hotel keeper at the Kingshouse Hotel, Glencoe, he was charged with the murder of his wife Agnes the previous March. Dunald McLeish, who worked at the hotel, testified that his employer, along with his wife, were often the worse for drink. Agnes had 'the appearance of a woman that had been must cruelly abused'. On 12 March Dunald McLeish arrived at the hotel to find the doors locked. He forced his way in and found Agnes lying in the lobby quite naked. At the time she was still alive. After going to summon help McLeish found the doors locked again and heard screaming. On entering the premises McDougall was discovered but then disappeared. He was captured the following day. Agnes was put to bed but died twelve days later from her injuries. In what became known as the Glencoe murder case, Alexander McDougall was found guilty of culpable homicide and sentenced to ten years' penal servitude.

The following year saw Alexander Robertson, sometimes known as 'Dundonnachie', brought before the Court of Session. His crime was somewhat less serious: he had crossed the Dunkeld Bridge over the River Tay in Perthshire and refused to pay the toll. The Duke of Atholl, who owned the bridge, had an interdict passed in 1871 prohibiting Alexander Robertson from using it as a crossing but he ignored it. Around about that time, however, he went to England. The dispute was resurrected on his return many years later when he crossed the bridge again in defiance of its keepers. The old warrant was then put into requisition and Robertson was locked up in Calton Prison in 1878. At his trial he defended himself, which created considerable amusement. The Lord President, however, found him guilty of the breach interdict and contempt of court, having in 1871 crossed the Dunkeld Bridge five times without paying. Having already undergone a short sentence of imprisonment and agreeing to avoid the Dunkeld Bridge in future, he was allowed to go 'scot-free'.

Some years later, in 1892, Dundonnachie turned up in Edinburgh again. This time he was involved in a legal case against Henry Hay, the surgeon at Calton Prison, demanding £500 in damages as he maliciously accused him of being a dangerous lunatic. Alexander Robertson had been confined for eight months in Morningside Asylum the previous year. The case was dismissed when he did not appear in court.

In the summer of 1889, 37-year-old Edward Rose set off from England for a walking holiday on the island of Arran. He was due home on 18 July but never returned. A few days later his brother came north to look for him. Over 250 men carried out a meticulous search of Goatfell Mountain from its base to its summit.

On 4 August, Edward Rose's body was found at the foot of a cliff near the summit. From the evidence it appeared that his death was not accidental. His skull had received several blows and an effort had been made to conceal the corpse.

Highland superstitions still seemed to have a grip on the area and the local policeman buried the victim's boots on the beach between the high and low watermark. If that were not done, it was believed that the murdered person's ghost would haunt the place forever.

The nationwide search got underway for the suspected culprit, John Laurie, who was last seen in the company of Edward Rose walking up the mountain together. Laurie had, in fact, returned to Glasgow wearing the deceased's tennis suit. On 3 September he was found lying under a bush by a police constable, close to his home town of Coatbridge. He had attempted to cut his throat with a razor.

On 1 November a number of prisoners arrived by train at Waverley Station from Glasgow. Among them was John Laurie, escorted by several warders. He was conveyed to Calton Prison in a cab while the others had to make do with the ordinary prison van.

The trial took place a few days later. A number of witnesses put forward a case that Edward Rose could have died accidentally in a fall from the mountain. The accused came from a good family and in his youth had been 'a foppish man' and a member of the Young Conservatives. The jury, however, found him guilty and he was sentenced to death. On his return to Calton Prison, a large crowd followed the prison van hooting and yelling. It had been many years since there had been a court case in Edinburgh that had aroused so much public interest.

The condemned man was removed from Calton Prison on 11 November to Greenock Prison where he was to be executed. There was concern, however, about John Laurie's state of mind when he murdered Edward Rose. It appeared to be a senseless crime in which little was stolen. A last-minute reprieve was granted and the sentence was commuted to penal servitude for life. After nearly twenty years' captivity John Laurie was released from Peterhead Prison in May 1909. He had once succeeded in escaping but was later recaptured by armed warders.

In August 1893 a prisoner by the name of Alfred Monson was removed in great secrecy from his cell in Greenock Prison. Mr Napier, the prison governor, assisted by a warder in plain clothes, travelled by train to Edinburgh with their charge. They alighted at Haymarket Station, hailed a cab and headed towards Calton Prison. Here the prisoner was placed in the care of Governor Christie. The *Glasgow Herald* of 7 November 1893 described his accommodation here at length:

> The cell which the prisoner occupies is on top of one of the blocks of buildings composing the Edinburgh Prison which are such a prominent feature in the architecture of the city. It is a large apartment lighted by a window high up in the wall and contains a fireplace, a table and an armchair. Adjoining the room is a small lavatory. The object of housing him in this part of the prison as much as possible [is] to keep him apart from the other prisoners At the end of one of the corridors, also on top of building, is what practically is a small cell, with an open iron grating instead of the roof. This has been assigned to Monson as his airing ground and he will be allowed to take exercises there under the care of a warder at stated periods. He is allowed a pint of beer with his other meals which are supplied from outside. Monson who is attired in a grey suit of clothes was in the airing cell when the visiting justices called and in their reply to their inquiry stated that he had no complaints of any kind to make in regard to the treatment he was receiving from prison officials, He has, it is understood, made a request to be allowed to get books from the outside and it was stated to him that there was a good library in connection with the prison and that he could have books from it. The Justices before leaving inspected Monson's cell in which a large fire was burning and on the prisoner's armchair was a bound number of Chamber's Journal open at a story which oddly enough, bore the title of 'A Legal Secret'.

Calton Jail's new prisoner was at the centre of what some newspapers headlined as 'The Ardlamont Mystery'. Alfred Monson, aged 33, was the son of a minister. He was married with three children and had until recently been a tutor to Cecil Hambrough, who came from a wealthy landowning family on the Isle of Wight. Hambrough, who was in his early twenties, was heir to a substantial fortune from his grandfather, who, according to his will, had appointed Alfred Monson as his guardian. The two men had spent the previous summer at Ardlamont House in Argyllshire. They had returned again in 1893. While on a shooting expedition on 10 August, Cecil Hambrough received a fatal injury. The doctor said it was his opinion that the death might have been caused by his holding the gun incautiously while negotiating a turf dyke. Less convinced were the insurance companies who stood to pay out large sums of money on the demise of Cecil Hambrough. They pressed for the case to be reopened and at the end of August Alfred Monson was arrested and taken to Greenock Prison.

The trial was the subject of great interest throughout Britain. Alfred Monson again had to be moved in secrecy from Calton Prison to the Sheriff Court to avoid curious members of the public. At his trial it was disclosed that on the day before the shooting, Alfred Monson and Cecil Hambrough had ventured out in a small boat in Ardlamont Bay. It began taking on water and started to sink. Cecil Hambrough could not swim but managed to cling on to some rocks. Monson made it back to the shore and returned to rescue his companion. The rowing boat was later examined and found to have holes drilled in it which had then been blocked up. Much of the evidence, however, was circumstantial. It was stated that the accused had little to gain by murdering Cecil Hambrough as he received an income for being his tutor. Hence the jury returned a verdict of 'not proven' and on 22 December 1893, the last day of the trial, Albert Monson was a free man again, much to the astonishment of the press and onlookers in the court.

22

PRISONERS FROM FOREIGN LANDS

Fredric Hill, who compiled the 1847 Inspectors Report on Prisons in Scotland and Northern England, stated that on a visit to Newcastle Prison he found that no less than one third of the prisoners were of Scottish and Irish extraction.

As a consequence he asked the governor of Calton Prison to undertake a survey to discover if there were large numbers of persons of English extraction in this Scottish prison. Not surprisingly it was found that only a small number of those detained within its walls came from south of the border. There were, however, a considerable number who had Irish connections, although it should be noted that in Victorian times all of Ireland was part of Britain.

From time to time the occasional foreigner ended up inside Calton Prison. By the end of the nineteenth century the port of Leith had steamer services to many countries on the opposite side of the North Sea. Also Edinburgh was a popular destination with the wealthy traveller in an age when the tourist industry was in its infancy. Crimes involving violence instigated by foreigners were rare, but when they did occur they often involved Italians. One such instance involved Benjamin Marco, Dominico Marco and Antonio Morgate, who all lived in the Grassmarket. They were charged with assaulting Patrick Reilly and Sophia Hutchison on 18 June 1874. A cabman had been playing on an accordion when Dominico Marco offered to play an Italian tune. On hearing the music the couple came out of a public house and began dancing. A quarrel erupted and Antonio Morgate rushed forward and struck Sophia Hutchison and Patrick Reilly with a short heavy weapon made from gutta-percha. This inflicted serious injuries on the two victims, who once on the ground were further assaulted and kicked. At the Burgh Court Antonio Morgate was sentenced to thirty days in Calton Prison.

Nearly three years later, on 29 February 1877, Antonio Statferi stabbed Hugh Smith in the West Port in the left arm, shoulder and the side of his face, causing an effusion of blood. The assailant was punished with a sentence of nine months in prison.

It was, however, a Belgium who was responsible for committing one of the more outrageous crimes. Charles Voodelkie moved to Glasgow in May 1900 with his French girlfriend, Amy Cagnard, who was in her early twenties and half his age. She had tried to leave him when they lived in London but he had threatened to kill her. On moving to Edinburgh, Charles Voodelkie sent her out to work as a prostitute while he sat at home drinking. On the night of 6 May 1901 he became involved in an argument with her when she could not give him any money. He threatened to kill her or, failing that, maim her so as to compel her to become a beggar. Some time later he shot Amy in the neck with a revolver. A doctor was called for but so intimidated by Charles Voodelkie was Amy that she said she had shot herself. The doctor became suspicious of this explanation and Charles Voodelkie decided to make his escape, not being finally captured until a few months later in Liverpool. He was then brought back to Edinburgh and locked up in Calton Prison to await trial. The court found him guilty and sentenced him to ten years' penal servitude. Amy survived the experience.

Fortunately most of the crimes committed by foreigners in Edinburgh were not as dramatic as this. They often involved fraud or theft. Charles Werner, a German by birth and described as a respectable-looking elderly man, appeared in court on six charges of fraud. During September 1884 he had answered six advertisements for a number of articles offered for sale, including a gun, silver spoons and two St Bernard dogs. He paid for them with cheques that proved to be worthless. In his defence it was stated that he had a business in Liverpool, working as a dental surgeon. He decided to move to Edinburgh and purchase a business here but it did not come up to expectations. Werner pleaded for leniency as his wife and five children were destitute. The sheriff, however, sentenced him to six months' imprisonment despite the fact that he had already been in Calton Prison for ten weeks awaiting trial.

Five years later a well-dressed young man appeared in a Hull court charged with stealing from three hotels in that town. He called himself Fredrick Pearson but he stated his real name was Henry Epel. The court was informed that he had come to England where he intended to earn his living as a musical performer. He had then travelled to Edinburgh where he was sentenced to eighteen months in prison for stealing jewellery from a hotel. Here he was convicted under the name of Frederickson.

In July 1903, 22-year-old Henrietta Devarrat, 'a tall well-dressed girl describing herself as a governess of Swiss nationality' found herself before the Edinburgh Police Court. She had stolen a gold bracelet and a gold neck chain from a house in Drumsheugh Place where she worked as a nursery maid. She also obtained board and lodgings by pretending that she was a French governess. Pending the completion of arrangements for return to Switzerland she was sent to Calton Prison for seven days.

A Polish swindler was sent to jail for thirty days a few months later for committing a similar offence. John Philip obtained board and lodgings at a house at Rosewell as well as stealing a miner's wage of £1 9s.

Some years later, another Eastern European ended up on the wrong side of the law. Stephen Norwich, a Lithuanian, pleaded guilty at Edinburgh Sheriff Court to having reset a quantity of jewellery at a shop at No. 15 Bridge Street, Leith, between 7 and 29 September 1923. He further admitted having in his possession a revolver for which he did not hold the necessary certificate. In his defence it was stated that he had previously been of high character and had several times acted as an interpreter in Edinburgh courts. Norwich received a sentence of two months in Calton Prison.

It was not only Europeans that occasionally ended up in the Edinburgh prison but Americans as well. On 25 November 1886, the *Edinburgh Evening News* related that 'a respectably dressed and intelligent looking young man named John Watson' was placed at the bar of the Sheriff Criminal Court. He was charged with stealing a silver watch and an aneroid barometer from the Balmoral Hotel and a field glass and a leather case from The Edinburgh Hotel. At his trial he stated he was an American and that he had been drinking ever since he left his country in July. He worked as an actor and had come to Scotland for an engagement but had been unsuccessful and had run out of money. The sheriff sent him to Calton Prison for six months which he considered a short time.

The following year, on Friday, 25 February, a man named Thomas Smith, who said he was a 'Yankee', appeared in the Edinburgh Police Court. This was the fourteenth time he had been brought up for sentence for begging in the city. Smith, whose clothes were all tattered and torn, stated he had been released just a couple of hours before from Calton Prison when he was arrested again for begging. The accused told the court that he had come to Scotland from America six months earlier in an effort to get work. He was a clerk by occupation but had found it very difficult to obtain employment. During the half year he had been in the country, most of his time had been spent in prison. He was sentenced to a further four days in Calton Prison but the magistrate told him to return to the court on his release so that they would consider what they could do to assist him.

An American named Clarence Perry, about 40 years of age, who was said to be a doctor, was sentenced to six months' imprisonment for a series of frauds committed in Edinburgh and Glasgow over a period of five years. They related to the fraudulent procuring of clothing and jewellery. He had also approached Sir Hector Cameron at his house in Glasgow in October 1905 claiming that he was Dr Perry from Toronto and had run short of money. There he obtained £3, but this was not the only occasion that this type of fraud was committed. Perry was said to have a degree in medicine which he obtained in New York but preferred to earn his living by dealing in jewellery. His downfall was attributed to drink.

PRISONERS FROM FOREIGN LANDS

Joe Fringer, a young fair-haired American, perpetrated a cruel fraud on a Leith family whose son had travelled to Algiers to join the French Foreign Legion. While in its service he befriended Joe Fringer, who learned of his family back in Scotland. After some five years' absence, in September 1924 the young man's family received a telegram from Newhaven in Sussex stating that he had arrived home and could they send him £7. This was followed by a further request for money from London. The elderly mother obliged, not realising that her son at the time was languishing in a French prison for desertion. Joe Fringer in fact had been the author of the telegrams. This only came to light when he travelled to Edinburgh and rather surprisingly presented himself at the Leith Police Station and asked for work. On investigation it was found that he was in contravention of the Aliens order and the fraud came to light. He received a sentence of three months in Calton Prison, perhaps the last foreigner to make its acquaintance before it closed.

A few years earlier, in 1919, demobilised American army officer Raymond Hiles and his wife Marjory were detained as the liner *Olympic* was about to sail to the USA and Hiles was placed in Calton Prison. The couple had eloped from England to get married in Scotland as the bride's parents had refused consent because of her young age. On arriving in Edinburgh it was found that they had to be resident in the country for twenty-one days before the marriage could take place. Unable to wait, they approached two porters who agreed to make false statements at the ceremony. This was soon discovered and was the reason for Raymond Hiles' incarceration in Calton Prison. At his trial in the Sheriff Court, the American's solicitor presented a memo to the Secretary of State for Scotland pointing out that the offence was in a different category from most. This met with a positive response and Raymond Hiles was officially given permission to leave the prison to marry Marjory in St Andrew's parish church. Immediately after the wedding the governor of the prison appeared and to the joy of the bride and bridegroom intimated that the Secretary of State had consented to the immediate release of Raymond Hiles.

In the years leading up to the First World War there was an increasing xenophobia against foreigners in Britain. Germans could find themselves detained on a trumped-up charge of being a spy. This suspicion, however, was not always without substance. In 1912 Armgaard Karl Graves was dispatched to Scotland to gather information on the new naval dockyard at Rosyth and collect information on ships in the Forth at Invergordon. Dressed in a well-cut lounge suit, he took up lodgings in Morningside. It is thought that he was born in Berlin in 1882 but his true name is not known. At the age of 16 he arrived in Australia but was accused of theft and harassing a woman; his stay was short-lived. In Germany he committed fraud which probably brought him to the attention of the German Naval Intelligence. While in Scotland he took few precautions to hide his true intentions, discussing the German Navy with his landlady. He also had a book on the world's navies. The British Secret Service began opening the letters he sent to Germany.

It was not long before Armgaard Graves was detained and locked up in Calton Prison. He spent 105 days there before being brought to trial in the High Court in late July 1912. The spy who stated he was an Australian doctor was convicted under the Official Secrets Act of communicating information regarding navy and land fortifications. There was a second charge of obtaining information on guns being manufactured at Beardmore's Ordnance Factory, of which he was found not guilty. A sentence of eighteen months' imprisonment was passed. The accused appeared to be quite well pleased with his sentence and while awaiting his removal to Calton Jail carried on an animated conversation with the warden.

His departure in the prison van was witnessed by a large crowd. One witness said that he had been told by Armaard Graves that the German invasion would come within the next twelve months. In fact during the First World War there were no plans by the Germans to invade Britain. Within a matter of weeks Armgaard Graves was freed from prison. He had convinced the British Secret Service that he would turn coat and work for them. His mission was to return to Berlin where he would collect a list of German spies in Britain. Once he received payment from his new employers he fled to America. There, to add insult to injury, he wrote a book on his exploits and projected the persona of a master spy. It is thought he died in America but not before he returned to a life of crime and at one point was accused of burning a woman alive.

From the outbreak of the First World War, German sailors who were taken prisoner began arriving in Edinburgh. They were, however, taken to Redford Barracks and not Calton Prison.

Shortly before the closure of Calton Prison, a man called Thomas Garin ended up in one of its cells. He was arrested in dramatic circumstances for having cut open a lockfast jewel case in a hotel in Princes Street. In addition he had assaulted a writer to the signet by striking him with a chisel. The police were suspicious that all was not what is seemed. Information was received from the Glasgow authorities that the prisoner was in fact Eddie Guerin, who, according to newspaper headlines, was renowned for making a sensational escape from Devil's Island, a penal colony in French Guiana. Despite his foreign-sounding name, he had in fact been born in London in 1860. At the age of 13 he immigrated to the United States where he started his life of crime. In 1890 he escaped in a horse and cart with a large sum of money from a bank. Not long after, Eddie Guerin made his way to France where he first gained notoriety in international circles. He took part in a robbery at a Bank of France in Lyon and got clean away. Ten years later, in 1901, he and his partner Chicago May, along with other accomplices, robbed the Paris office of the American Express Company. They were later arrested while on a train.

France wanted him out of the way and sentenced Eddie Guerin to imprisonment in their penal colony in French Guiana in South America. This comprised of three islands including the notorious Devil's Island. In fact Eddie Guerin was probably detained on St Joseph's Island and not Devil's Island as the popular press proclaimed. Four years into his sentence he escaped with three other inmates. They hollowed out a log to use as a boat. Then they began their 200-mile journey to the mainland. One of the fugitives developed fever and died. Another went insane and jumped overboard. The remaining two eventually reached the coast of Dutch Guiana. The other prisoner decided to paddle on in the canoe and was later recaptured by the French.

After a 70-mile trek, Eddie Guerin reached Paramaribo, the capital of Dutch Guiana. Chicago May met him there and nursed him back to health. Once back in the United States, Guerin told his exploits to mouth-dropping crowds in Broadway bar rooms. He was an excellent self-publicist. Not long after, he moved to England. While living in London, he had an argument with Chicago May, who disclosed his true identity. The French Government demanded his extradition but this was refused on the grounds that he was a British citizen. The Edinburgh Sheriff Court sentenced 'the only person to escape from Devil's Island' up until then to six months in Calton Prison. For the remainder of his life Eddie Guerin was in and out of trouble. In 1931, at the age of 71, he received a term of three years' penal servitude at the end of his trial in the Old Bailey, London.

23

DEATHS AND SUICIDES AT CALTON PRISON

As the year 1820 drew to a close, a middle-aged man lay dying in Calton Prison. His name was James McCoull, alias James Moffat, a notorious villain in early nineteenth-century Britain. The *Caledonian Mercury* grudgingly published an obituary in their newspaper as his exploits were too well known to be ignored. One newspaper dubbed him 'The Robber of the World' as his activities were not only confined to Britain but extended across Europe. James McCoull was born in London and started his life of crime at school. Well dressed and able to think on his feet, he was able to gain access to theatres and other events that were patronised by the higher echelons of society. He was then able to pick their pockets and other possessions. Being an avid gambler, James McCoull soon lost most of his proceeds. On one occasion he told a baker who was interested in astronomy that a new star had suddenly appeared in the sky. While looking upwards, the victim had his pocketbook stolen! Well known to the authorities in London, James McCoull left for the Netherlands. While living in Hamburg he was suspected of stealing and fled the city, arriving in Edinburgh in 1805. Here he established a tanning and dying business but this was thought to be a cover for his criminal activities. In 1809, caught picking a gentleman's pocket in a theatre, James McCoull ended up in Calton Prison. Unaware of his true identity, he was released after just a few weeks.

In 1811, he broke in and robbed the Paisley Union Bank in Glasgow with another well-known villain, Huffy White. This would be an act he would later regret. Not long after the theft James McCoull was detained in Glasgow Prison. Although he was eventually released due to a legal loophole and the bank managed to recover £10,000, they were determined to pursue the robbers.

Many years later James McCoull was brought to trial in Edinburgh charged with the robbery. Worse was yet to come as he was found guilty and sentenced to be executed on 26 July 1820. While in Calton Prison, however, his punishment was commuted to transportation. Before it could be put into effect James McCoull became ill and died a few months later. His wife – who he had not lived with since 1812 – paid for his burial in Calton Cemetery next to the prison.

James McCoull was perhaps the most famous criminal to die of natural causes within the walls of Calton Prison. Throughout the next century there would be one or two deaths each year and occasionally a suicide. Compared with other Scottish prisons, Calton Prison had a very low death rate in the mid-nineteenth century. This could be partly explained by the fact that it had a small hospital with its own surgeon. Also, seriously ill prisoners could be transferred to the Royal Infirmary. Prisons located in remoter areas of the county did not have these advantages.

In another well-publicised case, Elizabeth Burt from Kinross was accused of murdering Mrs Spark and her infant child by administering poison. At the time she was their nurse and denied all knowledge of the crimes. A druggist, however, stated that Elizabeth Burt had purchased the poison arsenic from his shop. After a preliminary investigation by the procurator fiscal, which seemed to have made a deep impression on her mind, she was taken violently ill on 7 March 1836. She recovered from this but her health was in decline when she was committed to Kinross Jail around ten days later. Later Elizabeth Burt was transferred to Calton Prison to stand trial. While confined here she declared herself pregnant by the husband of the poisoned woman. She suffered a miscarriage on the morning of 1 May 1836, dying later the same day.

On a Saturday night in April 1852, Peter Taylor, aged about 78, was released from Calton Prison after serving a short sentence of two days. He was met at the gate by his wife. Almost immediately he complained of faintness and, on reaching the General Post Office, sat down on the pavement, unable to proceed any further, and died.

At the end of 1859, the prison governor reported that no deaths had occurred in Calton Prison during the previous two years. For 1863, however, there were no less than seven deaths. This compared with fifteen in the House of Refuge, a staggering 109 in St Cuthbert's Poorhouse and 130 in the city's poorhouse.

In the latter part of the nineteenth century, deaths in Calton Prison tended to receive more publicity than in the past as it was necessary to hold a public inquiry under the Prisons (Scotland) Act of 1877.

Jane Mather died suddenly in the prison on 3 December 1879. She had been admitted on 25 November under a sentence for breach of the peace. She was found by the warders lying unconscious in her cell and died half an hour later. The prison doctor carried out a post-mortem of the body and certified the death to have been caused by a heart attack.

A more distressing case involved another woman, Mary Buchanan, aged 35. On 15 March 1881 she was fined £15 for shebeening (operating an unlicensed drinks establishment) with the alternative of three months' imprisonment. Mary Buchanan chose the latter. On admission to Calton Prison it appeared that she was paralysed down one side. Sarah Gibbon, who shared a cell with her, helped her to dress and undress.

After five days she caught cold and was troubled with diarrhoea. The fire was also removed from the cell around the same time. Both the inmates of the cell felt cold but were afraid to complain. The matron visited them once a week but did not speak to them. Meanwhile Mary Buchanan lay in a bed in filthy conditions.

The doctor passed along the lobby once a week and she managed to speak to him at the cell door. His remedy was to give her three days' bread and water. In fact she had already been put on this diet. She was also given a 'guard' bed to sleep on – a low wooden one. Mary Buchanan eventually succumbed to her illness on 5 June 1881. At the inquiry the prison doctor, James Sidey MD, stated that he did not intend the sentence of her being fed on bread and water to be carried out. Further he added there was no effective treatment for paralysis.

The previous year there was a somewhat similar case involving a male prisoner. John Goodwin was tried in the Edinburgh Summary Court on 3 May 1880 and sentenced to sixty days in Calton Prison for picking a servant's pocket. On arriving there he was found to be in a weak condition and suffering from an abscess on his neck. Inspector McEwan had him photographed, which was a practice adopted by all Scottish prisons in the 1870s. The picture was then circulated and it was discovered that the prisoner had several aliases including the name Rutherford Blanchard. He was a former convict who had spent much of his life in prison. On expiry of his sentence he was re-arrested for having failed to report to the police that he was a former convict on early release. On his return to Calton Prison his health continued to decline and he died in the hospital on 18 November, aged 39.

In 1887 there was a somewhat more curious case involving the death of Robert Hume, who was well connected in Edinburgh. His father-in-law had refused him access to his house at Portobello and this so enraged him that he produced a revolver and discharged three shots through a window. For this he had been arrested for the reckless use of firearms and was awaiting trial.

Some years before, a young lady had been shot in a villa in St John's Wood, London. Robert Hume was believed to be responsible but there was not enough evidence to charge him.

Calton Prison warders reported him to be somewhat excitable, as if recovering from a drinking bout. On 2 February 1887, he became very violent and overpowered a warder along with other prisoners who came to his assistance. Crockery was broken and clothes torn. The following day Robert Hume died in Calton Prison. The medical report stated that his 'whole brain was intensively congested and that must have led to an attack of excitement and this continuing for any time would lead to debility'.

A few months later there was a second death in the prison. Peter Connolly was jailed for seven days for travelling without a ticket between Glasgow and

Haymarket stations. When he arrived at Calton Prison he was in pain, which he attributed to cramp. The following morning one of his fellow inmates said Connelly was choking. A warder attended but did not have the correct keys and it took twenty-five minutes to open the door. Dr Henry Hay was summoned and instructed poultices be applied to the prisoner's stomach and that he was to receive a supply of milk. The doctor saw him again at 9 a.m., by which time Peter Connolly was in a state of collapse. He was given some brandy and hot-water bottles to keep him warm. When the doctor returned at 11 a.m. Peter Connolly was dead. A post-mortem found that the deceased had an ulcer in the bowels which had ruptured with fatal consequences.

On 9 January 1892, William Walker, an Aberdeenshire farmer, was committed to Calton Prison to await trial for alleged fraud upon banks. A few days later, when served with an order to attend court, he complained of feeling unwell. He was ordered to bed and was supplied with extra clothing but died later the same morning. A post-mortem was held by the police surgeon Dr Littlejohn, who concluded the cause of death was chronic heart disease. William Walker was 36.

A few months later, on 30 April, a female prisoner by the name of Fanny Pilkington also died in Calton Prison of heart disease and pneumonia.

John Smith arrived at Calton Prison on 20 March 1902 after being sentenced to fourteen days' imprisonment at Buckhaven Police Court, Fife, for sleeping out. On admission he complained of a tired feeling and was sent to the prison hospital, where he later died. The cause of death was due to a heart condition following advanced kidney disease.

At the end of that year James Waterson was sentenced to six months' hard labour. Though only 25, he had already spent nine years in prison. Pleading on his behalf, an agent stated that his confinement had injuriously affected his health and mind. James Waterson added that he had been sent to the convict prison at Peterhead where he found the conditions to be healthier than those at Calton Prison.

From time to time there were deaths in Calton Prison caused by suicide. Successful attempts were, however, relatively infrequent in Victorian times.

On 8 February 1812 Hugh Ross, an innkeeper in Ballantrae, was arrested for stealing a quantity of banknotes from a carrier's cart. Not long after the robbery he was apprehended on the instructions of the Paisley Bank but they could not obtain sufficient evidence to make a case against him. Hugh Ross sued them and was awarded substantial damages. Some six years later he was brought to trial in Edinburgh for the same crime but the jury found him not guilty. A few months later he was apprehended on the instructions of the Lord Advocate and placed in Calton Prison. Here he attempted to take his life by cutting his throat. Although the wound did not prove fatal, it 'reduced him to a miserable state'. He had succeeded in cutting his windpipe but his life was preserved by means of a silver pipe through which he now had to breathe. An elastic tube was also introduced at the wound in his throat through which he was fed. This had to be done initially by a doctor but he was later taught to feed himself.

William Pollock cheated the scaffold by committing suicide in Calton Prison. He had been sentenced to death for the murder of his wife. The execution was fixed to take place on 22 March 1826 but was found dead in his cell two days earlier. He had cut three strips from the back of his shirt, twisting them to form a rope, but it proved too short so he used a weaver's knot to attach it to a blanket. It was then attached to an iron gating above the cell door from which he hung himself. While in prison he paid little attention when the Bible was read to him by visiting clergymen, one of whom he informed, 'There is nothing you can tell me that I do not know. I know every part of the Scriptures.' Three suicide notes were left behind. One to Governor Young read: 'Excuse this rash act. When you consider all, you will see that there are good intentions, though not towards myself.' Another to the upper turnkey contained the following: 'I never could believe that I was the occasion of my wife's death and could not bear the idea of going to the scaffold.'

A prisoner called Patrick Gallacher under sentence of seven years' transportation hung himself with his handkerchief in May 1852.

In 1881 Alexander Watt, aged 52, also committed suicide in Calton Prison. He was sentenced to seven days' imprisonment for stealing a pair of boots he had been given to repair. Shortly after breakfast on 27 December he hung himself using a cord of shoemaker's thread which he used while at work in the prison.

When William Perfect, a brush maker, returned home after spending some time in the Royal Infirmary, he quarrelled with his wife when he discovered that she had joined the Christadelphian Society. Later he assaulted her, receiving twenty-five days' imprisonment. At 3.15 p.m. on the afternoon of Sunday, 13 July 1884, a prison warder looked through the spyhole in the cell door and all appeared to be well. Half an hour later he went back and found Perfect had hung himself with a handkerchief tied to the bell handle.

John Thomson, aged around 16, hung himself with an iron pin and hemp rope which he used for mat-making while in confinement. In October 1887, he had been sentenced to eighteen months in Calton Prison for forty acts of fire-raising in Aberdeen. At his trial it was stated in his defence that his mind had become corrupted by the reading of 'trashy literature'. In addition his father and mother were weak minded, but John Thomson was said to be aware of the gravity of his crimes.

A more dramatic suicide was made by John Williams on 12 September 1902. He had been sentenced to sixty days' imprisonment for indecent assault but was reportedly a good prisoner. When warder Robert Sime went to open his cell door at 6 a.m. he found that John Williams was already up. As he went to open the next cell, John Williams came out into the corridor and put his hand on the corridor railings, appearing to be looking for something down below. He then squeezed between the uprights and fell some 20ft into the corridor below. Death was instantaneous, his skull being fractured.

During the summer of 1908, a postman in prison for misappropriating a postal order informed the warders that he had swallowed a number of objects. At first they were not inclined to believe him but eventually he was sent to the Royal Infirmary where they discovered small stones, iron pins and pieces of a water jug inside his stomach. Surgeons succeeded in removing most of the objects and the prisoner seems to have survived the experience.

People who attempted to commit suicide outside the prison could also end up within its walls. Many were just half-hearted acts committed while under the influence of drink.

At two o'clock on a May morning in 1887, the wife of Thomas Smith reported that he had shut himself in his room with the intention of committing suicide. Police constables arrived at the house but the husband escaped by climbing up a drainpipe and onto the roof from where he threw slates at anyone in range. Two firemen got onto the roof along with two policemen but then Thomas Smith suddenly disappeared. He had fallen some 12ft into a disused attic and was removed to the Royal Infirmary. Sometime before this he had been sent to Calton Prison for attempting to cut his throat.

Maria Sherry was arrested after she had taken off some of her clothing and threatened to jump off a bridge and into the Union Canal at Leamington Place. In court it was stated that she was a chronic drunkard. The sheriff thought the best course of action was to put her under control for some time to let her recover her mental balance. She was sentenced to seven days' imprisonment. It was her fifty-second court appearance.

On 3 May 1895 the *Evening Telegraph* had the somewhat alarming headline 'Suicidal mania in Edinburgh'. There had been several cases of attempted suicide, most of which had been the consequence of drinking to excess. They included William Bird, aged 46, who had drunk a quantity of laudanum but pleaded not guilty when he was taken to court. Margaret Stewart, on the other hand, admitted her guilt to having threatened to commit suicide by climbing onto a wall in front of Princes Street Station and threatening to throw herself off, a drop of 15ft. Dr Williamson said he frequently had to examine the prisoner, who had given him a great deal of trouble. She was sent to Calton Prison for sixty days.

In November 1903, George Brown was charged with attempting to commit suicide by drinking a quantity of Laudanum. Sir Henry Littlejohn, the police surgeon, recommended that the best course of action would be to send him to prison for a short period in order to recover from the effects of poison and drink. The sheriff passed a sentence of seven days.

24

ESCAPES

Escapes from not only the Edinburgh Tolbooth in the High Street but those in other towns the length and breadth of Scotland were all too frequent. This type of building almost invited their prisoners to attempt to escape, located in the main street often with no perimeter wall to deter those intending to make a break for freedom. Often only a few iron bars or a single cell door separated the offender from freedom. His friends and accomplices were in a position to offer assistance, being able to approach the outside of the building from a public street.

All this was about to change as purpose-built prisons began to replace the traditional places of confinement in the early nineteenth century. From now on those deprived of their liberty would be confined in solidly constructed buildings, located away from the everyday bustle of life. Many resembled medieval fortresses with high perimeter walls and turrets, with the interior accessed through a gatehouse. It would be thought that escape from such austere structures would now be almost impossible. Despite being confined behind these grim walls many still dreamed of escape and breakouts from Edinburgh's Bridewell and the new prison on Calton Hill were surprisingly frequent in the early years of their operation. This appears attributable to the fact that the advances in prison architecture were not initially accompanied by similar improvements in prison practices. When, however, the traditional turnkeys were replaced by a professional prison warder service in the mid-nineteenth century escapes from Scottish prisons became a rare occurrence.

In the twilight years of the Georgian age there were several high-profile escape attempts by prisoners confined in the institutions on Calton Hill. In early 1815, James Kelly, who was confined within the Bridewell for sheep stealing, made an unsuccessful escape attempt. While attempting to flee he knocked down a turnkey and severely cut his head with an improvised weapon. For this the sheriff depute sentenced him to thirty lashes under the Bridewell Act. This punishment was administered to his naked back by the hangman while the other prisoners were made to watch.

A more successful break for freedom took place in January 1820. At noon on a Monday three men and three boys confined in the same cell in the Bridewell effected their escape in the following manner: when a turnkey opened the door he had a quantity of snuff thrown in his eyes. He was immediately set upon by the prisoners who forced him to the floor. They then put a rope around his neck with the intention of hanging the unfortunate turnkey. The noose of the rope entered his mouth, preventing him from yelling out and raising the alarm. Fortunately for him, he was a stout man and this fact prevented the prisoners hanging him. Instead they opted for locking him in another cell. They then made their way along one of the passages and escaped over the back wall of the Bridewell. Their liberty, however, was short-lived. Within a few days all six had been recaptured. A man called Adams who had haboured them in his house was also committed to the Bridewell for sixty days.

In October 1820, on the day of the races at Dumfries, two prisoners made their escape from the local gaol. A turnkey, Thomas Morrin, was beaten about the head with a large stone in a sack and subsequently died. One of the prisoners was recaptured not long after but the other, David Haggart, remained at large. A reward was offered leading to his capture. Several months went by and nothing was heard of him. In April 1821, a man who said his name was David Bryan was arrested for pickpocketing in Downpatrick, Ireland. For this crime he was sentenced to transportation to New South Wales in Australia. The local magistrate, however, thought that this prisoner answered to the description of David Haggart listed in *The Hue and Cry*. A police officer was sent from Dumfries to see if his suspicions were correct. By the time he had arrived in Ireland the suspect had been moved to Kilmainhaim Goal in preparation for his transportation. The magistrate's hunch was proved correct and David Haggart was escorted to Edinburgh by two sheriff's officers. On the evening of Friday, 25 May he arrived at the new Calton Jail securely manacled in irons to await his trial.

By sheer coincidence there had been a major escape attempt from the adjoining Bridewell earlier the same day. At about four o'clock a desperate attempt was made to break out by a number of prisoners during which they attempted to strangle a turnkey. After stealing his keys, they managed to reach the outer yard and two of their number succeeded in climbing over the boundary wall. The others, thirteen in number, were less lucky. The turnkey who they had assaulted had now regained his senses and grabbed a hatchet and trapped the remaining prisoners in one the lower passageways through which they had intended to make their escape. The exit in front of them was blocked by a locked door. Police officers and a military guard arrived at the Bridewell and returned all the prisoners to their cells.

David Haggart had more to worry about than just imprisonment. He was found guilty of murdering the turnkey at Dumfries Gaol and was sentenced to death. Apparently he had evaded justice on several previous occasions by escaping from other prisons. On 19 July 1821, this tall, slender young man aged around 19 was lead to the scaffold in Liberton Wynd. The hood was pulled down over his head but was removed briefly as David Haggart wished to address the large crowd of onlookers. He implored them to avoid the fault of disobeying their parents, inattention to the Holy Scriptures and being idle and disorderly. The hood was then replaced over his head and he was launched into eternity. 'His struggles were long and violent. Everyone present seemed deeply impressed with the awful exhibition' according to the *Caledonian Mercury* newspaper.

On 18 March 1823 a daring escape was made in broad daylight by three prisoners from Calton Jail, next to the Bridewell. James Curley – who had been sentenced to transportation for life for circulating forged Bank of Scotland notes – along with Matthew Adie and a man named Hughes, was instructed by a turnkey to carry coals from the roundhouse to the lodge near the main gate. Here they climbed up a staircase that led to the top of the turrets on either side of the prison's entrance. They then descended onto the roof to the top of the wall and dropped down into the enclosed ground next to the main street. For Matthew Adie and Hughes their freedom was short-lived as they were apprehended in Newcastle on Wednesday, 26 March 1823.

Escape attempts often took place when construction or renovation work was being undertaken on the buildings. Thomas Hamilton, who was confined in Calton Jail for the crime of pickpocketing, succeeded in escaping in early 1824. Three painters were engaged in renovating his cell. He covered himself in paint and walked out of the prison carrying a pot of paint; two of the painters appear to have been in on the deception.

The *Caledonian Mercury* reported that at about two o'clock on a Tuesday morning in June 1825:

> ... the peacefulness of the Bridewell was disturbed by a daring outrage as we have had on record. The court was entered by three fellows who had climbed over the outer wall. Such an occurrence it seems was by no means uncommon in itself, as the Bridewell had frequently been entered the same way, under the cloud of night by persons desirous to convey meat and drink to some of the prisoners, in consequence of which a watchman has recently been stationed there by order of the authorities.

The three intruders actually encountered the watchman concerned. When he refused to let them approach any of the prisoners he was savagely assaulted by them. As he lay on the ground the intruders kicked him and attacked him with a knife. The victim was found with a dreadful cut on his head and another on his hand. Two of the culprits were later apprehended and the identity of the third was known to the police.

Only three months later there was another serious incident at Calton Hill Prison. No less than eight prisoners managed to get clean away. All of them had been confined in one cluster of cells which faced onto the airing ground to which there was access for the turnkeys by an iron gate. John Murray, who had been sentenced to transportation for life, was imprisoned with the escapees. He informed Captain Young, the governor of the jail, that a plot had been hatched by his fellow inmates to escape later the same day. This information was communicated to the turnkeys who were given strict instructions not to open the gate to the airing ground unless two of them were present. At around half past three in the afternoon when one of the turnkeys happened to be absent, a prisoner called to the remaining member of staff on duty to remove a bundle of clothes from his cell which he wanted to be washed. Disregarding his orders, the turnkey opened the gate alone. The trap was sprung and he was instantly knocked down. Eight prisoners then rushed out along the centre passage which had an iron gate at each end. Conveniently one was standing wide open. It was later discovered that this escape took place with the connivance of one of the turnkeys. When they reached the perimeter wall they struck the turnkey on duty at the entrance door with a broom shaft. Using his keys they opened the last barrier to their freedom and spilled out onto the street. Casting off their prison clothes they ran off in the direction of Arthur's Seat. The prison staff immediately gave chase but lost them in the narrow lanes near Gibbet Toll (on the east side of Dalkeith Road, just north of the entry to Holyrood Park Road). On reaching the Radical Road at the foot of the Salisbury Crags they split up and went their separate ways. A few days later one of the escaped prisoners, A. MacKay, gave himself up but refused to give any account of the others. They included J. Mitchell and J. Sharp, both of whom had originally been sentenced to death but had been commuted to transportation for life. At the end of September 1825, not long after the mass escape, Captain Young received information concerning some of his missing prisoners. He set off for the Wellington Inn, located 2 miles to the south of Penicuik, accompanied by two policemen. The two fugitives were found in a hayloft and these 'desperadoes' were soon confined in their former quarters.

With two serious breaches of security within a few months questions began to be raised about the prison and its management. The *Caledonian Mercury* newspaper made the following criticism of it:

> The insecure state of the jail, from which so many escapes have been made, demands most serious consideration. It was destined entirely for a criminal jail but to the shame of humanity, be it said, it continues to be used for the confinement of debtors, who have the precise same accommodation in it as the worst of criminals.

At a council meeting held in late October 1825, the Jail Committee, as a result of their investigation into the recent escape of prisoners, recommended the removal of Mr Young, the prison governor. This proposal was agreed to. There was apparently no shortage of applicants to fill the vacant post!

The following year William Forrest, who had escaped from the Bridewell in May 1821, was recaptured. He had been imprisoned for three months before he managed to make a successful bid for freedom. He was returned to the Bridewell to carry out the remainder of his sentence. Escapes from here were also common as with Calton Prison.

There was, however, a further escape from the Bridewell on 19 December 1826. At about nine o'clock, six prisoners who had been on a treadwheel suddenly attacked the inner turnkey who was escorting them back to their cells. They stuffed a handkerchief into his mouth and at the same time covered his head with an improvised hood made out of bedding. They then dragged their victim to one of the sleeping cells where they bound him hand and foot. On obtaining his keys they then went about unlocking the cells where some of their companions were confined. All this was done in perfect silence. The prisoners next proceeded to the outer iron gate of their ward. Here they were in for a shock as the keys they had stolen would not open it. However, they managed to force open the iron gate despite a brave attempt by the outer turnkey to halt their progress. Once they had overcome these obstacles the prisoners broke out into the open ground surrounding the Bridewell. By this time the alarm had been raised and Governor Rose and the turnkeys managed to detain five of the escapees. Nine of their associates, however, succeeded in climbing over the boundary wall and disappeared into the surrounding streets. One of their number was captured a few days later in Edinburgh.

The notorious poisoner and robber John Stewart, mentioned in chapter six, had planned to cheat death by breaking out of Calton Jail before his execution. Early on in his criminal career he was arrested for sheep stealing and locked up in Stranraer Gaol. Within a short time John Stewart had broken free but his narrow escape from justice made a lasting impression on him. He turned to other forms of crime, including pickpocketing, and became highly proficient at them. When eventually detained in Glasgow Prison on suspicion of murder, John Stewart was convinced his death on the gallows was inevitable unless he effected his escape. According to the *Cambridge Chronicle and Journal*, 'He instantly resolved to make every possible exertion, to run all hazards and even to shed more blood, if by additional murders he could accomplish his design.' The prison authorities got word of John Stewart's plot and he was subsequently confined in one of the 'iron rooms' until he was transferred to Calton Jail to await his trial. This failure did nothing to discourage his determination to escape. Here he plotted with eight 'ruffians' to make another bid for freedom. Their initial plan was to grasp an opportunity when most of the turnkeys were attending to prisoners in other parts of the prison. John Stewart and his accomplices would then murder the sole turnkey in their part of the building along with the deputy governor and use their keys to get out of Calton Prison. Unable to implement this atrocious scheme, they thought up another plot. One of the large seats was loosened with its mountings. The prisoners were going to use it to knock out the stanchions of the windows at the foot of the stair and then break the interposing cast-iron barriers, forcing their way to the outer gate. If the turnkey here offered any resistance he was to be immediately dispatched with small spikes from the tops of railings, which had been sharpened to form blades. Once outside all the escapees would then flee in different directions, being bound by oath never to disclose the names of the ringleaders. The plot, however, was uncovered before the prisoners could put it into action. Security was tightened and John Stewart was watched with redoubled vigilance. 'His hope turned into black despair and he resigned himself to his fate.' After being tried he was found guilty and executed.

Local prisons which were beginning to be phased out of use in the 1830s had an even poorer reputation for security. A local journalist described the example at Stranraer in an article that appeared in the *Caledonian Mercury* in October 1833 as follows:

> Our jail is likely to become as noted as that of Lanark where the prisoners used to walk out after dinner after amusing themselves, return when they found it convenient. Within the space of eighteen months no fewer than seven prisoners have escaped from it. On Sunday evening last, Robert Brown, convicted at Ayr Assizes of forgery and sentenced to transportation for life and Hugh McMicken sentenced to eighteen months imprisonment for assault, quietly walked out of jail and by the means of a false key opened the main door, which they coolly locked after them. Brown took his departure just in time, for next day he was to have been removed to the Calton Jail for greater security, he thought proper, however, to save his keepers this trouble.

During February 1835 a scheme was concocted by some of the inmates of Calton Prison to escape from their confines. They put their plan into action at about half past three on a Sunday afternoon when the governor was at church. Numbering no less than thirty-two, of whom around half were described as felons of a desperate character, they contrived to prevent the spring bolt of their dayroom from locking properly at the usual time of shutting up. When the turnkey went to serve them their supper they rushed out through this door and succeeded in getting as far as the main gate.

Due to the quick thinking of the gatekeeper, who immediately went out of the prison and locked the door behind him, the escape attempt was foiled. He then raised the alarm and within a few minutes Captain Stuart arrived with the police accompanied by a number of public-spirited citizens. Meanwhile, inside the prison the turnkeys, assisted by some of the prisoners – namely the debtors – succeeded in driving the would-be escapers back into the yard. A few of the more desperate characters offered some resistance by hurtling any available object they could lay their hands on at the staff. Order, however, was very soon restored and all the prisoners returned to their cells. The *Caledonian Mercury* reported that, 'It is due to the debtors to state, that they rendered their assistance in the most prompt and efficient manner and that by their cool and judicious conduct the whole affair was quashed without personal violence or any damage done to property.'

This appears to have been the last serious disturbance within the walls of Calton Prison. From 1839 onwards, Central Government took control of Scottish prisons from the burghs, reducing the opportunity for corrupt staff to assist in escapes. The prison staff were now also becoming much better trained and professional.

More unusually, in late September 1858 there was a break-in to the prison. Early on a Friday morning a warder opening up the clerk's office situated next to the entry gate found that the lock on the outer door had been picked. Once inside he discovered that a desk had been forced open and £20 in notes and gold had been stolen. There was evidence that a ladder been used to scale the perimeter wall in Regent Road. Detectives were assigned to the case and later the same day they apprehended two suspects. One of them was Robert Campbell, a housebreaker who had only just completed his sentence on 18 September. His accomplice was James McGowan, who had in fact been a prison warder and had only left his job two weeks previously.

A month later two prisoners succeeded in breaking out of Calton Prison, which by this time was a rare occurrence. A little after seven o'clock they managed to gain access to the airing grounds. Part of the east wall was under repair at the time and the two men effected their escape by using a plank of wood as an improvised ladder to scale the perimeter wall and drop down the other side. One of the felons, however, was captured the same evening by a policeman.

As it was beginning to get dark on the evening of 16 November 1859, Governor Smith was sitting in his office when he heard a dull intermittent sound coming from the west end of the male quarters. It appeared to be timed to take place when the noise of carts coming and going in the prison yard obscured it. Accompanied by several warders, Governor Smith traced the source of the noise to a cell in which there were two newly tried convicts. At a given signal the door was flung open, catching the two prisoners attempting to escape. They had used a small saw to cut through an iron bar on which their hammocks were strung. In every cell there were two such bars attached to the wall. Once they had detached the iron bar the two prisoners had levered the inner window from its iron case. A large stone had also been removed from the middle sash of the window. There was only one more stone to be removed and they would have been able to climb out of the building. One of the prisoners, Peters, was transferred to Chatham Convict Prison where he received notoriety as one of the ringleaders in the 1861 riot.

An attempt to escape was made by a prisoner who went by the name of Creamor in 1883, while major building work was underway. When in the yard for exercise he noticed an unattended ladder propped up against the wall that overlooked the North British Railway. Deciding not to waste this opportunity, he made a desperate attempt to escape. On reaching the parapet, Creamor either fell or jumped from the wall and rolled some distance down the jagged rockface. Prison staff quickly picked him up and took him to the prison hospital in an unconscious state where they treated severe cuts to his head and other serious injuries.

Due to the secure nature of Calton Prison, offenders sometimes ended up there because they had successfully escaped from detention elsewhere. On 22 June 1896, six girls who were inmates of Dalry Reformatory School were brought before the Police Court on a charge of escaping from this institution. Such an offence gave the magistrate the power to send the offenders to prison for a term not exceeding three months. For the previous year and a half, girls had frequently absconded from the reformatory school but on being detained were 'welcomed back there'. The magistrate overseeing this case said such leniency sent out the wrong signal to those intending to run away from this institution. Two of the girls, Mary Ann McGonnigal and Beatice Day, who had been found guilty of the same offence in court in March 1895, were sentenced to forty days in Calton Prison. A further two, Maria Burgess and Jemima Hamiton Findlay, who were found on Calton Hill in the company of a man, received a sentence of fourteen days' imprisonment. The final two, Catherine Cowper and Jane Ann Aikin, who were absent from the reformatory all night, received a sentence of ten days' imprisonment. In passing these sentences the magistrate stated that it had been to him the most painful duty that he had been called upon to discharge in that court.

The 16 May 1900 saw a most unusual event – a successful escape of a prisoner from within the confines of Calton Prison. Some of the older staff declared it to be the most daring dash for liberty from this prison. Shortly after chapel service, William Wilson, a labourer from Leith, was exercising with the other prisoners. He managed to break away from the group undetected and made for the west wall, some 18ft in height, near the old prison gate. It is believed Wilson was able to climb over this obstacle utilizing a piece of wood. He then dropped over the wall and into Waterloo Place. The alarm was only raised when a member of the public informed the warder at the gatehouse that he had witnessed a man in prison clothes running away. The city was soon being scoured by police officers in horse-drawn cabs, on bicycles and on foot. There was, however, no trace of William Wilson, who had in fact fled into Lower Greenside. In this squalid area he found some friends or accomplices and was able to cast aside his prison uniform. In spite of changing into a rough jacket suit, a number of gossiping women recognised him as he made his way along the lanes of Greenside towards Leith. By sheer bad luck a public-spirited member of the public overheard the women talking and decided to follow the escaped prisoner. The amateur detective eventually caught up with his quarry at Gayfield Place. Here he feigned friendship and told Wilson to 'run for God's sake'. In response Wilson asked him where he should go. The pair headed for Granton, from where the fugitive intended to take a ferry to Burntisland. When they got as far as Newhaven, his companion called at an acquaintance's house. Here he requested the lady to inform the police of William Wilson's location and his intended escape to Fife – but not before they had lunch here.

On arrival at Granton, the pair had some time to spend before the arrival of the Burntisland boat. There were a couple of constables in the vicinity, which made William Wilson somewhat uneasy. He decided to wait at the end of the pier but was trapped here when Superintendent Lamb and Sergeant Barnett of the Edinburgh detective force arrived in a horse-drawn cab. Wilson's 'friend' pointed out where to find him. The party then returned to Edinburgh and the escaped prisoner was safely locked up again in Calton Prison. The *Edinburgh Evening News* reported that, 'The police complimented the enterprising young man on his successful tracking of one whom they recognise to be a dangerous customer.'

With little prospect of any chance of escape once locked inside Calton Prison, some prisoners attempted to make a bolt for freedom before they reached its walls. One of the original arguments against the location of a prison here was that it involved transporting convicted criminals some distance from the courts in the High Street, giving them the window of opportunity to flee. In the eighteenth century the old prison in the Tolbooth was only a stone's throw from the buildings where justice was administered. In May 1850, John Hunter was charged with sheep stealing. He was noted to be a fast runner and a good gymnast. A horse-drawn van was used to transport him from the police office to Calton Prison. During his arrest Hunter had offered considerable resistance, and so two sheriff's officers accompanied him and his hands were manacled together. On reaching Calton Prison, one of the sheriff's officers got out of the cab to knock on the door for admission. Carelessly the vehicle's door was left open and John Hunter leaped out into the street. Throwing off his shoes he sprinted in the direction of the Royal High School with the sheriff's officers in close pursuit. The escaped prisoner then ran up Calton Hill and down to Greenside. Several times he skillfully doubled back in an effort to shake off anybody following him. At Bonnington, Hunter reached open countryside and ran across the grounds of several nurseries. Later that day he was seen in Duke Street with his hands bleeding, probably from his efforts to release them from the manacles. Towards the end of 1850 a warrant of fugitation was issued against John Hunter but his whereabouts after fleeing from the gates of Calton Prison remained unknown.

Many years later, in 1913, there was a similar escape from a horse-drawn prison van. This took place on the George IV Bridge. It was standing with its doors open ready to transport three prisoners from the Sheriff Court to Calton Prison. Two had already been placed in it but the third, described as a little man, broke loose and ran off into Chambers Street. The driver of the prison van whipped up his horse and gave chase. Unlike John Hunter this prisoner did not remain at liberty for long, being captured in the Cowgate and then successfully transported to Calton Prison.

Not all felons had the luxury of being driven to prison in a horse-drawn van. It was a common occurrence to see prisoners being taken from the Sheriff Court on foot, either handcuffed together or to a detective officer. There is evidence that sometimes they received public ridicule. One of their number complained to Sheriff Glyere in March 1905 as he left the dock, 'I hope my Lord you will get a conveyance to take us over and not drag us through the streets strapped together like dogs.' To this the sheriff made no comment.

In the latter years of the nineteenth century a number of prisoners attempted to escape from their escorts with varying degrees of success. In the winter of 1874, Issac Glossop and John Smith were found guilty of breaking into a grocer's shop in Forrest Road. They were sentenced to fifteen months' and twelve months' imprisonment respectively. While the prisoners were being conducted to Calton Prison, John Smith succeeded in freeing his hands from the handcuffs that held the two together. Both ran off but the officer in charge gave chase and soon caught John Smith. Issac Glossop, however, with the iron handcuffs still attached to his hands, got clean away. He remained at liberty for just over three months until he was detained by the police in Glasgow.

Another escape bid was made by two soldiers being transferred from Calton Prison to Edinburgh Castle on 17 June 1879. On reaching the top of the Lawnmarket both fled from their escort, which was composed of a corporal and two privates. One soldier was captured in the Grassmarket while his associate got as far as Princes Street before being detained by a policeman.

The 23 March 1898 saw an even more desperate escape attempt from the cells at the High Court by 22-year-old convicted housebreaker John MacLeod. While being transferred between floors in preparation for his removal to Calton Prison, he suddenly bolted into the jailers' office. He threw open its windows and squeezed himself out between the stanchions. This accomplished, John MacLeod leaped some 35ft to the ground. He landed in Old Fishmarket Close but injured himself and was now only able to crawl. Police detectives found him hiding nearby in the premises of Neill & Co. printing works. John MacLeod was removed to the Royal Infirmary a short time later with a broken leg and serious internal injuries.

While prison escapes in the latter days of Calton Prison were virtually unknown, this was not the case with its replacement at Saughton. The new prison was very different from its predecessor, being situated in open countryside. Gone were the austere fortress-type walls and towers. Here comparatively low railings enclosed large recreation grounds and gardens. This was to prove too much of a temptation for some inmates. Even before the prison was completed two youths were detained by the Lanarkshire police at Plains dressed in the uniform of a borstal institution. On making inquiries it was discovered that they had escaped from the prison extension at Saughton and were making for Glasgow, their home town.

Three years later, in 1925, its role as Edinburgh's new prison got off to a somewhat inauspicious start. There were no less than two successful escapes from it. John Devine, alias Cedric Norval, made off from a work party and remained at liberty for seven hours. Detective Inspector Stewart and Detective Constable Gibson arrested him as he walked down Arthur Street. The fugitive had by this time managed to change out of his prison clothing consisting of blue and red overalls and corduroy trousers, which he concealed in a lavatory in The Meadows. John Devine, who was aged 56 at the time, was serving a sentence of eighteen months. No stranger to prison, he had an unusual mania for stealing paintbrushes. In fact Devine had trained as a painter when he was a young man. Keeping in touch with his fellow tradesmen he would get to learn of any big house that was being decorated. In the evening he would go to it and steal the paintbrushes – but nothing else.

In the summer of 1925, 37-year-old Stewart Couper, a notorious cat burglar, climbed over the railings at the back of Saughton Prison. It was sometime before his absence was discovered. When the alarm was raised the warders immediately set out in search of him. Two on motorcycles caught sight of him crossing an open field but Couper managed to disappear into a wood at Craiglockhart. On one occasion he had broken into a house in Great King Street that belonged to a former doctor of Calton Prison. He gained entrance by climbing a rhone pipe and getting in by a skylight. One slip and he would have fallen to his death. Another of his exploits involved scaling 80ft up the outside of what was then the tallest building in Princes Street. Unfortunately he dropped the key to his lodging house while inside and the police were able to trace him from this. When he broke out of Saughton Prison he was serving a two-year sentence for attempting to rob a house in Edinburgh's West End. About a week after Stewart Couper had absconded from Saughton Prison, a house was burgled in Inverleith Row. The police thought that this was his handiwork. The following day two policemen walked into a public house in Leith and discovered their man playing a game of dominoes with some of his associates. Stewart Couper had remained at large for nine days. On his arrest he was described as being worn and weary and relieved to be caught.

With these lessons learned, security at Saughton improved and escapes became a rare occurrence.

25

THE CELL DOORS CLOSE FOR THE FINAL TIME

By the beginning of the twentieth century it was apparent that Calton Prison was becoming increasingly unsuitable for purpose. Its site did not allow further expansion and most of the activities for the prisoners were confined to the gloom of its stone buildings. Several sites were examined for the site of a new prison for Edinburgh. They included locations near Craigleith Quarry and Granton Gasworks. Negotiations for ground at East Pilton reached an advanced stage but broke down. In 1913, 40 acres of ground were purchased at Saughton and construction work began the following year. The outbreak of the First World War, however, slowed its completion. Much of the building work was carried out by the prisoners themselves. From 1916 onwards they would work for part of the week at Saughton and then return to Calton Prison. Many prisoners requested to be sent to work there. Built on low-lying ground, *The Scotsman* newspaper commented that the new jail would not overshadow the city with its sinister presence like its Victorian counterpart. The contrast between the two could not have been more different: there were not even walls around Saughton Prison, just a fence. On 6 November 1919 it was appointed a legal place of detention but it was far from finished. While some prisoners were held here, many others were still detained in Calton Prison, which did not finally close until 1925. Those who had served a long sentence were transferred to Saughton for the last month or two of their confinement in order to get them fit and healthy for their liberation. During this time both were officially known as the Edinburgh Prison. Work on Saughton Prison was officially completed in 1930 when it had 158 male and 84 female cells. Other buildings included the Governor's House, officers' quarters, a hospital block, stores and office buildings.

The controversy over the fate of the future of the Calton Prison site raged over many years and generated a large number of letters to local newspapers. Edinburgh town council approved one plan for offices likened by one critic as a 'cross between the Lamassary in Lhassa and a Kirkcaldy linoleum Factory'. The Fine Art Commission objected to further designs that were submitted. Questions were raised in Parliament about the future of the site. The famous novelist John Buchan called for an 'outward and visible design of Scottish nationhood'. Both the King and Queen as well as the prime minister Ramsay MacDonald were drawn into the controversy.

For a time it looked as if the new Sheriff Court might occupy the former prison ground or even the National Library of Scotland. On 1 November 1929, the Edinburgh Dean of Guild Court granted a warrant for the demolition of Calton Prison. All the buildings were to be razed with the exception of the outer walls. Few raised any objections to the loss of this impressive structure, which was sometimes mistaken for Edinburgh Castle by travellers arriving at the city. There was little interest in preserving examples of Gothic architecture, which in some quarters was regarded as being in bad taste. Most were glad to see the demise of the Calton Prison as it was regarded as an embarrassment, having buildings full of felons dominating the skyline. One letter to *The Scotsman* applauded its end:

> It was characteristic of the age to erect such a huge laundry for the washing of the dirty linen on the second most conspicuous situation in the town, such places are in fitting surroundings in a mean street, so when one takes into account the painful associations, is not a clean sweep the most desirable course!

By 1935 this had been realised. Calton Prison was no more. Much of its stonework was used to construct a dam for the new Hopes Reservoir in the Lammermuir Hills. After many years of debate an art deco-influenced design by Thomas S. Tait was selected.

The foundation stone was laid on 28 April 1937 by the Duke of Gloucester and was completed in early 1939. It then had the distinction of being the largest metal-framed building in Europe. The south side was designed to merge into the contours of Calton Hill. Initially its cream-coloured stonework made it stand out from the surrounding buildings. Being close to Waverley Station, the smoke from steam locomotives soon darkened it, making it blend in with the neighboring structures. The new office complex was named St Andrew's House. It was officially inaugurated by King George VI and Queen Elizabeth on 26 February 1940. Initially it housed the Scottish Office and the Secretary of State for Scotland.

Today, the sole-surviving building of Calton Prison is the Governor's Tower, erected in the early nineteenth century. It was originally intended to demolish this as well and it narrowly escaped this fate more by accident than any intention to preserve it. There were even letters written to the local press demanding its removal. The following appeared in *The Scotsman* on 12 May 1939:

It is gratifying to note that the Cockburn Association raises no objection to the removal of that white elephant, the Old Governor's House from the Calton Hill. At present it completely spoils the view of the fine new national building from the North Bridge and even from Jeffrey Street. It is unthinkable that the appearance of a fine modern building should be ruined by this piece of sham medievalism, which was never a decent piece of domestic architecture at any time and is today not only useless but an eyesore. It should have gone with the jail to which it belonged. Some people would advocate the retention of a piggery in the finest site of the city, if only the piggery were a hundred years old.

The southern boundary wall also still exists and can similarly be seen directly below St Andrew's House but it has been reduced in height. There are further gruesome reminders of the former prison. The bodies of ten prisoners unfortunate enough to suffer capital punishment still lie buried on the hillside with the ground above them now a car park for workers in St Andrew's House. The door to the death cell still survives in The Beehive Inn in Edinburgh's Grassmarket.

In the final years of the twentieth century, Saughton Prison was itself redeveloped. Over the next decade all the original buildings, described as 'harled with red sandstone dressings with gables and crenellations' were swept away, cutting the last links with Calton Prison.

APPENDIX 1

PRISONS IN EDINBURGH-SHIRE IN 1825

Calton Jail – the National Jail of Scotland	
Number of prisoners capable of being housed	106 persons
Number of cells for criminals	54
Number of cells for other prisoners	14
Number of prisoners committed in 1825	
Male criminals	54
Female criminals	57
Male debtors	529
Female debtors	27
Greatest number of prisoners confined in 1825 at any one time	141
Number of persons employed as keepers and under keepers	9
Airing ground	yes

The Lock-Up House, Lawnmarket, Edinburgh	
Number of prisoners capable of being housed	24
Number of cells for criminals	7 (plus a 'black hole')
Number of cells for other prisoners	0
Number of prisoners committed in 1825	
Male criminals	366

APPENDICES

Female criminals	292
Greatest number of prisoners confined in 1825 at any one time	45
Number of persons employed as keepers	1
Airing ground	none

Bridewell (House of Correction) for the City and County of Edinburgh

Number of prisoners capable of being housed	132
Number of cells for criminals	184
Number of cells for other prisoners	0

Number of prisoners committed in 1825

Male criminals	396
Female criminals	707
Greatest number of prisoners confined in 1825 at any one time	205
Number of persons employed as keepers and under keepers	7
Airing ground	yes

Canongate Tolbooth, Royal Mile, Edinburgh

Number of prisoners capable of being housed	30
Number of cells for criminals	2
Number of cells for other prisoners	8

Number of prisoners committed in 1825

Male criminals	20
Female criminals	2
Male debtors	304
Female debtors	30
Greatest number of prisoners confined in 1825 at any one time	38
Number of persons employed as keepers and under keepers	3
Airing ground	none

Leith Jail in the town of Leith (demolished in 1824)

Number of prisoners capable of being housed	19
Number of cells for criminals	3
Number of cells for other prisoners	5
Number of persons employed as keepers and under keepers	2
Airing ground	none

Musselburgh Jail in the town of Musselburgh

Number of prisoners capable of being housed	26
Number of cells for criminals	2
Number of cells for other prisoners	2

Number of prisoners committed in 1825

Male criminals	2
Female criminals	0
Male debtors	15
Female debtors	3
Greatest number of prisoners confined in 1825 at any one time	5
Number of persons employed as keepers and under keepers	3
Airing ground	none

Dalkeith Jail in the town of Dalkeith

Number of prisoners capable of being housed	10
Number of cells for criminals	2
Number of cells for other prisoners	0

Number of prisoners committed in 1825

Male criminals	11
Female criminals	3
Greatest number of prisoners confined in 1825 at any one time	2
Number of persons employed as keepers	1
Airing ground	none

APPENDIX 2

CRIMES COMMITTED BY PRISONERS IN THE BRIDEWELL

Most of the prisoners were sentenced to confinement in the Bridewell by the Police Court of Edinburgh. Some, however, came from the magistrates of Leith and small numbers were delivered up by the Sheriff of the County of Edinburgh, the Justices of the County, the High Court of Justiciary and military court martials.

1812

Robbery	4
House or shop-breaking and theft or with intent to steal	5
Theft, pickpocketing and attempts to steal	160
Reset of theft	7
Swindling and fraud	9
Having in possession base money and materials for making it	2
Vending base money	12
Garden breaking	11
Assault	22
Assault with intent to commit rape	2
Rioting	6
Harbouring vagrants and disorderly persons	3
Enlisting while contracted to apprenticeship	1
Improper behaviour in military service	1
Dereliction of duty as a police officer	1

Wanton cruelty to animals	1
Vagrancy, drunkenness, riotous and disorderly conduct on the streets and other breaches of the peace	243
Returning from banishment under previous convictions	5
Breaches of the articles of war	4
Total	499

1824

House or shop breaking and theft, or with intent to steal	2
Theft, pickpocketing etc., and attempts to steal	443
Reset of theft	14
Swindling, falsehood and theft	26
Having in possession base money and materials for making it	3
Vending base money	2
Issuing forged notes	1
Embezzlement and breach of trust	1
Entering premises with false keys	1
Wounding and maiming	5
Assault	31
Keeping disorderly house and harboring vagrants and disorderly persons	1
Begging	93
Vagrancy, drunkenness, riotous and disorderly conduct on the streets and other breaches of the peace	505
Rescuing and attempting to rescue prisoners	1
Contempt of court	1
Garden breaking	3
Deserting service or apprenticeship	2
Selling unstamped almanacs	2
Exposing diseased butcher meat to public sale	1
Breaches of the articles of war	3
Returning from banishment under former convictions	164
Total	1,333

APPENDIX 3

THE NATIONAL GAOL OF SCOTLAND (CALTON PRISON) 1830

Apartments	
Sleeping Cells	58
Day Rooms	6
Infirmaries	4
Kitchen	1
Bath room	1
Store room	1
Chapel	1
Total	72

Dimensions of Apartments (to nearest ½ foot)

Function	Length × Breadth × Height	Number of Airing Windows	Ground
Used by Male Criminals			
9 sleeping cells	8½ feet × 6 feet × 9 feet	2 windows	–
22 sleeping cells	8½ feet × 6 feet × 9 feet	1 window	–
4 dark cells	8½ feet × 6 feet × 9 feet	no windows	–
3 sleeping cells	11½ feet × 6 feet × 9 feet	2 windows	–

2 condemned cells	11½ feet × 6 feet × 9 feet	1 window	–
2 day rooms	16 feet × 15 feet × 10 feet	2 windows	68 feet × 28 feet
1 day room	15 feet × 8½ feet × 10 feet	2 windows	76 feet × 17 feet
1 day room	20 feet × 9½ feet × 10 feet	2 windows	68 feet × 22 feet

Comment: the thirty-four sleeping cells and two condemned cells are well ventilated by the windows but have no heating. Each day room has a fireplace and water closet attached, together with a water pipe and trough in the airing ground and is well ventilated by the windows and fireplace.

Used by Female Criminals

3 sleeping cells	11½ feet × 6 feet × 9 feet	2 windows	–
2 sleeping cells	11½ feet × 6 feet × 9 feet	1 window	–
2 sleeping cells	8½ feet × 6 feet × 9 feet	1 window	–
1 sleeping cell	8½ feet × 6 feet × 9 feet	1 window	–
1 infirmary (used as a day room)	23 feet × 19 feet × 11 feet	4 windows	100 feet × 9 feet
1 day room	19½ feet × 15 feet × 10 feet	2 windows	89 feet × 16 feet

The sleeping cells were well ventilated by the windows but they had no heating. The infirmary and the day room, however, each had a fireplace as well as a water pipe in their airing grounds.

Used by Male Debtors

4 sleeping cells	11½ feet × 6 feet × 9 feet	2 windows	–
6 sleeping cells	11½ feet × 6 feet × 9 feet	1 window	–
1 infirmary room	23 feet × 19 feet × 11 feet	4 windows	–
1 infirmary room	12½ feet × 15 feet × 11 feet	2 windows	–

| 1 day room | 20 feet × 15 feet × 10 feet | 2 windows | 96 feet × 22 feet |

The sleeping cells were all heated by stoves and were well ventilated by their windows. The infirmary and two day rooms each had a fireplace and the airing ground has a water pipe.

Used by Female Debtors

| 1 infirmary room | 12½ feet × 15 feet × 11 feet | 2 windows | – |

The infirmary room has a fireplace and is well ventilated by the windows.

General

1 kitchen	22½ feet × 9½ feet × 10 feet	1 window	–
1 bathroom	11½ feet × 9½ feet × 10 feet	1 window	–
1 store room	9½ feet × 5½ feet × 10 feet	no windows	–
1 chapel	34 feet × 27½ feet × 31½ feet	10 windows	–

The kitchen had a fireplace, boiler and water pipe. The bathroom had a boiler and hot and cold water pipes. There was no heating in the chapel.

APPENDIX 4

NUMBER OF PRISONERS COMMITTED TO CALTON PRISON FOR THE YEAR 31 JULY 1828 TO 31 JULY 1829

Year 31 July 1828 to 31 July 1829

	Male	*Female*	*Total*
Total number of prisoners committed	998	170	1,168
Number committed under revenue statutes	22	4	26
Number of debtors committed	423	35	458
Number of criminal prisoners	575	135	710

Greatest number of prisoners at any one time: 36 debtors, 111 other prisoners = 147

Year 29 September 1838 to 28 September 1839
Calton Prison, Lock-up House and Bridewell

	Male	*Female*
Greatest number of criminals at any one time	214	278
Least number of criminals at any one time	105	231
Greatest number of debtors at any one time	16	0
Least number of debtors at any one time	6	0
Greatest number of male prisoners of all kinds at any one time	140	173
Least number of female prisoners at any one time	78	123
Greatest number of female prisoners of all kinds at any one time	95	136
Least number of female prisoners of all kinds at any one time	32	95
Greatest aggregate number of prisoners at any one time	223	278
Least aggregate number of prisoners at any one time	113	231

APPENDIX 5

NUMBER OF PRISONERS IN CALTON PRISON AND THE BRIDEWELL FOR THE YEAR 29 SEPTEMBER 1838 TO 28 SEPTEMBER 1839

	Calton Prison and Lock-up House	*Bridewell*
Greatest number of criminals at any one time	214	278
Least number of criminals at any one time	105	231
Greatest number of debtors at any one time	16	0
Least number of debtors at any one time	6	0
Greatest number of male prisoners of all kinds at any one time	140	173
Least number of female prisoners at any one time	78	123
Greatest number of female prisoners of all kinds at any one time	95	136
Least number of female prisoners of all kinds at any one time	32	95
Greatest aggregate number of prisoners at any one time	223	278
Least aggregate number of prisoners at any one time	113	231

APPENDIX 6

AGE OF CRIMINAL PRISONERS ADMITTED TO CALTON PRISON AND THE BRIDEWELL FOR THE YEAR 29 SEPTEMBER 1838 TO 28 SEPTEMBER 1839

	Calton Prison and Lock-up House		*Bridewell*	
	male	*female*	*male*	*female*
Under 14 years old	125	20	14	83
14–16 years old	129	48	83	38
17–29 years old	427	342	260	302
30–39 years old	127	127	89	116
40–49 years old	61	41	47	55
50–59 years old	41	15	22	20
60 and upwards	15	10	8	8
Total	950	623	593	553

APPENDIX 7

COST OF RUNNING CALTON PRISON AND THE BRIDEWELL FOR THE YEAR 29 SEPTEMBER 1838 TO 28 SEPTEMBER 1839

	Calton Prison and Lock-up House	*Bridewell*
Food, including cost of cooking	£936 7s 10d	£1,059 7s 2d
Clothing	£131 7s 2d	£176 3s 8d
Bedding	£8 10s 6d	£63 8s 7d
Washing	£49 12s 4d	£86 9s 8d
Lighting	£41 4s 7d	£52 7s 0d
Fuel	£96 5s 7d	£80 8s 10d
Furniture	£4 16s 0d	£79 17s 8d
Salaries	£949 1s 2d	£821 1s 1d
Repairs	£98 3s 6d	£62 6s 3d
New buildings and alterations	£15 4s 0d	£109 2s 6d
Sundries	£138 10s 6d	£144 5s 1d
Gross expense	£2,469 3s 3d	£2,735 7s 6d
Portion paid by the burgh	£2,064 4s 4d	£725 19s 7d
Portion paid by the counties	£336 6s 4d	£554 17s 5d
Paid for military prisoners	£11 10s 0d	£188 4s 8d
Paid by sundry parties	£19 8s 5d	£42 13s 0d

APPENDIX 8

AVERAGE WEEKLY ALLOWANCE OF FOOD FOR CRIMINAL PRISONERS IN THE BRIDEWELL AND EDINBURGH PRISON 1839

Food	Calton Prison	Bridewell
Bread or oakcake	80oz	58oz
Oatmeal made into porridge	37oz	75oz
Barley made into broth	24oz	24oz
Meat (when cooked) either given alone or in broth	13½oz	14oz
Bones boiled with the broth	0	3½oz
Cheese	0	4oz
Beer	1 pint	6 pints
Sweet milk	11 pints	0
Salt and vegetables	6½oz	0
Other solid food	155oz	185oz
Average daily cost of food per prisoner including cooking	3¾d	2¾d

APPENDIX 9

CRIMES AND OFFENCES FOR WHICH PRISONERS WERE COMMITTED TO CALTON PRISON IN THE YEARS ENDED 30 NOVEMBER 1845 AND 30 NOVEMBER 1846

	Ending 30 Nov 1845			Ending 30 Nov 1846		
	Male	Female	Total	Male	Female	Total
Theft and fraud	823	749	**1,572**	961	868	**1,829**
Disorderly conduct and assault	1,102	1,282	**2,384**	1,090	1,177	**2,267**
Mobbing & rioting	8	0	**8**	49	0	**49**
Murder or culpable homicide	9	6	**15**	5	6	**11**
Incest	1	1	**2**	0	0	**0**
Assault with intent to ravish	6	0	**6**	4	0	**4**
Fire-raising	0	4	**4**	3	0	**3**
Assault with intent to kill	2	0	**2**	1	0	**1**
Forgery	10	0	**10**	11	2	**13**
Concealment of pregnancy and exposing children	1	4	**5**	0	0	**0**
Perjury	1	0	**1**	0	0	**0**
Uttering base coin	3	5	**8**	14	6	**20**
Bigamy	1	0	**1**	1	0	**1**

APPENDICES

Bestiality	1	0	**1**	2	0	**2**
Sodomy	2	0	**2**	2	0	**2**
Indecently exposing their person	13	8	**21**	11	9	**20**
Neglecting to ailment their wives or children	0	0	**0**	6	1	**7**
Writing threatening letters	2	0	**2**	0	0	**0**
Keeping improper houses	5	0	**5**	0	0	**0**
Road offences	53	0	**53**	40	0	**40**
Breach of engagement	3	0	**3**	14	0	**14**
Poaching	9	0	**9**	4	0	**4**
Committed as dangerous lunatics	5	11	**16**	0	0	**0**
Begging	77	35	**112**	49	34	**83**
Beating carpets in the street	0	0	**0**	0	2	**2**
Selling coals without proper weights	2	0	**2**	0	0	**0**
Porters plying without a license	7	0	**7**	2	0	**2**
Allowing their chimneys to take fire	2	0	**2**	4	1	**5**
Playing at pitch and toss	0	0	**0**	1	0	**1**
Firing a small cannon	0	0	**0**	1	0	**1**
Assisting soldiers to desert	0	0	**0**	5	1	**6**
Soldiers for military offences	137	0	**137**	56	0	**56**
Total	2,297	2,105	**4,402**	2,386	2,107	**4,443**

APPENDIX 10

TRADES AND OCCUPATIONS OF PERSONS COMMITTED TO CALTON PRISON IN THE YEAR 1 OCTOBER 1845 TO 30 SEPTEMBER 1846

	Male	Female
Agents	9	0
Bakers and millers	58	0
Barbers	5	0
Basketmakers	7	0
Bookbinders and book folders	12	1
Brokers	2	5
Brothel keepers	13	26
Butchers	37	0
Cabmen	58	0
Clerks and schoolmasters	22	0
Comb makers	8	1
Corkcutters	3	0
Dyers	4	0
Engineers	10	0
Fishermen and women	7	4
Gardeners	13	0
Glassblowers	7	0
Hatters	6	0
Hawkers	58	28

Housewives	0	417
Jewellers and silversmiths	30	0
Labourers, carters and miners	529	0
Masons	33	0
Mill girls	0	5
Outwork	0	25
Painters	48	0
Painters and map colourers	22	2
Police Officers	4	0
Porters	34	0
Prostitutes	0	573
Publicans	8	0
Sailors	49	0
Servants	16	79
Shopmen	9	0
Sewing	28	0
Shoemakers and shoe binders	92	5
Skinners	5	0
Smiths, founders and plumbers	108	0
Soldiers	100	0
Surgeons	4	0
Spinners	5	0
Sweeps	27	0
Tailors	63	0
Tobacconists	4	0
Typefounders	15	0
Washing	0	23
Weavers and winders	34	4
Wrights and coopers	89	0
Miscellaneous	27	3
No occupation (tramps, etc.)	248	188
Total	1,940	1,417
	3,357	

APPENDIX 11

SENTENCES OF CRIMINAL PRISONERS COMMITTED TO CALTON PRISON IN THE YEAR 30 JUNE 1856 TO 30 JUNE 1857

(A)

Length of Sentence	Male	Female
Ten days and under	91	198
Eleven to sixty days	677	909
Above sixty days and less than six months	32	13
Six months and under one year	19	23
One year and under two years	0	0
Above two years	0	0

(B)

Imprisonment for Indefinite Periods	Male	Female
Until caution be found to keep the peace after conviction on criminal charge	156	220
Until or instead of payment of fine or penalty on conviction or offence, prosecuted for the public offence	351	781

To Transportation	Male	Female
Fourteen years	2	0
Fifteen years	2	0
Twenty-one years	1	0
Life	2	0

To Penal Servitude	Male	Female
Four years	18	6
Above four years to six years	17	4
Death sentence	0	1*

(*sentence commuted to transportation for life)

APPENDIX 12

NUMBER OF STAFF AT CALTON PRISON AT 31 MARCH 1883

	Male	*Female*
Governor	1	0
Chaplain	1	0
Medical Officers	1	0
Stewards	1	0
Clerks	3	0
Matron	0	1
Teachers	1	1
Warders	21	10
Assistant Warder	0	1
Total	29	13

(One female warder acted as sick nurse)

APPENDIX 13

COST OF RUNNING CALTON PRISON FOR THE YEAR FROM 1 APRIL 1888 TO 31 MARCH 1889

Salaries and wages	£4,329 4s 6d
Uniforms for officers	£51 5s 0d
Victualling for prisoners	£1,114 15s 11d
Clothing for prisoners	£154 13s 8d
Bedding for prisoners	£11 19s 11d
Medicines, Surgical instruments	£43 19s 6d
Gratuities to prisoners	£126 1s 8d
Furniture, Kitchen Utensils, Crockery, etc.	£58 0s 11d
Fuel, light and water	£429 19s 5d
Soap and cleaning materials	£59 6s 0d
Rents and feu duties	£1 7s 6d
Repairs to buildings	£691 10s 0d
Incidental expenditure	£94 13s 6d
Total	£7,166 8s 2d

APPENDIX 14

MISCONDUCT OF CRIMINAL PRISONERS IN CALTON PRISON FOR THE YEAR 1 APRIL 1888 TO 31 MARCH 1889

Offence Reported	Male	Female
Disobendence of Governor's or Officers' orders	16	4
Disrespect to Officers or Visitors	21	18
Idleness or negligence at work or refusal to work	163	11
Irreverent behaviour during divine service or prayers	14	3
Swearing and using improper language	10	4
Indecent in language, act or gesture	11	0
Assaulting any person	2	1
Talking with another prisoner without authority	127	5
Singing, whistling or making unnecessary noise or giving unnecessary trouble	34	9
Disfiguring or damaging any part of the prison or any article	45	6
Having forbidden articles in his or her possession	20	1
Refusing or neglecting to conform to rules and orders	54	10
Offending against good order and discipline	13	4
Total	530	76

BIBLIOGRAPHY

Reports

A Return of the Number of Persons in Great Britain and Ireland to Which Persons who are Committed for Criminal Offences are Confined and the Number of Escapes which have Taken Place From Each During the Last Five Years (The House of Commons, 1856)

An Account of all the Gaols, Houses of Correction, or Penitentiaries In the United Kingdom – As Far as Relates to Scotland, March 1819 (Report prepared for Parliament)

Annual Report of the Prison Commissioners for Scotland For the Year 1911 (London: His Majesty's Stationery Office, 1912)

Annual Report of the Prison Commissioners for Scotland for the Year 1913 (Edinburgh: His Majesty's Stationery Office, 1914)

Annual Report of the Prison Commissioners for Scotland for the Year 1918 (Edinburgh: His Majesty's Stationery Office, 1919)

Annual Report of the Prison Commissioners for Scotland for the Year 1920 (Edinburgh: His Majesty's Stationery Office, 1921)

Annual Report of the Prison Commissioners for Scotland For the Year 1925 (Edinburgh: His Majesty's Stationery Office, 1926)

Convicts – Return of the Number of Convicts Sentenced to Death or Transportation and of the Number of Persons imprisoned for Misdemeanors Throughout the United Kingdom during the years 1847, 1848, and 1849 (The House of Commons, 1850)

Fifth Report of the Inspectors to Visit the Different Prisons of Great Britain IV: Scotland, Northumberland and Durham (Her Majesty's Stationery Office, 1840)

Eighth Report of the Inspectors to Visit the Different Prisons of Great Britain IV: Scotland, Northumberland and Durham (Her Majesty's Stationery Office, 1843)

Twelfth Report of the Inspectors to Visit the Different Prisons of Great Britain IV: Scotland, Northumberland and Durham (Her Majesty's Stationery Office, 1847)

Sixteenth Report of the Inspectors to Visit the Different Prisons of Great Britain IV: Scotland (Her Majesty's Stationery Office, 1851)

Seventeenth Report of the Inspectors to Visit the Different Prisons of Great Britain IV: Scotland (Her Majesty's Stationery Office, 1853)

Eighteenth Report of the Inspectors to Visit the Different Prisons of Great Britain, IV: Scotland (Her Majesty's Stationery Office, 1853)

Twenty-Fourth Report of the Inspectors to Visit the Different Prisons of Great Britain III: Northern District (Her Majesty's Stationery Office, 1859)

Twenty-Eighth Report of the Inspectors to Visit the Different Prisons of Great Britain, II, Northern District (Her Majesty's Stationery Office, 1863)

Thirty-First Report of the Inspectors to Visit the Different Prisons of Great Britain, II, Northern District (Her Majesty's Stationery Office, 1866)

Thirty-Fourth Report of the Inspectors to Visit the Different Prisons of Great Britain, II, Northern District (Her Majesty's Stationery Office, 1870)

Thirty-Fifth Report of the Inspectors to Visit the Different Prisons of Great Britain, II, Northern District (Her Majesty's Stationery Office, 1871)

Thirty-Sixth Report of the Inspectors to Visit the Different Prisons of Great Britain, II, Northern District (Her Majesty's Stationery Office, 1872)

Thirty-Eighth Report of the Inspectors to Visit the Different Prisons of Great Britain (Her Majesty's Stationery Office, 1874)

Report from Committee on Petition of Royal Burghs of Scotland respecting the Providing of Jails (The House of Commons, 1818)

Report From the Departmental Committee on Scottish Prisons: The Minutes Of Evidence, Appendices, and Index are Published Separately: Scottish Prisons Inquiry, Scotland, Departmental Committee on Scottish Prisons (London: Her Majesty's Stationery Office, 1900)

Report from the Select Committee on the State of Prisons in Scotland (The House of Commons 1826)

Reports of the State of the Several Gaols, Houses of Correction and Penitentiaries throughout the United Kingdom (The Home Department, 1820)

Second Report of the General Board of Directors of Prisons in Scotland (Her Majesty's Stationery Office, London, 1841)

Eighth Report of the General Board of Directors of Prisons in Scotland (Her Majesty's Stationery Office, London, 1847)

Nineteenth Report of the General Board of Directors of Prisons in Scotland (Her Majesty's Stationery Office, 1858)

Twenty-Ninth Report on Prisons in Scotland being in Continuation of the Reports of the Late General Board of Prisons – The Seventh Annual Report of the Managers appointed under the Prisons Administration Act 1860 (Her Majesty's Stationery Office, 1868)

Thirty-Ninth Report on Prisons in Scotland including the Seventeenth Annual Report of the Managers appointed under the Prisons (Scotland) Administration Act 1860, II. Report for the Year 1877 (Her Majesty's Stationery Office, 1878)

Fifth Annual Report of the Prison Commissioners for Scotland (in continuation of the reports of the late General Board of Prisons and the managers appointed Under the Act of 1860) – The Forty-Fourth Annual Report of Prisons in Scotland, 1882–83 (Edinburgh, 1883)

Eleventh Annual Report of the Prison Commissioners for Scotland (in continuation of the reports of the late General Board of Prisons and the Mangers appointed under the Act of 1860) –The Fiftieth Annual Report Of Prisons in Scotland 1888–89 (Edinburgh: His Majesty's Stationery Office, 1889)

Books

Anonymous, *Memoir of the Life and Trial of James Mackcoull, or Moffat, Who Died in the County Jail of Edinburgh on 22nd December, 1820* (first published 1822, reprinted by MOML, digital print editions 2014)

Brodie, Allan, Croom, Jane and O'Davies, James, *English Prisons* (Swindon: English Heritage, 2002)

Brown, William, *A Week in Jail by William Brown, lately Prisoner in the Calton Jail, Edinburgh* (Edinburgh: William Brown, 1859)

Cameron, Joy, *Prisons and Punishment in Scotland from the Middle Ages to the Present* (Edinburgh: Canongate Publishing Ltd, 1983)

Eddleston, John J., *The Encyclopedia of Executions* (London: John Blake Publishing Ltd, 2004)

BIBLIOGRAPHY

Edinburgh Bridewell, *Returns of Commitments to the Bridewell of the City and County of Edinburgh* (The House of Commons, 1828)

Gallacher, William, *Willie Gallacher's Story; the Clyde in Wartime. Sketches of a Stormy Period* (1919; digital reprint by Lightning Source UK Ltd, Milton Keynes, 2014)

Gaols, Scotland (The House of Commons, 1830)

Gifford, John, McWilliam Colin and Walker, David, *The Buildings of Edinburgh* (Middlesex: Penguin Books Ltd, 1984)

Grant James, *Old and New Edinburgh*, 3 vols (New York: Cassell, Petter, Gaplin & Co., no date)

Gurney, Joseph John, *Notes On a Visit Made To Some Of The Prisons in Scotland and the North of England; in Company With Elizabeth Fry; With Some General Observations on the Subject of Prison Discipline* (1819, MOML Print Editions 2014)

Marston, Edward, *Prison: Five Hundred Years of Life Behind Bars* (Kew: The National Archives, 2009)

Neild, James, *The State of Prisons of England, Scotland and Wales* (first published 1812, Cambridge University Press, 2011)

Prisoners (Corporal Punishment) Return of the Number of Prisoners Punished since 21 July 1864, under the Act 26 and 27 Vict. c.44, and certain other Acts, by Whipping, the Place of Punishment and the Number of Stokes Ordered and Inflicted in Each Case and by What Instrument and by Sentence Of What Presiding or other Judge, at what Assizes or other Court, and the Age of each Prisoner so Punished (The House of Commons, 1871)

Robinson, Frederick William, *Memoirs of Jane Cameron, Female Convict By a Prison Matron, Author of Female Life in Prison* in two vols (1864, reprinted by Amazon.co.uk Ltd, 2014)

Rules for Prisons in Scotland, Settled and Approved by the Secretary of State under the Prisons (Scotland), Act, 1877 (The Home Office, 1878)

Skelton, Douglas, *Dark Heart-Tales from Edinburgh's Town Jail* (Edinburgh: Mainstream Publishing Company, 2008)

Smith, David R., *The Dalkeith Tolbooth and Market Cross* (Midlothian Library Service, 1998)

Steuart, David, *The Lord Provost, General Heads of a Plan for Erecting a New Prison and Bridewell in the city of Edinburgh. Offered to the Consideration of the Public, by the Right Honorable, the Lord Provost Of the City of Edinburgh and Archibald Cockburn, 1783* (Ecco Editions, Lightning Source UK Ltd, Milton Keynes, 2014)

Thun, Catter (H. MacKenzie Campbell), *The Calton Ballads* (Edinburgh: J. Munro Bell & Co., 1898)

Verne, Jules, *Backwards to Britain* (Edinburgh: Chambers, 1992)

Wilson, David, *Pain and Retribution: A Short History of British Prisons, 1066 to the Present* (London: Reaktion Books Ltd, 2014)

Young, Alex F., *The Encyclopedia of Scottish Executions 1750–1963* (Orpington: Eric Dobby Publishing Ltd, 1998)

Websites

www.britishnewspaperarchive.co.uk
archive.scotsman.com